BRITISH MACROECONOMIC POLICY SINCE 1940

British Macroeconomic Policy since 1940

JIM TOMLINSON

CROOM HELM
London • Sydney • Dover, New Hampshire

©1985 J. Tomlinson
Croom Helm Ltd, Provident House, Burrell Row,
Beckenham, Kent BR3 1AT
Croom Helm Australia Pty Ltd, First Floor,
139 King Street, Sydney, NSW 2001, Australia

British Library Cataloguing in Publication Data

Tomlinson, Jim
    British macroeconomic policy since 1940.
    1. Macroeconomics   2. Great Britain—
    Economic policy—1945-
    I. Title
    339'.0941   HC256.6

    ISBN 0-7099-2485-2
    ISBN 0-7099-2497-6 Pbk

Croom Helm, 51 Washington Street, Dover,
New Hampshire 03820, USA

Library of Congress Cataloging in Publication Data

Tomlinson, Jim.
    British Macroeconomic Policy since 1940.

    Bibliography: p.
    Includes index.
    1. Great Britain—Economic Policy. 2. Macroeconomics.
I. Title.
HC256.4.T585   1985   339.5'0941   85-3748
ISBN 0-7099-2485-2
ISBN 0-7099-2497-6 (Pbk.)

Printed and bound in Great Britain
by Billing & Sons Limited, Worcester.

CONTENTS

Contents

Contents

TABLES

ACKNOWLEDGEMENTS

For comments on particular points in this book I am
grateful to Professors A.W. Coats and A.S. Milward,
to J.F. Wright, G. Routh and Keith Smith. For more
extended discussion of some of the issues I am
grateful to David Higham and Geoff Hodgson, and
especially to members of the Birkbeck College
"Politics and State" seminar, most of all to
Athar Hussain and Grahame Thompson.
    Mrs. Christine Newnham and Shirley Dodd typed
various versions with their usual speed and
efficiency.

To Kathryn, Isobel and Eleanor

INTRODUCTION

In the 1980s the question of what objectives governments should give priority to in their economic
policy-making is a central political issue. This has
not always been the case, even in the post-war
years. For a couple of decades after 1945 the policy
objective of full employment was given an almost
unquestioned priority, whilst in the late 1970s
policies against inflation had come to have an
almost equal pre-eminence.

These disputes raise the general question of
how and why particular objectives become those at
which government macro-economic policy is aimed. The
focus of most discussion in macro-economic policy-
making is not on this question but on how particular
policies are pursued, the success or failure which
has accompanied such pursuit. Thus for most purposes
the literature in this area takes for granted the
existence of the objectives which are to be pursued.
Most accounts will list those objectives which have
become conventional to macro policy, but not
establish how that conventional status came into
being.

Typical is Black (1979, p.1) who argues that
"Macro-economics is so-called because it studies the
behaviour of economic aggregates. These include the
size of the national income; the levels of employment and unemployment; the rate of growth of the
economy over long periods; the degree of fluctuation
in the level of national income; and the rate of
inflation of prices and wages".

With the addition of some balance of payments
objective,[1] this covers the standard repertoire of
macro-economic policy objectives attributed to
British governments in the post-war period. These
may be summarised as involving policies on unemploy-

ment, the balance of payments and the exchange rate, the price level and the rate of growth of the economy.

Given the failure of British policy in the post-1945 period it is not perhaps surprising that so much attention has been focussed on the means of attaining these objectives. In a comparative sense Britain clearly has been deficient in the attainment of some or all of these objectives much of the time, and in turn these have been accepted across a broad consensus as the appropriate concerns of policy.

To try and approach policy from a slightly different angle of vision is not just an attempt by an author to differentiate his product. Nor is it simply that to discuss what is widely taken for granted is often a fruitful exercise. The possible benefits of focussing on the status of the objectives of policy in fully understanding economic policy are outlined in the rest of this introduction.

I

Clearly these objectives have not always existed. Fifty years ago the U.K. government could not sensibly be said to have had macro-economic objectives in the modern sense. This is not to suggest that governments at that time were indifferent to such questions as growth, unemployment and inflation, but it is to suggest that they cannot be said to have attempted to <u>manage the economy</u> in order to attain such objectives.

This distinction is similar to that drawn by the Radcliffe Committee (1959, paragraph 58) in talking of economic growth: "As a broad objective of policy this, like employment is not wholly new; it would be ridiculous to impute to Victorian political economists any lack of interest in economic progress. But it is newly explicit as an objective of Governments......".

Of course it is hardly new or very profound to point out the recent arrival of macro-economic management. But the existing literature, whilst of course fully aware of the recent historical arrival of macro-management, does not I suggest adequately account for this arrival. The predominant accounts of the genesis of macro-management above all greatly exaggerate the role of economic theory, especially the "Keynesian Revolution". I have attempted to subvert such accounts elsewhere (Tomlinson 1981A and 1981B). Equally, and in the context of this book even more importantly, accounts of the rise of macro-management do not normally consider that the question of the objectives towards which the economy is to be managed is at all problematic. Inflation, unemployment, balance of payments disequilibrium and stagnant living standards are seen as the obvious concerns of policy once Keynes had vouchsafed the possibility of managing the economy. (The only major exception I know to this generalisation is Arndt 1978).

One of the problems of the dominant approach is that the meaning and significance of these objectives is seen as unchanging. Once brought into being they remain constant as objectives, albeit of course differentially difficult to attain at various times. One of the major thrusts of this book is to try and show how the objectives listed have changed in their meaning and significance over the post-war period, how the continuity of a word or phrase has in some cases hidden substantial changes in substance.

II

This focussing on the status of objectives of policy may be seen as complementary to the more traditional concern with how those objectives are to be attained. A concern with ends rather than a concern with means to those ends. But as all social scientists readily recognise, such a separation of ends and means is always doubtful, ends and means cannot be satisfactorily separated. This point can readily be made in the context of the ends and means of economic policy. The attempt to clearly separate ends and means in economic policy is perhaps best known in the work of Tinbergen (1956). He attempted to formalise the objectives of policy in relation to the instruments for their achievement. Such a formalisation has its uses, but as Cairncross (1970, p.21) has emphasised, the implication in this framework, of politically determined objectives being served by 'technically' determined instruments is unsatisfactory, political dispute enters discussion of the instruments of policy also. As Beckerman (1972, p.35) notes, this is partly because "there are hardly any pure 'instruments' of policy that do not have some end value". But we may go further than this and say that, in some cases at least, the status of the objective is itself only understandable in relation to the instruments perceived to be necessary to achieve it.

3

This argument may be briefly illustrated by the case of inflation (see also on this Higham and Tomlinson 1982, and Chapter 8 below).

Concern with inflation is clearly one of the most long-standing of government objectives. Reasons given for this opposition to inflation are many and complex, though the analytic strength of these reasons may well be questioned. Nevertheless, whatever the strength of the anti-inflation arguments, inflation's status as a problem is rarely questioned. This is partly I would suggest because opposition to inflation is nearly always effectively linked to a notion or notions of its causes, and therefore the means to end it. Thus the recurrent arguments of anti-inflation policy have tended to be that inflation is caused either by excessive worker power in collective bargaining, or the profligacy of governments. Now if one sets aside any question as to the truth of such accounts of the causes of inflation, what is apparent is that focussing on inflation as a 'problem' cannot be treated separately from what are seen as its causes and cures. The obvious point that in Britain the more conservative a government is, the more concerned it is with defeating inflation as a policy end, cannot be disentangled from the fact that the conservative's predominant means to achieving that end have always cut across the Left's commitments to strong trade unions, free collective bargaining and to the expansion of government expenditure.

The point illustrated by this brief example is that in macro-economic policy as elsewhere one cannot neatly separate off accounts of ends and means. This implies that the arguments of this book whilst mainly complementary to the normal concern with the means of policy, may occasionally cut across accounts of those means, precisely because they question the separation of 'means' and 'ends'. Whilst most of this book focusses on specific policy issues, and is not a general theoretical treatise, it clearly relates to certain general pre-suppositions. For example the problem of means and ends raises the problems of what have been called rationalist accounts of social action (Hindess 1977A, Ch. 7 and 1977B, Ch. 6). Such rationalist accounts are arguably endemic in the social sciences, and are nowhere more prominent than in orthodox neo-classical economics.

Rationalism means conceiving social action in the form of a setting into motion of thought. Thus social action is the result of a separate activity, an activity of the mind which leads on to an activity of the flesh. More prosaically in the case of economic policy-making, rationalism will tend to conceive of a two-stage process whereby objectives are established and then material means to their attainment constructed. These means will be a product of, and therefore subordinate to, the objective. In this way ends will simply subordinate means, the means will be constructed to attain those ends. Against this may be asserted the irreducibility of any means in economic policy-making to a specific end. The means will always have their own conditions of existence and effects, which will make them always insubordinate with respect to the end they are supposed to achieve.

Again this point may be made by way of an example.[2] Recent attempts to apply the "economics of politics" approach to public expenditure expansion in the U.K. have suggested that the expansion has been the product of politicians' and bureaucrats' calculations. Each group has the objective of maximising their respective interests in votes and budgets. Both groups it is argued generally gain from government expenditure growth and this mechanism therefore explains why public expenditure has indeed grown in the last few decades. (Though on whether this growth has been a real one, see Beck 1979). One striking aspect of this literature is that it renders any discussion of institutional mechanisms regulating public expenditure entirely besides the point - those institutions are merely shells within which these maximising calculations make themselves felt. Thus all the debates about mechanisms of control of public expenditure in the U.K. cannot be treated as important in this argument. Only constitutional mechanisms constraining the effects of such maximising will be effective (see Buchanan, et al. 1978).

Any detailed account of the public expenditure process (e.g. Pliatzky 1982, Heclo and Wildavsky 1981) would seem to provide overwhelming evidence of the unhelpfulness of such approaches to understanding public expenditure. These books show the many and often contradictory calculations which underlie public expenditure decisions. They show that, like all large organisations, government is not a simple hierarchy where the top level makes decisions and those beneath simply obey. For both these reasons it seems difficult to accept that there is one essential principle (or form of calculation) which underlies public expenditure.

III

The points made at the end of the previous
section imply a focus on institutions, institutions
seen as irreducible elements in the policy-making
process. Irreducible to any single form of calculation as well as irreducible to any external 'idea'
or 'interest'. Irreducibility to any single calculation in particular is stressed here, because so many
social science accounts of institutions are precisely subject to criticisms on the grounds of such
rationalism. For example recent work in neo-
classical economics like the 'transactions cost'
approach (for a good outline of this see Williamson
1981) would seem to be a prime example of rationalist notions being applied. Organisational diversity
is seen as the product of differences in the nature
of transactions which organisations engage in, with
a form of natural selection imposing adjustments on
organisational patterns to minimise transaction
costs. Organisational activities are then a reflection of rational efficiency calculations, a whole
host of the organisations practices being explicable
in this way. Forms of organisation are calculations
made flesh.

To stress the 'irreducibility' of institutions
is to assert the impossibility of a general theory
of institutions, for what could any general theory
be but an attempt to reduce institutions to the
operation of a government principle? Thus many of
the arguments deployed against the dominant notions
of the enterprise (Tomlinson 1982, Thompson 1982)
are also applicable here, for they too deny that the
practices of enterprises can be reduced to the
operation of a governing principle, whether it be
profit-maximising or any 'managerial objective'.

To deny the possibility of an adequate general
theory of institutions is not to deny the use of
general concepts in analysing those institutions.
Thus, for example, a central focus of much recent
heterodox Marxism has been on the forms of calculation of economic and political agents (see Cutler,
Hindess, Hirst, Hussain 1976 and 1977; Thompson
1978). Calculation is seen as a crucial and under-
analysed aspect of the practices of such agents and
this point may be extended to the institutions
active in the area of economic policy-making. For
example to bring out the forms of calculation
employed by the Treasury in the inter-war period is
to stress an aspect of policy-making at that time
underplayed or distorted by many accounts (Middleton

1982). Below, a similar attempt to show the importance of institutional calculation is made in discussing the post-1940 period.

IV

In part this book is a sequel to a previous book (Tomlinson 1981A). However there are major differences in the organisation of the arguments as well as of course the materials deployed. Above all the previous book was hegemonised by an attempt to undercut an "ideas versus vested interests" notion, which was seen as strongly present in the literature on economic policy-making in that earlier period, but unhelpful.

The role of "ideas" in economic policy-making was argued to have been exaggerated relative to structural changes in the economy, the changes having highly diverse origins. In particular the argument was that the whole notion of a 'Keynesian revolution' in twentieth century economic policy-making had been based on a great exaggeration of the role of economic theory in policy changes. Against this, it was suggested, more focus should be put on such elements as the rise of government expenditure's share in National Income, the development of national income accounting[3] and the lower level of integration in the world economy consequent on departure from the gold standard. All these, it was argued, provide a background without which the triumph of 'Keynesianism' would have been unthinkable.

The other half of the dichotomy was that of 'vested interests', which Keynesian writers have suggested is the only alternative to stress on "ideas" (Winch 1972, pp.24-5). It can be agreed that vested interest explanations of policy are often crude and unsatisfactory. This is true both of Marxist accounts, which stress class interests, and neo-classical arguments which stress individual agents maximising their interests. Both seem inadequate to the complexities of policy-making. However these do not seem the only possible alternatives. 'Problems of British Economic Policy', no doubt in a sketchy, incomplete way attempted to construct an approach which avoided both poles of this dichotomy. It did so by focussing on the construction of 'problems' both discursively and for institutions within which policy was pursued. This was not posed as an alternative 'general theory' of policy-making.

Introduction

Whilst these latter points are retained in this book (and developed further below) the stress on "ideas versus vested interests" is much more muted in this book. The main reason for this difference is that discussion of post-war policy has by and large seen much less emphasis on the crucial role of economic theory at least until the arrival of "monetarism". This theme is of some importance in Chapter 1 because of its obvious importance in accounts of the rise of full employment policy. It is also of some importance though in a rather different way in Chapter 10, where it is argued that much of the discussion of monetarist policy in the U.K. has greatly overstated the significance of monetarist economic theory to that policy. Elsewhere, however, it is not so important, not only for the reason given above, but also because of the dangers of too indiscriminate a use of such arguments. Clearly there is a danger that too much stress on attacking the role of "ideas" in policy-making will be open to be construed as stressing the importance of brute "reality" against the ephemeral status of ideas. Nothing could be further from my intentions. Throughout I try to make clear that in economic policy-making, as elsewhere, "the facts" never speak for themselves, they are only 'known' through know-ledge, they do not exist as knowledge separate from the concepts which organise them.

V

As already stressed this book takes the insti-tutions of policy-making seriously, never treating them as the simple instruments of an external grand design. Equally it takes seriously the discourse of economic policy-making. By this is meant that the way in which certain terms have been deployed in policy-making, treating those terms "in their own right" rather than as simply signs of something else.
One could I believe write a very valuable book which simply focussed on the deployment of certain terms, common in economic discussion, in various contexts. For example there would be a great deal to be gained from doing for a term such as "efficiency", or "market forces" what Pitkin (1967) does for representation and which Tribe (1978) has done for certain aspects of economic thought. This however is not such a book. Whilst it does treat forms of the deployment of certain words as a problem, as a focus of interest, it also attempts to link these

discourses to their institutional loci. It attempts
to show how particular discourses attained a certain
status in policy-making by linking institutional
practices to discursive forms. This undoubtedly
creates problems, and may indeed lead to a "falling
between two stools" where an adequate account is
given neither of discourses or institution. Nevertheless it seems an objective worth attempting.

A corollary to this focussing on discourses and
mainly governmental institutions is that political
forces in the guise of classes, trade unions,
employers organisations and political parties play a
relatively minor role. This is because the book is
concerned with policy-making very much at the
central governmental level, so in part it is simply
a question of the agencies directly relevant to this
level. This level does not it seems to me directly
reflect activities at other levels - it is not
simply a reflection of 'larger forces' whether they
be ideas or classes or even political parties. This
point does not mean that I believe that in some
ultimate sense these other political agencies do not
impinge on policy-making - but that they do it only
at several removes.

In particular this book does not make a great
deal of the changes of party political regime in
this period. This is not because I believe these
differences in some _general_ sense unimportant, but
that in relation to macro-economic policy objectives
and policy-making the similarities are often more
striking than the differences. As Coats (1981,
p.394) suggests "it is not too much to say that
there has been a fundamental consensus - admittedly
with some significant changes of emphasis and
differences in detail - on the basic objectives of
economic and social policy". This consensus is most
apparent for the 1950s and 1960s, to which period
the title "Butskellism" has commonly been applied.
But that consensus in many ways, albeit under
challenged, continued into the 1970s, as will be
argued below.

The focus on similarities (or rather the
ignoring of differences) arises from the stress on
discourses of economic policy-making to which in a
sense both parties have been prisoner. Equally a
focus on institutions of economic policy-making
which does not reduce their operation to a single
'principle', 'ideology' or 'interest' must bring out
their relative immunity from the often short-lived
political pressures brought about by changes in the
colour of governments.

IV

The book is divided into halves. The first of
these focusses on how a new policy regime was constituted during and after the Second World War
around the four objectives of macro-policy. It is
stressed that this was a very different regime of
policy-making than that in existence before 1939,
and that much of it was in place before the war
ended. At the end of the chapters on the individual
objectives I try and summarise what this new regime
was in toto and how it is best to be characterised.

The second half looks at the disintegration of
this new regime. The evolution of the four objectives discussed in the first half is continued up
until the late 1970s. This is followed by a
discussion of "monetarism".

In some ways the policies pursued after the
election of the Conservative government in 1979 may
be seen as a culmination of the breakdown of the
consensus surrounding the installation of the "new
regime". This forms one theme of this chapter. But
monetarism has commonly been treated not so much as
a particular mode of dealing with the very severe
constraints on the British economy, but as a kind of
ideologically-based import, to be explained largely
in terms of the acceptance by government intellectual and political ideas fundamentally distinct from
those dominant in the post-war period (Gould et al.,
1981, Ch. 2). This view it is argued greatly
exaggerates both the "newness" of post-1979 monetarist policies and also the possibility of pursuing
radically different policies by simply changing the
ideology of policy-makers.

Finally the last chapter briefly summarises the
arguments of the book and the implications of these
for British policy in the 1980s, especially in
relation to the objective of full employment.

NOTES

1. Some commentators exclude the balance of
payments from a list of objectives, believing it to
be more appropriate to treat this as a constraint
in pursuing other policy objectives.

2. For more details see J. Tomlinson, "The
Economics of Politics and Public Expenditure",
Economy and Society, 10, 4, (November 1981),
pp. 383-402.

Introduction

3.   Since the appearance of <u>Problems of British Economic Policy</u> the Inland Revenue Report on National Income for 1929 has been brought to my attention. R. Stone, <u>Inland Revenue Report on National Income 1929</u> (C.U.P., Cambridge, 1977). Here Stone notes that this report could have served as a stimulus to a "statistical revolution" like that in the U.S.A. in the 1930s (p.V). Had it done so of course my stress on the separate (non-Keynesian) foundations of National Income Accounting would have been wholly uncontentious.

PART ONE

THE NEW REGIME

Chapter One

FULL EMPLOYMENT[1]

A commitment to full employment is commonly treated
as the most important single distinguishing feature
of economic policy in the U.K. after World War Two.
This chapter attempts to explain how that objective
came into being. The chapter is organised around an
analysis of the context of ideas and institutions
from which emerged the publication of the 1944 White
Paper on Employment which is treated as a crucial
sign of this new commitment. In looking at this
context I have focussed on three "elements" which it
will be argued were crucial to the genesis of the
full employment policy commitment.

Keynesianism
The three arguments focussed upon here are Keynesian
economic theory, technocracy and total war. The
first and obvious point about the role of Keynesian
economic theory is that even if the major reason
for the change in the means of economic management
were changes in economic theory, this would not of
itself account for the commitment to full employment
i.e. a change in the ends of policy. But in fact the
'rise of economic management' was predicated on many
other changes than the growth of new theoretical
concerns - the forced departure from the gold standard in 1931 loosening the constraints of the international economy; the growth of government expenditure giving government budgets a significant
leverage over the whole economy- the growth of
National Income accounting providing a framework for
the assessment of the impact of macro-economic
policies (Tomlinson 1981A, pp.120-134).
    Of course the availability of certain means to
full employment policy, whatever their origin, may
be said to have encouraged a commitment to such a

policy, by making it appear realistic and plausible
to make such a commitment. But this does not seem
clearly to have been the case in the war period
prior to the 1944 White Paper. This can be illustrated by looking briefly at some of the developments
in economic theory and institutions in this period.

The initial intellectual impetus to the
governmental use of Keynesian methods of National
Income accounting in the Second World War came from
Keynes' articles and later pamphlet on How to Pay
for the War (Keynes 1978). This was an attempt by
Keynes to use the rudimentary, private National
Income figures available at that time (notably of
Rothbarth) to demonstrate "to the working classes
that borrowing and heavier taxation of the rich
alone were not feasible or desirable methods of
financing the war from their point of view" (Winch
1972, p.260). But the attraction of this approach
for the Treasury was its highlighting of that most
longstanding of Treasury objectives, the prevention
of inflation. As Keynes himself stressed "The
importance of a war budget is not because it will
'finance' the war.... Its importance is social; to
prevent the social evils of inflation now and
later...." (Keynes 1978, p.218). The focus on
inflation undoubtedly aided the use of government
resources to provide more adequate and official
National Income estimates - though not without
resistance on the part of some government depart-
ments.2 In this way was founded the basis of the
'Keynesian' budget of 1941 and its successors, a
basis far removed from concern with unemployment.

Whilst the Treasury willingly embraced the use
of National Income accounting as a guide to non-
inflationary war finance, this institution was
itself being displaced from its normal central role
in economic policy making. Partly this was a consequence of the feeling that finance should have a
less dominant position in government policy,
especially following the accession of Labour
ministers to the Cabinet in 1940, and added to by
the increasing use of physical controls as the war
proceeded (Chester (ed) 1951, p.6; Roseveare 1969,
pp.273-4). Parallel to this decline of the role of
the Treasury was the concentration of economists in
other parts of Whitehall, notably in what was
originally the Central Economic Information Service,
this being split into the Central Statistical Office
and the Economic Section of the Office of the War
Cabinet in early 1941. It was particularly amongst
economists in this latter grouping that work on

questions of employment was concentrated (see Robbins 1971, Ch. IX; Keynes 1980, Ch. 5). For example, as early as 3 November 1940, this committee had produced a memorandum on "Internal Measures for the Prevention of General Unemployment" which focussed attention on 'demand deficit' unemployment, (P.R.O. 1941A) and generally this secretariat may be seen as a conduit for Keynesian ideas into policy making, avoiding the Treasury where there was, right through the war, strong opposition to Keynesianism.[3]

However, an important point to be made is that the focus of the literature on the evolution of Keynesian ideas within the government machine, is of course largely the product of economists themselves, with their characteristic and no doubt understandable focus on the translation of theory into policy. This focus readily fits in with the notion that the availability of "Keynesian means" was central to the acceptance of full employment as a policy end, and that once we have noted the evolution of these means, the end of hardly something that requires much explanation. However this may well misrepresent the position. The policy end of full employment had other and arguably more powerful origins than simply the availability of the means (see especially Section III below). Equally much of the original wartime stress on the goal of full employment was predicated not on Keynesian, or any other, economic theory, but on a belief in the possibilities of extending wartime planning into the post-war period. For example, Beveridge's[4] support for full employment at this time was based on a combination of increased acceptance of state intervention in the economy, coupled with agreement with the long (if thin) history of proposals for full employment by socialists such as the Webbs and Cole. Cole (1944) in particular had stressed that the extension of wartime control over production to peacetime could bring full employment. Beveridge like many others recognised the force of this argument, given the perceived successes of wartime manpower planning (Hancock and Gowing 1949). Thus Beveridge's cure for unemployment was "based on state control of production and on detailed planning of deployment of labour rather than on monetary and fiscal regulation of consumer demand" (Harris 1977, p.430). Later Beveridge became converted to the Keynesian version of how to maintain full employment, but the important point in the present context is to register that commitment to full employment in wartime Britain

17

could exist entirely independently of any changes in economic theory. In this instance he who willed the end could will a variety of means.

Technocracy

The strength of this stress on planning as a means of solving economic problems was due to a number of elements. Part of it was no doubt due to the (eventual) Russian successes against Nazi Germany which could be argued, however problematically in retrospect, to demonstrate the strength of a planned economy. More important to the specific case of full employment was the ideology of 'technocracy', which had been so strong in Britain from the First World War right through the inter-war period.

The term technocracy seems to have first been used in the U.S.A. after the First World War, to describe "a system of economic thought inspired by the kind of rational analysis at the basis of the physical sciences" (Meynaud 1958, p.12). Three major aspects of this technocratic trend were the belief that 'problems' in society are given independent of political argument,[5] the veneration of science and the denigration of politics. Technocracy saw the way to a better future through the application of science to social affairs, but politics was seen as an anachronistic blockage to such an application (Ibid., p.96). In Britain the especial focus was that of involving experts in policy formulation. Such ideas are apparent in the reconstruction movements of both world wars, the "rationalisation" movement in industry in the 1920s, as well as the periodic attempts to bring economic expertise into government departments (Howson and Winch 1977, p.7).

In the Second World War the technocratic movement may be said to have had two main thrusts. One was through the work of Keynes and his allies, who saw economic policy making in highly rationalistic terms, a question of defeating intellectual outdatedness and educating the elite into more adequate thinking. This of course went along with a footlooseness in politics. Keynes "encouraged or collaborated with any person or group who seemed to be working along the right lines to solve problems that were, in his view, mainly of an intellectual character. While he could feel respect for individual politicians, his view of this as a breed is perhaps summed up by his definition of politics as "the survival of the unfit" (Winch 1972, p.339).

A parallel thrust to this technocracy of the liberal intelligentsia was that of the planners. The idea of planning as a non-political technique can be traced back, paradoxically perhaps, at least to Marx's dictum of the "administration of things replacing the administration of men" under communism, but it received a powerful impetus from the perceived successes of Soviet Five-Year Planning, and later the success of planning in the British war effort. Even by socialists this planning was commonly seen as merely a rational response to changes in society, a means applicable to a variety of different political ends. Thus for example in 1942 a Labour Party document[6] could speak of the increased role of the state as irreversible, the only question being who was to use it, the few or the many. This conception of planning as a non-political means was strong across the political spectrum, as Marwick (1964) notes in his discussion of the 1930s, and lasted at least until the publication of Hayek's Road to Serfdom in 1944, which heralded a new era.

These technocratic beliefs and their particular embodiment in Keynesianism and planning ideas, existed like all beliefs by and through institutions. It is of note that when, for example, the Official Committee on Post-War Internal Economic Problems was outlining its programme of work, it was able to draw on work going on in a range of institutions, many of which had not existed in the First World War - Political and Economic Planning, the National Institute of Economic and Social Research, the Oxford Institute of Statistics, the Nuffield Reconstruction Survey, were all founded by the 1930s (P.R.O. 1941B). Each of these of course had its own particular conditions of existence, but it is symptomatic of the time that so many agencies for the dissemination of economic expertise had come to exist in the inter-war period. They provided at one and the same time both a source of such expertise and supporters for its use in government.

As already noted both the Keynesian and the planning methods could be called upon by proponents of full employment, and both may be labelled technocratic. Both aspired to the application of disinterested expertise to social affairs, and both claimed to evade the claims of politics. Now this 'politics' which they attempted to escape was a particular one, a politics conceived fundamentally as a dispute over private versus public ownership. A typical example of this view is given by Robbins

(a member of the War Cabinet Economic Secretariat)
(P.R.O. 123/48):

> "In reflecting, during the last two years, upon
> the principal problems of economic reconstruc-
> tion, I have been more and more convinced that
> the main practical problems with which we shall
> be confronted are problems which tend to fall
> outside the categories of pre-war political
> controversy. The problems of equilibrium in the
> balance of payments, of maintaining full
> employment, or raising the standard of life by
> increased productivity, are problems which do
> not raise, at any rate in the first instance,
> the old issues".

Such a view was of course based on a particular
view as to what constituted pre-war politics -
public versus private ownership - which clearly
over-simplified these politics. But it was enough of
the truth to provide a rationale for a persistent
theme in debates over full employment. For example
it was a theme stressed by Bevin in his House of
Commons introduction of the Employment White Paper
in 1944.[7] In this way the triumph of technocracy
reflected and played upon a particular kind of
political debate, one about public versus private
ownership, which was itself a highly particular
feature of Britain, never so prominent in most other
non-Communist countries.[8] Without this foil, it is
doubtful if technocratic ideas could ever have come
to have such a powerful grip in Britain.

Full employment could thus be presented as an
economic policy which cut across the old divisive
shibboleths of politics and presaged the rule of
science and expertise rather than vested interest
and division. It was a policy "all reasonable men"
could agree upon.[9]

Total War
In the debate on the King's Speech in December 1939
Anthony Eden argued that "The war will bring about
changes which may be fundamental and revolutionary
in the economic and social life of the country. On
that we are all agreed" and he went on "The truth is
that war presents an audit of the nation; it exposes
weaknesses ruthlessly and brutally, and this war is
going to do that too. These weaknesses will call for
changes" (Hansard, 6 December 1939, Col. 756).

This is one of the earliest statements of a thesis which was to become stronger and stronger as the war progressed (and to be reiterated endlessly after the war). Modern wars, "total wars", such as the Second World War necessarily produce social changes. The governmental promise of full employment was commonly presented in this light - a recognition of necessity imposed by the exigencies of war. In the same debate in which Eden spoke, Attlee recalled the belief in the previous World War that unemployment would not be tolerated by returning soldiers - and drew the not necessarily obvious conclusion that this time it would not be tolerated. From this he drew the further implication that "peace aims and reconstruction cannot be postponed till the end of the war" (Ibid., 28 November 1939, Col. 23). In the face of considerable reluctance on the part of both Chamberlain (Ibid., Col. 31) and Churchill[10] this was to become a major part of the political rhetoric of the war.

If we are sceptical of such historical necessities it is worth examining in some detail this ideology of total war and the way it operated.

First we may note that as a matter of historical fact much of the impetus of the 'total war' notion came from an inaccurate portrayal of the enemy. Nazi Germany was presented as a country whose commitment to war was total, and therefore to match this effort required a wholesale mobilisation of British resources. We now know that this was grossly inappropriate as an account of the Germany war economy - civilian consumption in particular was protected from the claims of munitions production to an extent which in retrospect appears astounding. As Carroll (1968, p.10) notes "the strategy of blitzkrieg was precisely Hitler's justification for opposing, and means of avoiding, "total mobilisation" of Germany's resources for war". (see also Milward 1965, Chs. 1, 2, pp.131-61 and Speer 1962).

Secondly we can see that the alleged link between social changes and total war in the Second World War period is complex, at least four elements being distinguishable. Two of these are stressed in Titmuss's famous account of social policy in the war. Changes in the scope of welfare services he argued "did not happen in any planned or ordered sequence; nor were they always a matter of deliberate intent. Some were pressed forward because of the needs of the war machine for more men and more work. Some took place almost by accident. Some were the result of a recognition of needs hitherto hidden by ignorance of social conditions" (Titmuss 1976, p.507).

The first of these links, the amelioration required directly by the wartime need for fit and healthy personnel for war, is of course one with a long history - almost every war in the modern period in Britain has sparked off a debate about the health of the population and its fitness for contemporary forms of warfare. There is perhaps nothing very remarkable in this itself, but two points can be made about this link between governmental concern with the numbers and health of the population and warfare. On the one hand war is only one axis around which such concerns have circulated - others have suggested a more profound, underlying, change which is said to begin with European states' concern with population, dating this broadly to the eighteenth century (Foucault 1979, I). On the other hand the health of the potential fighting population was much less serious a problem for the authorities in the Second World War, because the general health of that population seems to have substantially improved (albeit from very low levels) since the First War. This was not mainly due to policy changes, despite the furore created by such work as Boyd Orr's Food, Health and Income, but to the unevenly distributed but substantial rise in the standard of living over that period.[11] Thus it is not clear why this link should be of particular concern in the Second World War.

On the question of the revealing of previously hidden social evils, we may perhaps again make two points which serve simply to suggest that a particular feature of World War Two is being over-generalised. Social evils are not only revealed by war - the history of poverty for example is a history of periodic "re-discoveries" of the problem which do not necessarily coincide with wars (Williams 1981). Secondly the fact that a problem is 'revealed' to policy does not means policy solves the problem - whilst action was taken during the war, for example the development of school meals, school milk, and medical services, there was along-side this an unplanned redistribution of income and consequence rise in living standards of the working class during the war, which served to ameliorate substantially pre-war poverty (see further below). The general point again is that the role of war per se is exaggerated in its effects on social policy.

The total war thesis further argues that wars
like that of 1939-45 were different from previous
wars because of the involvement of the bulk of the
population, both as victims of the bombing and as
providers of munitions. Wars' effects were no longer
limited to combatants. This has two consequences.
First the concern felt in previous wars for health
and fitness was generalised to a large proportion of
the adult population. This linkage is the general
theme of Andrzejewski's <u>Military Organisation and</u>
Society, which argues that the proportion of the
total population engaged in military activity in
wartime is a major determinant of the amount of
social reform following from that war.[12] He denies,
however, the general applicability of his 'military
participation ratio' analysis to Britain, and in
particular confines his discussion of the effects of
the Second World War to the bringing to power of the
Labour Party with its programme of "soaking the
rich" (Andrzejewski, pp.70-1).

Secondly, and more importantly, the civilians
who were now part of the war effort had to be
motivated. It was this latter argument which was
pre-eminent in wartime discussions of full employment and deserves detailed attention. Titmuss made
the general point succinctly ... "the war could not
be won unless millions of ordinary people, in
Britain and overseas, were convinced that we had
something better to offer than had our enemies -
not only during but after the war" (Titmuss 1963,
p.82).

This linking of post-war policy and wartime
morale was evident right from the beginning of the
war. In 1940 a War Aims Committee was established.[13]
Part of its remit was to state clearly Britain's
case against Hitler, but this rapidly became linked
to the question of post-war domestic objectives and
the question of employment. A memorandum of November
1940 discussed methods of achieving full employment,
partly it would seem because Hitler was seen as
having a convincing case "upon the material side"
(e.g. solving unemployment) even though "totally
bankrupt in moral criticism" (P.R.O. 1940A). Now it
is worth stressing that a war aims committee does
not inevitably concern itself with post-war measures
of social change. It might well for example have
focussed on anti-fascist themes and the political
consequences of Hitler. But such matters rapidly
become secondary (Addison 1977, p.183). Symptomat-
ically the War Aims Committee was quickly absorbed
by a Committee on Reconstruction Problems which in

various guises (a Minister of Reconstruction coming in November 1943) survived the rest of the war. Not merely survived, but became a focus of enormous efforts which before VE day were to lay the basis of most of the 1945 Labour Government's social legislation. (This is a major theme of Addison, 1977).

The singularity of this is worth stressing; a war begun to defend Poland against aggression became a war which could only be won by promises of a 'new deal' at the wars end.[14] This is not easy to explain. One major aspect was clearly a popular, but arguably highly peculiar, view of morale and war effort. Success in war was conceived of as linked to individual commitment to the war, if this could not be guaranteed the war could not be effectively fought. This view was popular across the political spectrum, although it receives its strongest formulation in the works of socialists like Wintringham, for him the war could only be won by Peoples War in which everyone was fully committed to a socialist future following the defeat of the enemy. In Cromwell's phrase "we can only fight well if we know what we fight for and love what we know" (Wintringham 1942, p.89).

The formula in both strong or weak versions is both generally implausible and empirically ill-founded. Generally implausible because it ignores the capacity of organisations (be they armies, factories or universities etc.) to generate results despite the diverse objectives, interests and purposes of their participants. In other words it raises what may be seen as one part of the conditions for an organisation's success into a sine qua non. This argument in its most general form has been applied to armies by Keegan (1976). A more specific and directly relevant case is the Allied bombing of Germany. Brodie (1959) makes the well-known point that up until the last months of the war this bombing had notably little impact on German industrial output. He further argues that this was despite the fact that the bombing "did indeed seriously depress the morale of Germany civilians" (Ibid., p.131). This is only paradoxical if one believes (as many in wartime Britain appear to have done) that morale is the key to production. In Nazi Germany it was well recognised that Stimmung (attitude or feeling) is very different from Haltung (behaviour), and that the latter might remain largely unaltered despite the bombing's effect on the former. The level of industrial production was sustained despite the drop in morale because of "need combined with habit ... coercion ... propaganda ... in descending order of imports (Ibid., p.133). In Britain the third of these elements was obviously much less powerful, but even in the German case its role should not be exaggerated in comparison especially with 'need' and 'habit'.

To apply this point to Britain, is there any good reason to suppose that a munitions worker will produce more if he or she is motivated by a belief that victory in war will produce full employment, than if he or she believes for example that war work provides a good opportunity to work long hours and earn good wages? Appropriate individual incentives undoubtedly do help output, but output is constrained by an enormous range of factors other than individual effort, let alone individual morale. And in any case why should the incentive of a future promise by politicians be stronger than the incentive of good wages? There is indeed evidence of the scepticism with which workers in wartime Britain greeted promises about the post-war period, a strong and understandable feeling that it had all been heard before (Calder 1969, p.631; Addison 1977, p.229-69).

More surprisingly perhaps, the wartime government in Britain knew a great deal about what the populace thought, in a way new in that war. Assessments of civilian concerns and morale were systematically fed to the government. These assessments showed not only the scepticism about post-war promises, but also suggested that moral was affected much more by such questions as food availability, help with the consequences of bombing and the progress of the war, than promises of future social amelioration (Calder 1969, p.542; Addison 1977, pp.195, 215-6). Despite both theoretical implausibility and lack of empirical support, the linking of post-war objectives to the war effort was a most successful "strategy", and perhaps the most important element in the creation of an objective of full employment.

The Politics of Full Employment
To refer to the linking of full employment and other post-war objectives to be the war effort was a 'strategy' may be misleading if that word is taken to imply that there was ever one agency which attempted and succeeded in making this link against an opposition which sought to defeat this aim. Rather the striking feature of the period was the almost unanimous agreement to the link being made,

and this, I stress, despite the implausibility and lack of empirical support available.

Without looking at the evidence we might be tempted to see this linkage as a political one, as a successful attempt by the Left to use the war as a way of advancing the interests of its working class constituency. Such suspicions were indeed voiced by anti-Socialists at the beginning of the war. Prior to the formation of the Wartime coalition of 1940, and whilst he was still Prime Minister, Chamberlain accused Attlee of suggesting "that the war was a good time to introduce socialism and that the best way in which we could win it would be by ourselves all turning into socialists" (Hansard, 28 November 1939, Col. 29). But as we have already noted, the striking feature of the war was that this linking of post-war aims and wartime effort rapidly established itself more or less across the political spectrum. In this sense it is truer to see the Left (and the Labour Party in particular) as the bene-ficiaries rather than the originators of this factor (Addison 1977, esp. Ch. X). It was not the conse-quence of a clear political calculation, a way of dishing the Tories.

Nevertheless Labour did play upon one aspect of this linkage, the argument that planning could provide both the means of wartime success and post-war prosperity. Here the previous point about the common linkage between planning (rather than Keynesian economic theory) and full employment for many outside the ranks of economists is important. The Tories were not only besmirched by their asso-ciation with pre-war unemployment, but also by their suspected hostility to planning. Here there is need to be careful; some Conservatives, notably Macmillan and Boothby, as already noted, had been very important in the creation of the conception of planning as a politically neutral 'means' to various ends. But alongside this went the view that Labour was the 'natural' party of planning and thus the party likely to embrace enthusiastically the means to full employment.

Employment as an Objective of Policy

Finally we may summarise the general points about the formation of objectives of policy which may be drawn from this example.

First that the emergence of full employment as a central objective of policy does not seem to have depended upon a clear case having been made for its desirability in economic and social terms, as an overly rationalistic account of policy objectives might suggest.

The closest to such a case was made in the arguments over the reform of social policy, especially around the Beveridge Report of 1942. In that Report, full employment was argued to be one of the pre-conditions for the social welfare proposals, partly because of the importance of "productive employment" for human happiness, but more specifically because full employment would greatly aid the financing of the scheme (Beveridge 1942, paras. 440-443).

Also whilst not argued in the report, its author had strongly in mind during its drafting that inter-war unemployment was a major cause of the poverty his report was designed to combat. Rowntree's study of York in 1936 was especially important, showing as it did that, unlike at the time of the previous Rowntree Report of 1899, the major cause of poverty was unemployment plus inadequate provision for childhood and old age (Harris 1977, pp.379, 393).

Beveridge's sensitivity in this way to the costs of his policy may have helped convince sceptics in the Treasury. But overall, the impression one gets of war time debates is that the desirability of full employment was largely taken for granted rather than argued through, a point which is of some significance when considering the withering of the full employment commitment in the 1970s and 1980s.

Secondly economic theory played a relatively minor role in creating the objective of full employment. Its role in making possible economic management via budgetary manipulation has been commonly exaggerated, and in any case many initially saw the way to full employment as being by other means.[15]

Even in the White Paper the firmness of commitment to the objective of a high and stable level of employment is not matched by the clarity of its discussion of the means (Winch 1972, pp.269-73).

When one looks away from the predominant Keynesian accounts of these events one finds a paradox. Both in the case of Marxist and neo-classical accounts there is on the one hand explicit recognition and criticism of the rationalism of

Keynesian explanations. Buchanan and Wagner (1977; see also Tomlinson 1981C) for example point to what Harrod (1952) called Keynes' rationalistic "pre-suppositions of Harvey Road" and argue against these pre-suppositions, that government policy is best understood as the consequence of maximising behaviour by politicians and bureaucrats, rather than the disinterested pursuit of the public good by a small and enlightened elite. Equally Sweezy, from a Marxist position, derides Keynesian ideas of the neutrality of the capitalist state and criticises "The Keynesians (who) tear the economic system out of its social context and treat it as though it were a machine to be sent to the repair shop there to be overhauled by an engineer state" (Sweezy 1968, p.349).

Yet when it comes to explaining how governments come to take on the objective of full employment both return to the very rationalism they had otherwise criticised. Full employment was, they both argue, taken on board by governments because of the influence of Keynesian theory (Buchanan and Wagner 1977, p.37; Sweezy 1968, pp.348-52). In other words neither the neo-classical nor the Marxist approach accepts the adequacy of Keynesian ideas, but both agree with the Keynesian view on how policy develops.

In the absence therefore of a developed account from either of these position of how full employment was put on the agenda which is true to their theoretical perspectives it is difficult to criticise sensibly such positions.[16] All one can say, is that in a general way, it is difficult to see a convincing explanation for a policy of full employment as simply a consequence of representation of interests, either the interests of politicians and bureaucrats as in a neo-classical framework, or of the working class as in a Marxist framework. Of course politicians did come to believe that full employment was something they needed to promise to gain votes, but it would seem clear that what has to be explained is why then, why did the perceived "tastes" of electors change during the Second World War? Secondly career bureaucrats seem to have been the main obstacle to full employment policies being pursued rather than avid supporters. It was the temporary wartime draftees into the civil service who made the running against often dogged resistance from some of the permanent civil servants. I do not see how this can be explained in neo-classical terms.

Finally in relation to Marxist arguments, whilst the workers clearly could be said to gain from the <u>fact</u> of full employment, what has already been said about the Labour Party does not suggest we can see the full employment objective as simply the political representation of a pre-given working class interest. This is not to dispute the boost given by the war to working class political representation, but to argue that the way in which this interest was construed cannot be understood without considering the three sets of ideas discussed above. They provided a new stage upon which interests could be represented and fought for, a stage built on the broad and diverse foundations indicated above.

The Significance of Full Employment

This chapter started from the assumption that the publication of the 1944 White Paper heralded a policy commitment which is fundamental in understanding post-war policies. This assumption seems to me an appropriate one, but the reasons need to be clarified.

This policy commitment was not significant because it led directly to the <u>fact</u> of full employment in the 1950s and 1960s. Matthews (1968) has convincingly argued the negative case that the full employment of the period up to the mid-1960s was not the consequence of the fiscal policy of the period. This was because fiscal policy was normally deflationary in this period. He argues that rather than being fiscally induced "the explanation of the rise in investment must lie at the heart of the explanation of the rise in the level of activity" (p.560).

It must be recognised that there are problems with Matthews' argument. (See also Ch. 5 below). His measure of fiscal stance excludes government capital expenditure, and is therefore at variance with those measures which are more akin to the current focus on the financing of the public sector. For example the figures used by Neild and Ward (1979, Table 4.1, p.39) as the basis for their constant employment calculations, show actual positive balances in only two years between 1949 and 1964, in sharp contrast to Matthews. However it would seem that Matthews' basis of calculation is appropriate to the Keynesian framework he adopts, which sees the determinants of government capital and current expenditure as fundamentally different, and the balance of current expenditures and receipts as the relevant measure of fiscal stance.

Here it should perhaps be stressed that there are several valid definitions of budget balance depending on the purpose in hand (Chelliah 1973, p.775). For the purposes of Matthews argument his measure does appear to be the appropriate one.

We may reasonably characterise post-war fiscal policy as being adjustments around full employment rather than central to its attainment. This of course does not mean that the commitment to full employment did not itself aid the achievement of the high levels of investment which were crucial by maintaining confidence (a point made by Matthews). But given the impossibility of measuring this reason for high investment, it is perhaps worth stressing the more 'objective' reasons for high investment after the war, above all the accumulation of investment opportunities resulting from the peculiar historical circumstances of the first half of the century. As Matthews puts the point (p.568) "there were in any case powerful forces independent of government action making for an investment boom of unusual proportions".

Despite this view of the importance (or lack of it) of fiscal policy for full employment it is also important to note that 'fiscalism' did become deeply entrenched in Britain in this period. Budgetary policy became the centre piece of macro-economic policy to an extent to which no other country can compare (Dow 1964, p.178). So the question of the efficacy of those techniques clearly needs to be separated from the question of their importance for policy. The latter may have been placed on claims as to the former which in retrospect appears hardly justified. (Though also based on the perceived failings of monetary policy, the major alternative, on which see Dow, Ch. IX).

The full employment policies of the post-war period were not those either of the 1930s nor of the 1944 White Paper. In the 1930s the main Keynesian employment creating proposals had focussed on public works, low interest rates and perhaps direct credits to consumers. Only with How to Pay for the War did the tax level become the focus of attention (Dow, pp.179-80). Equally the emphasis on changes in government expenditure in the 1944 White Paper, soon became a focus on tax changes given the administrative barriers to and economic arguments against short-run variations in most items of government expenditure.

Neither of the above points is intended to imply that the 1950s and 1960s were somehow just the same as the 1930s except for a fortunate intense cyclical boom (which is one possible reading of Matthews' argument). The commitment to full employment did matter to policy, and the 'fiscalism' which accompanied it is also central to understanding the post-war period. Acceptance of full employment, largely based on the forces discussed above and on electoral considerations rather than other elaborated reasons, constrained policy in the 1950s and 1960s is an entirely new way. Equally the new emphasis on fiscal policy both largely derived from its perceived centrality to full employment and constrained the use of other policy measures. In Prest's (1968, p.2) somewhat sardonic view the "predominant view of the time (was) one of being roughly 101 per cent certain of the rightness of the principles of Keynesian fiscal policy and 99 per cent certain of their practicality". On such certainties was the 'new regime' founded. In Chapter 9 their crumbling away is discussed.

NOTES

1.   I am grateful for helpful comments on the ideas in this chapter from members of seminars at the Institute of Historical Research, London University and the University College of Wales, Aberystwyth.

2.   Ibid., pp.325-6; R. Stone, 'The Use and Development of National Income and Expenditure Estimates', in D. Chester (ed), Lessons of the British War Economy, (C.U.P., Cambridge, 1951), pp.83-101. On Treasury opposition to inflation see also W.K. Hancock and M.M. Gowing, The British War Economy, (H.M.S.O., London, 1949), pp.47-9.

3.   For example P.R.O., CAB.87/63, EC.43/6, 16 October 1943.

4.   Beveridge's Full Employment in a Free Society, (Allen and Unwin, London, 1944) was a thorough-going Keynesian document. But two years earlier, at the time of his Social Insurance and Allied Services, (H.M.S.O., London, 1942), he was already assuming the possibility of full employment after the war - this was one of the three basic assumptions of his report.

5.   "So those in political societies who apply the technologists style of thought to the business of government have, in fact, taken for granted the political devices by which some things emerge as problems, and some other things are submerged as irrelevancies. Politics defines what the inhabitants of a state think should be the problems to be solved", B. Crick, In Defence of Politics, (Penguin, Harmondsworth, 1964), p.10.

6.   The Old World and the New Society. G.D.H. Cole in similar vein wrote "socialism stood for rationality - indeed, it was rationality - for it represented a co-ordinated social control of economic life aimed at the maximisation of plenty. In other words, socialism meant planning - the incarnation of rationality", A.W. Wright, G.D.H. Cole and Socialist Democracy, (Clarendon Press, Oxford, 1979), p.199.

7.   Hansard, 21 June 1944, Col. 213. Some on the Labour benches did not take kindly to this line of argument, Cols. 246-8, 363.

8.   For example in Scandinavia, F. Castles, The Social Democratic Image of Society, (Routledge and Kegan Paul, London, 1978). This peculiar emphasis on nationalisation in British socialist politics is discussed in J. Tomlinson, The Unequal Struggle? British Socialism and the Capitalist Enterprise, (Methuen, London, 1982).

9.   The White Paper "has been produced by an all party government and it merits as such that, malcontents apart, any reasonable man should be willing to accept it at least as a basis for further exploration", Economist, 146, 3 June 1944, p.739.

10. For example on a copy of a statement by Keynes on war aims in 1941 Churchill wrote: "I should not have thought it was a very good moment to launch this economic manifesto when all our minds are concentrated, or ought to be concentrated, on the struggle", P.R.O., PREM 4, 100/5, 24 May 1941. Also A. Calder, People's War, (Panther, London, 1969), p.616.

11. On the standard of living see S. Pollard, The Development of the British Economy 1914-67, (Arnold, London, 1969), pp.289-96. On nutritional standards see J. Boyd Orr, Food, Health and Income, (Macmillan, London, 1936), esp. pp.18-9, J. Burnett, Plenty and Want, (Nelson, London, 1966), pp.224-57. For a less "optimistic" view see C. Webster, "Healthy or Hungry Thirties?", History Workshop 13, (Spring, 1982), pp.110-29.

12. The inapplicability of this argument to the First World War is argued by P. Abrams, "The Failure of Social Reform 1918-20", Past and Present 24, (February, 1963), pp.43-64).

13. By a War Cabinet decision of 23 August 1940.

14. It was not true of the First World War. Social amelioration was offered (especially in housing) as an after the event "reward" for the war effort, or probably more important as a means of defusing unrest especially amongst demobilised soldiers. See for example M. Swenarton, Homes Fit For Heroes, (Heinemann, London, 1981), Ch. 4.

15. A similar discounting of the role of economic theory in generating the economic growth objectives normally associated with development economics is apparent in D. Rimmer, "Have Not Nations: The Prototype", Economic Development and Cultural Change, 27, 2, (April, 1979), pp.307-25 and H.W. Arndt, "Economic Development: A Semantic History", Economic Development and Cultural Change, 29, 3, (April 1981), pp.457-66. See also Chapter 4 below.

16. The closest I know to an explicit Marxist discussion of the policy of full employment is Kalecki's account of why capitalists would oppose such a policy, M. Kalecki, "Political Aspects of Full Employment", Political Quarterly 14, 4, (Winter, 1943), pp.322-31. On North America see N. Apple, "The Rise and Fall of Full Employment Capitalism", Studies in Political Economy 4, (Autumn, 1980), pp.5-39 and R.B. Duboff, "Full Employment: The History of a Receding Ideal", Politics and Society 17, 1 (Autumn, 1977), pp.1-25.

Chapter Two

THE BALANCE OF PAYMENTS AND THE EXCHANGE RATE

At first sight to ask why governments "worry about" their balance of payments may appear absurd. Clearly it can be argued that as long as separate monetary areas exist then there will exist a balance of payments problem, a problem of maintaining some kind of equilibrium between international receipts and expenditures. It may be objected that this concern can be abolished via floating exchange rates; in practice there seems to have been no case where a country's authorities have not "taken a view" as to the appropriate exchange rate. So countries may be said to have always either a balance of payments or an exchange rate policy.

However if we look back to the later part of the nineteenth century, it is clear that at that time neither governments nor anyone else perceived the existence of a balance of payments or exchange rate problem in anything like their modern guise. In Britain in the second half of the nineteenth century the conduct of policy in this area was almost entirely with current or prospective gold flows.[1] Under the gold standard as it existed at that time, the Bank did not simply allow international flows of gold to determine domestic monetary conditions, but intervened, especially by use of the Bank Rate, to regulate these flows. Excessive gold flows functioned as signs of a threat to the standard and Bank Rate, in British circumstances, was an effective weapon to repel any such threats, given the central position of the U.K. in the international economy (Keynes 1972, Ch. 2).

Thus the gold standard system did not mean that national objectives were wholly absent, though clearly the scope for their pursuit was greatly circumscribed by the close link between domestic and international economic activity given the central

position of the U.K. in the international economy.[2]
But adherence to the standard did mean that the
authorities' concern was focussed on the 'residual'
of gold flows, rather than on any of the components
of international transactions, and the exchange rate
treated as 'given'. The 'Balance of Payments' only
existed insofar as it showed up in the movement of
gold into and out of London. By contrast, modern
balance of payments policy is largely based on
concern with other than simply the 'bottom line' of
international transactions, and in conditions where
to a greater or lesser extent the exchange rate is
also a policy variable.

Broadly speaking, we may ascribe the creation
of a balance of payments and exchange rate policy
problem in its modern sense to the breakdown of the
gold standard system, combined with the growth of
domestic economic management. The breakdown of the
gold standard undercut the semi-automatic workings
of international transactions and thus the focus of
concern on gold flows. The breakdown of that
standard was partly conditioned by the unwillingness
of certain countries to accept the consequences of
adherence to the standard for their own economies,
to abide by the "rules of the game" (e.g. France and
the U.S.A. in the 1920s).[3] This implies that a
desire for domestic economic management was one of
the reasons for the breakdown of the gold standard.
Equally, the breakdown of the standard unintention-
ally opened the way for economic management in
countries like Britain. These two forces interacted
to make focus on the balance of payments necessary
both because gold flows no longer functioned as
simple signals of international equilibrium, and
because the transactions that underlay these flows
impacted on domestic economic activity, and therefore had to be somehow incorporated in schemes for
managing that level of activity. (This was of course
especially true in open economies like Britain, and
it is hardly surprising that so much of the pioneering work on the balance of payments was done in the
U.K. - see further below).

Once the balance of payments had emerged as a
separate policy problem there was still a great deal
of latitude in the way in which that problem was and
is conceived. So this chapter will attempt to do two
things. First to look in more detail at the story
sketched above about how the balance of payments
came into existence as a problem, (which will
involve in this case going back considerably before

1940 if the account is to make much sense). Secondly to look at the ways in which this new problem functioned in economic policy discussions, especially around the Second World War and the immediate post-war years. Chapter Seven will look further at the later development of the balance of payments problem.

The Origins of the Problems of the Balance of Payments

The general absence of concern with the balance of payments in the nineteenth century is reflected in the absence of balance of payments statistics "The only official statistics on the items making up the balance of payments collected before 1914 were the monthly import and export figures. Private surveys also provided a few very tentative estimates of some of our invisible earnings in particular years, as well as series showing the volume of new loans on the London market by overseas borrowers" (Foot 1972, p.346).

The collection of import and export figures may be seen as a result of the pre-free trade concern with the balance of trade, a term which Viner (1937, p.9) says originated in 1615 in the "mercantilist" era. In the nineteenth century the visible trade figures were put to some use by economists, not in the context of the 'balance of payments', but in relation to the predominant economists concerns of the time - the gains from trade, the relation of trade to banking mechanisms and the adjustment of trade under simple specie flow mechanisms (see Viner 1937). Of course the trade figures were deployed in policy controversies, notably that on protectionism, but the 'space' for such controversies was greatly restricted by the agreement on adherence to the gold standard and the arguments themselves were often around the effect of trade on Britain's gold reserves (see Tomlinson 1981A, Ch. 3).

Changes in the quality and quantity of statistics on foreign transactions mirrored the demise of the nineteenth century gold standard system. Most importantly, growing concern with these transactions reflected growing concern with Britain's ability to export capital, which the gold standard system had both relied upon, by providing sterling in foreign countries, and greatly aided, by providing a stability of exchange rates.

The Balance of Payments and the Exchange Rate

This point is evident in a number of ways. When the first "current account" figures were produced by the Board of Trade early in the 1920s this term was not used, rather the heading was "income available for investment overseas" (Foot 1972, p.358). Equally when the Board of Trade set up a Trade Figures Committee in 1925, the terms of reference were "to report on the existing estimates of the annual balance of payments, with particular reference to the powers of this country to make overseas investments" (P.R.O., T160, 1926, para. 1).

In the nineteenth century the scale and financing of foreign investment had rarely been perceived as a problem. There were no official figures on income from overseas investments, and after the First War the first official 'guesstimates' were still based on Paish's estimates of 1909 and 1911 (Ibid., para. 3).

Concentration on gold flows in the nineteenth century, means that as long as Britain could sustain the willingness of foreigners to hold sterling, and thus not threaten Britain's slender reserves, the underlying transactions were not of concern. As Lindert (1969, p.79) aptly states "Before 1914 the international community displayed an aggregate willingness to accumulate sterling, and the Bank of England likewise saw little wrong with the process as long as its own gold reserves were not declining relative to its own liabilities. Under these conditions the declining competitive position of certain British export industries and the rapid rise in imports were not countered so vigorously with deflationary measures as they would have been if the Bank had adopted the payments equilibrium goals of the post-war era".

Lindert's stress on the Bank's focus on its own liabilities brings in a further illustration of the veil of semi-ignorance which to modern eyes enveloped contemporary discussion. In 1913 Keynes had argued that one of the peculiarities of Britain's position as a gold standard country, and which made that standard work much better for her than for other countries, was that she was "predominantly a creditor in the international short loan market...." (Keynes 1971, p.13). In 1931 the Macmillan Committee could lament the loss of this position "Before the War London's short-term position with the rest of the world was probably well balanced. Today her gross liabilities for foreign short-term bills and deposits are largely in excess of her claims in respect of her acceptances" (CMND. 3897, para. 349).

Yet the basis of these statements does not seem to have been correct, and Britain was a short-term debtor even before 1931 (Ford 1952, p.181; Lindert 1969, pp-56-7).

Yet this 'ignorance' is of course relative only to particular conceptions of what is to count as knowledge. Broadly speaking, before World War One, the functioning of the gold standard, and the related ease of export of capital, did nothing to generate problems which would force a rethink of the appropriate manner of assessing Britain's international economic position and performance.

By the time the official committee on the Trade Figures was established in 1925, the gold standard could of course no longer be treated as <u>datum</u>. Whilst after floating since 1918, Britain had achieved the objective of returning to the standard in April 1925, it was now generally perceived that being on the standard was both problematic as a desirable objective and also problematic of attainment. In particular, the scale of British foreign investment was seen as a policy problem in a manner quite unlike the nineteenth century, and the major thrust of the Committee's Report was to try and put discussion of this problem on a more rational basis, by pressing for improvements in the data on which such decisions could be made. Actual regulation of foreign investment had been introduced in 1914 as a war contingency. It was maintained in the post-war period, largely for internal, mainly debt management reasons, though in times of foreign exchange crises also for external reasons, in 1925, 1929 and 1931 (Atkin 1970). However these controls were very reluctantly agreed by the authorities, were usually quickly removed (as in 1925), and the weight of official opinion was against them.[4]

Thus the late 1920s may be characterised as a period of continued attachment to the gold standard, intellectual as well as institutional, but on terms which forced a new concern with the correlates of that policy. In particular, a new concern with the transactions which underlay Britain's world financial position. The Macmillan Committee reflected this. It defended on pragmatic grounds the gold standard system, and argued that the authorities should "try and make the existing system work" (para. 254). At the same time, it reflected upon the greater demand for foreign lending than before 1914 relative to the surplus Britain had for that purpose (para. 349). Whilst anxious to maintain this foreign lending position, the Report of the Committee

stressed the strains this imposed, especially in
conditions where much of this lending was financed
from short-term credits. The new scale and volatility of these credits required above all a much
larger Bank of England reserve than had traditionally been considered appropriate. Thus on the eve of
the gold standard's demise, Macmillan re-inforced
the traditional gold standard concern with the state
of the reserves, though now these were seen in a
slightly different context as having an 'optimum'
amount relative to the other items in the balance of
payments, rather than as simply the sole sign of the
health of Britain's international transactions.

Unsurprisingly, the Macmillan Committee also
recommended the collection of more balance of payments statistics, especially relating to short-term
liabilities and assets. When in a few weeks in 1931
over £200m. disappeared across the exchanges from
London, the Bank of England was stimulated to
collect such figures for the first time.[5] Such
figures were also of interest when the Bank wanted
to assess the appropriate value for sterling in the
period of floating in the 1930s (see further below).
But as Sayers (1976, p.473) stresses, "These figures,
while useful when assessing the adequacy of the gold
reserves, were too small a corner of the total
picture to throw any sure light on the valuation of
sterling". More generally, it is of note that in
Sayers' account it is precisely in this period of
the 1930s that the Bank began "thinking also in
terms of the balance of international payments",
(p.473) as a different approach from the previously
popular purchasing power parity notion, to the idea
of the appropriate valuation of sterling. Thus it
was as a relatively minor evaluative device that the
notion of the balance of payments in something like
the modern sense entered Threadneedle Street.

In 1931 of course the gold standard collapsed.
Control over foreign investments was tightened and
maintained (Richardson 1936, pp.69-75), though this
was probably not the main reason why in the 1930s
the net flow of capital was into Britain.[6] The
exchange rate became the object of policy for the
first time. Previously, in the period up to April
1925, official action was aimed at returning to the
gold standard, for which a given exchange rate was
seen as a pre-condition rather than an end result.
Indeed the discussions prior to the 1925 decision
show how far we are removed from 'modern'
(especially 1960s) discussions of the exchange rate.
Strikingly those discussions did not involve a

discussion of the exchange rate in the sense of
involving an assessment of the effects of changes in
relative international prices on the different
components of the balance of payments. Such an
attempt does not seem to have been made until that
of Moggridge (1972, Appendix I). As he notes (p.245)
"At that time, no attempt was made to attach very
precise estimates as to the effects of appreciating
the exchange to $4.86......".

By the 1930s Britain had some of the elements
of a balance of payments policy, as well as the
concern with the exchange rate there were also of
course general import controls from 1931. However
these latter were introduced for a whole series of
reasons, and not just for 'balance of payments'
reasons in the modern sense (see also Tomlinson
1981A, Ch. 7). Generally, the 1930s was a period
when the demise of the gold standard allowed a
'space' for the re-orientation of economic policy
concerns towards the domestic economy. The possibility of managing that domestic economy was greatly
enhanced by the loosening of the external constraint
of the gold standard, especially under conditions
where Britain was in the very unusual position of
being a net receiver of capital, and was able to use
some of the foreign exchange accruing in this way to
accumulate reserves.

The Balance of Payments and Economic Management

I have discussed elsewhere (Tomlinson 1981A, Ch. 8;
1981B) the conditions under which economic management grew in the period after 1931. One of the
points stressed was the relatively small part played
by economic theory in this growth, especially
compared with the space given to developments in
economic theory in many accounts. The same general
point may be made in the current context. Whilst
changes in economic theory relating to the balance
of payments did come in the nineteen thirties, the
major integration of the balance of payments into
modern macro-economic theory is really a post-war
phenomenon (see further below).

At the most general level the rise of concern
with the balance of payments, in something like the
modern sense, can be seen simply as a logical
correlate of domestic demand management, in an
economy where international transactions are a substantial element in total economic activity. But
this linkage was certainly not one forged overnight,

and seems in Britain to have been the result of a
series of partial transformations.

Under the peculiar nineteenth century conditions of Britain's attachment to the gold standard
there is little evidence of direct short-term
conflict between Britain's adherence to that standard and domestic employment (e.g. Lindert, p.43).
Certainly there is little evidence of a policy perception of such a conflict, partly because unemployment was not largely seen as an 'economic' problem
(Tomlinson 1981A, Ch. 1). Fundamentally, the main
instrument of international adjustment under the
gold standard was seen in Britain as the Bank Rate,
the effects of changes in that Rate being thought of
as largely exhausting themselves in the short-term
money markets. (The effects on other countries'
domestic activity of course may well have been less
neutral, for example, Argentina (Ford 1962,
Chs. 7-9).

A shift towards concern with the domestic
implications of changes in the Bank Rate is apparent
in the early 1920s. One of the major reasons for the
maintenance of control over the export of capital
after the end of the First War was because of the
concern with debt management. This was especially
on the part of the Bank of England, which after 1919
took over from the Treasury as the main agency concerned to control (albeit by 'suasion') the export
of capital. The Bank of England was, as Howson
(1975, Conclusions) stresses, "obsessed" by the
enormous debt accumulated by the end of the war,
though we may think this is a perfectly explicable
'obsession' given the Bank of England's institutional function as manager of the National Debt.

Whilst this concern with the debt remained
throughout the inter-war years, it receded somewhat
in the wake of the conversion of a large part of
that debt to a long-term basis in the early 1920s.
Once however it was conceded that the level and
changes in Bank Rate had any domestic repercussions,
then these could relatively easily be extended to
embrace domestic investment, and therefore employment. In 1919-24 this was definitely not a concern
of the authorities (Atkin 1970, p.332), but the
separation of the domestic economy from the effects
of Bank Rate changes became the more difficult to
sustain as both concern with unemployment mounted,
and the Bank Rate mechanism appeared to lose its
ability to 'solve' Britain's external balance
problems without incurring domestic unemployment as
a consequence.

The Balance of Payments and the Exchange Rate

Nevertheless in the period of the restored gold standard (1925-31), it was concern with the stability of the exchange rate which dominated. As Winch argues (1972, p.99) "In the history of the idea of "conscious and deliberate management" of the economy, the return to gold in 1925 was a backward step. This is not to say that British governments did not make efforts to alleviate unemployment during this period; but fears, real and imaginary, for the external stability of the pound meant that efforts in this direction were severely hampered".

As has already been argued, to suggest a two-fold origin of modern concern with the balance of payments in the breakdown of the gold standard and the rise of concern with domestic economic management, especially employment, is not to point to two separate causes. Rather the gold standard system came under challenge partly because of the (potential or actual) conflict it created between domestic and international policy. Equally the demise of the gold standard gave a great opening for 'experimentation' with forms of economic management previously excluded by adherence to the gold standard.

After 1931, and especially after 1935, the exchange rate became an object of policy and was managed, at least in part, in order to maximise exports for employment reasons. Of course it is important to stress that the fall in the exchange rate after September 1931 was not a deliberate policy of devaluation; it was forced on the authorities. Equally the Exchange Equalisation Account did not so much actively attempt to reduce the exchange rate, rather it prevented a rise which would otherwise have taken place especially in the 1935-38 period (Waight 1939; Sayers 1976, pp.416-30, 463-75). In addition it must be said that holding the exchange rate down was also implied by a policy of reserve accumulation, so it was not only for employment reasons that such a policy was pursued. In many ways, therefore, the management of the exchange rate was like the policy of cheap money. It originally arose accidentally rather than from a deliberate government design. It could be, and was, justified in terms of employment effects, but had other objectives as well, in the same way as cheap money was predominantly a policy concerned with debt management rather than employment (Winch 1972, p.213).

Exactly the same points may be made about that other great break in external policy of 1931, the imposition of general tariffs and Imperial

Preference. This could be and was justified on
employment grounds, but it obviously had many other
objectives. Winch (p.214) stresses governmental
concern to use tariffs to bargain for industrial and
agricultural re-organisation. Many in the Conservative Party seem to have viewed protection as important mainly as a step on the road to Imperial
Preference and greater Empire integration, though
this latter could also be rationalised in terms of
employment creation, as it was for example by Amery.

Overall the 1930s saw policies being more and
more justified, if only post hoc, on grounds of
employment effects, and this included external
policies as much as purely domestic ones. A shift
was taking place in the objectives of the institutions of policy-making. This is illustrated by a
rather trivial but suggestive case. In 1919 for the
first time there was introduced into Britain an
Export Credit Insurance Scheme - on a temporary
basis. This scheme staggered through the 1920s, with
little effect. After various reorganisations a new
temporary scheme was introduced in 1930, on the
basis of Employment creation. In 1937 this was made
permanent - though in the face of considerable
reluctance on the part of the Treasury (Aldcroft
1962).

A commentator (Abrams 1946, p.3) could suggest
that unlike the 1940s, exports in the 1930s were
encouraged to create work. This has a certain truth,
but only a limited one. Certainly it cannot be said
that in this respect the government acted vigorously
to manage foreign trade to aid employment. Indeed,
of course, the 1930s was a period of marked decline
in the share of British National Income derived from
trade, and thus fitted in with policies which
focussed on domestic policies, especially of fiscal
retrenchment and industrial rationalisation, which
largely defined the parameters within which policy
operated. Broadly the 'management' of foreign
transactions was concerned to insulate these domestic policies from external influences.

These changes in the parameters of policy-making were followed,[7] rather than caused, by changes
in economic theory, culminating in Meade's systematic integration of balance of payments theory into
macro-economics (Meade 1951).

Earlier Keynesian work was mainly concerned
with balance of payments adjustment via international trade multipliers, thus applying new concepts to
a very traditional problem. Meade broke with this by
focussing on policy as opposed to automatic adjust-

43

ment mechanisms, as well as integrating price and income effects in the discussion of adjustment (Corden 1965, pp.10-12). The policy orientation of Meade's work led him to assume policy objectives of domestic and foreign balance as the basis for his discussion. This led to criticisms (Corden, pp. 12-13) that he had injected 'value judgements' into his theoretical constructs. By the time Meade wrote his book however these objectives could be treated as 'natural', as not requiring a defence. (However the related question of the status of the balance of payments as an object in its own right is returned to in Chapter 7 below).

However whilst these changes in economists' theory are not entirely beside the point, (they presumably are at least some kind of index of changes in policy perceptions), they are not I would suggest central changes such as those that had occurred prior to the Second World War. Some assessment of the role of economic theory in balance of payments policy thereafter is given in the next section.

The Post-War Payments Problem
In 1959 the Radcliffe Committee in outlining the major objectives of British economic policy focussed on two particular objectives relating to the balance of payments. One was "some contribution, implying a margin in the balance of payments, to the economic development of the outside world", the other, "A strengthening of London's international reserves, implying further margin in the balance of payments" (Radcliffe 1959, para. 69).

The first objective, the capacity to export long-term capital on a substantial scale, was seen by Radcliffe mainly based on "broad international policy, but is also based on a belief that the prosperity and growth of the British economy itself depends upon steady and rapid growth in the less developed parts of the world" (para. 59). The second objective, the strengthening of the reserves, was seen as crucial to the maintenance of the exchange rate of the pound in the face of periodic sterling crises. "This country stands, determined to maintain a fixed and stable exchange rate" the Chancellor of the Exchequer had said in 1956. (House of Commons, 26 July).

These dual objectives shaped the evidence given by the Treasury to the Radcliffe Committee, and in particular its view that Britain should attempt to run a current account surplus of up to £450m. per annum in order to accumulate reserves, the better to defend sterling, and to allow for the desired scale of foreign investment (Radcliffe Committee, Minutes of Evidence, Q13358).

The balance of payments objectives, of large scale capital exports and a fixed exchange rate, were arguably predominant throughout the period from soon after the end of the Second World War until into the nineteen sixties. They in turn emerged from the revolution in the British balance of payments brought about by the Second World War, and the parallel developments in the perceptions of the balance of payments. This section of this chapter will be concerned with these developments up until approximately the publication of the Radcliffe Report.

Revolution is an appropriate term to describe the changes in the British balance of payments during the Second World War, for in three major areas there was a change of tremendous proportions (Bloomfield 1945). These were the enormous deficits accumulated on the visible account, the scale of loss of foreign investments and thereby the loss of invisible receipts, and the accumulation of new liabilities, especially in sterling, the "sterling balances". Some idea of the scale of the first of these is given by changes in Table 2.1.

Table 2.1:   British Trade During World War Two (£m.)

Total Exports	Year	Total Imports
533	1938	920
486	1939	886
437	1940	1152
378	1941	1145
276	1942	997
240	1943	1234
281	1944	1309
450	1945	1104

Source: Central Statistical Office: Statistical Digest of the War, (H.M.S.O., London, 1951).

The Balance of Payments and the Exchange Rate

The deterioration in the trading position of the U.K. reflected the change in the use of domestic resources brought about by the scale of mobilisation in the war. At the beginning of the war there may have been some hope of at least a residual "business as usual" but this quickly disappeared. "After some early vicissitudes, however, the Treasury came to accept the almost complete diversion of resources from the export industries" (Sayers 1956, p.267). The Bank of England had been concerned with the current balance even before the war began, and after 1940 it focussed attention mainly on external policy including the current balance (Sayers 1976, p.588).

After the war some looked back in astonishment at the extent to which the authorities had down-graded considerations of exports; noting the "single minded, almost reckless, disregard of consideration of post-war prospects" (Balogh in Worswick and Ady 1952, p.477). From the summer of 1940 "Britain's military effort had been discordant with her economic strength; the resources necessary for victory could not be mobilised without casting away resources necessary for the nation's likelihood when victory was achieved" (Hancock and Gowing 1949, p.522). This of course was unsurprising in the face of the problems of 1940, policy was guided by the notion that "the future must be entirely sacrificed to the overwhelming needs of the present" (Ibid.).

This policy was not sustainable for ever of course, and only the introduction of Lend-Lease made possible the continuation of the scale of resources devoted to the war effort. However Lend-Lease raised new difficulties, because one of the conditions for the grant of such aid was that Lend/Lease goods were not to be embodied in exports (Sayers 1956, pp.398-403). British attempts to expand her exports, especially towards the end of the war, thus raised conflict with those in America who had never really liked Lend/Lease, and were certainly determined to prevent it being used to compete with America's own exports. Nevertheless, in the short-run Lend-Lease was vital to the British trading position, given that by 1943 British exports were down to under one-third of the pre-war volume.

By the time Lend-Lease was fully effective in 1943/44, Britain had already greatly depleted her reserves, sold a large proportion of her readily saleable dollar assets, and over the war as a whole was to sell approximately one quarter of her over-seas assets, worth about £1,118m. in current prices.

Finally there was the accumulation of sterling liabilities. These arose mainly because certain underdeveloped countries, notably India and certain countries in the Middle East, were net dollar earners whilst at the same time running surpluses with the U.K. Britain was thus able to finance a considerable proportion of her imports by persuading these countries to accept credits on Britain rather than current payments.

These three aspects defined the major circumstances in which Britain's balance of payments position existed by the end of the war. Central to policy discussions was also the role of the United States. For the obverse of the weakening of the British balance of payments as a result of the war, was a strengthening of the American. And, in addition, the granting of Lend-Lease gave to America a leverage over British policy which was central to British policy discussions for most of the 1940s, both during and after the war. This is notably recognised by the creation as early as 1941 of an "Official Committee on Post-War External Economic Problems and Anglo-American Co-operation", appointed by the War Cabinet, which held its first meeting in 1941. At the first meeting of this Committee James Meade spelt out the close link between the balance of payments problem Britain would face after the war and American policies, especially on multilateral free trade (PRO CAB. 87/60, 1941).

It would be inappropriate here to tell the tale of the lengthy negotiations which led to the creation of the Bretton Woods system and the more gradual but effective creation of a world free trade system. Inappropriate, both because the tale has been much told (for example Gardner 1956; Harrod 1952, Chs. 13 and 14; Keynes 1980B), and because we are only concerned here with the aspects relating to the evolution of British policy objectives.

The American objectives in these negotiations were broadly to create a system of free movement of capital and free movement of goods internationally. This was seen as economically advantageous for the United States, but also as politically important in preventing the re-emergence of authoritarian regimes like those against whom the war was fought, and whose origins were seen as partly in the discriminatory capital and trade policies of the 1930s.

The Balance of Payments and the Exchange Rate

The arguments for free trade came to prominence in discussion of the Article VII of the Mutual Aid Agreement which followed on and codified Lend-Lease. This article committed Britain and the U.S.A. to non-discrimination in trade with each other, and after acceptance in 1942 generally became known as the 'Consideration' for Lend-Lease (Sayers 1956, pp.405-13).

There was considerable ambiguity in what exactly Britain had committed itself to in signing the Mutual Aid Agreement. It was on one hand an acceptance of multilateralism; on the other hand the acceptance of this was hedged around with certain qualifications, which at least in part reflected British misgivings about the short-term possibilities of multilateral Free Trade. These misgivings were certainly initially shared by Keynes, who for example in his advocacy of free capital movement was strongly to assert the separation of that issue from the question of free trade (see Keynes 1980A, Ch. 2).

Around the question of free trade there emerged during and after the war four main policy positions.

First there were those who may be said to have been "more Keynesian than Keynes". Prominent amongst these was Balogh whose argument was essentially a defence of the kind of trade (and exchange) controls which had been employed in the war as a necessary correlate of the policy of full employment. In a number of places (e.g. in Worswick and Ady 1952; in Oxford 1944) he expressed hostility to the American policy of multilateral free trade and especially its enforcement on Britain via the loan agreement of 1945.

Whilst often linked to the Left of the political spectrum, this position differed mainly in rhetoric rather than substance from that of proponents of a much strengthened Imperial Preference. Amery argued for Imperial Preference rather than a "resuscitated internationalist laisser-faire" (Amery 1947, p.XV; also Page Croft in PRO PREM. 4/95/4, 1945). Balogh too stressed the centrality of the Sterling Area to Britain's trade prospects (Worswick and Ady 1952, p.487).

For Balogh trade controls were the direct way of linking full employment and balance of payments equilibrium (Ibid., p.495). Others argued that the link between trade and employment had been severed by the work of Keynes, inadequate domestic demand was the cause of unemployment. Exports were desirable "not to create employment but to obtain

desirable imports" (P.E.P. 1947, p.2; see also
Abrams 1946, p.3). Trade was not the way to more
employment, rather employment was the way to more
trade.

Fourthly there was the view which Keynes
personally seems to have adhered to, that whilst in
the short-run the balance of payments position might
necessitate deviations from free trade, in the
longer run such a regime was desirable. This view
saw not a direct subordination of trade and payments
policies to employment, but rather was concerned
with policies for the encouragement of the general
growth of world output and trade.

These positions are sketched not because we are
directly concerned here with the differing positions
of economists, but in order to make two points.
First, and unsurprisingly, discussion of the balance
of payments in this period usually meant some
reference to employment creation. But secondly that
this was often an indirect or merely rhetorical
reference point. For strikingly whilst employment
was enshrined on (almost) every banner, the direct
link between such an objective and the balance of
payments was strikingly little analysed and
discussed, except by the small band of 'Keynesians'
around Balogh. This comes over very much in the
Employment White Paper of 1944 (CMND. 6527). Whilst
the very first paragraph stresses Britain's dependence on imports and therefore exports, the main
policy to aid this was seen as international
economic stability, for which a prime condition was
"reasonably stable rates of exchange" (para. 3).
This of course avoided any possible new policies
to encourage exports for employment reasons, in
favour of the most traditional of policy objectives,
the maintenance of the exchange rate. This reflected
many discussions in official circles during the war,
such as the Report of the Steering Committee on
Post-War Employment which in 1944 reported on the
"International Background" and which foresaw grave
dangers of a post-war slump in the wake of an
initial boom. As remedies to this it focussed on the
encouragement of international investment, the
stabilisation of primary produce markets and the
need for maintaining demand in all the world's major
countries (CAB 87 63, 1944, paras. 33-6).

The Balance of Payments and the Exchange Rate

The Sterling Area and Foreign Investment
Such a perception of Britain's position problems
meant that post-war policies focussed particularly
on matters related to the Sterling Area and the
exchange rate. Britain still suffered from what
Strange (1971, p.47) has called the 'Top Currency
Syndrome', the belief that "the interest of the
British economy necessarily always and very closely
coincided with that of the international economy".
Thus external economic policy in the early post-war
years mainly circulated around the related issues of
the convertibility of sterling, the exchange rate,
Britain's reserve position and the sterling balances,
rather than directly on matters relating to
employment.

The question of convertibility was, with multilateral free trade, the issue upon which the United
States attempted to use its bargaining power arising
from Lend-Lease and the Washington loan of 1945 to
enforce policies on Britain. The Agreement on the
latter had as one of its clauses the return of
sterling to free convertibility within a short
period of its signature. As is well-known, this
policy was pursued to a disastrous conclusion by the
British government and was soon reversed (e.g. Kirby
1981, pp.98-100).

Part of the reason for the failure of this
policy was that many holders of sterling balances
liquidated these balances. But these balances were
themselves an important aspect of British policy in
their own right.

By the late 1930s the sterling system had three
main features. Firstly there was the widespread
practice of transacting in sterling, which spread
far outside the Commonwealth. Secondly, there was
the holding of reserves in sterling, which was
common in the Commonwealth but by no means confined
to it. Thirdly, there was the practice of making a
local currency convertible into sterling rather than
gold, which was general in the Commonwealth but also
occasionally adopted elsewhere (Harrod 1963, p.120).
This was the system which in America seems to have
aroused so much opposition. However, rather than
representing any Imperialist grand design, it seems
to have emerged piecemeal from the disintegration of
the gold standard system.

Within this sterling system the holding of
sterling as a reserve asset was not central, and was
certainly not itself a hangover from the old pre-1914
days of Britain's dominance of the gold standard,
because in that period foreign exchange holdings as

reserve assets were relatively little known especially outside the Empire. (This remains true, though work by Lindert (1969) suggests that foreign exchange was a larger proportion of international reserves - around 16 per cent - than was commonly thought before his work).[8]

The accumulation of large sterling balances during the Second World War was largely the 'accidental' consequence of the large scale military expenditures by Britain in India and the Middle East, who because of their ability to export to the U.S.A., were willing to accept sterling liabilities in return for their supply of resources to Britain's war effort. Thus there grew up a system whereby Britain operated a policy arrangement for all the sterling area (= the Commonwealth - Canada + Egypt + Palestine + Iraq) dollar receipts. During the war this policy worked to Britain's advantage, as it effectively enabled her to finance dollar purchases indirectly via the receipts of other members of the area. Once the war ended, however, these countries, many of which were traditional capital importers and had a large accumulation of unsatisfied demand, would quickly turn this policy into a liability. This view was strongly argued by Keynes in a Memorandum circulated to the War Cabinet (P.R.O. CAB. 66 (52), 1944).

He coupled a generally pessimistic view of the post-war impact of the sterling balances, with a proposal that the capital value of the sterling balances should be discharged by exports over a prolonged period. "This system should provide a most serviceable aid to the policy of full employment since we could offer to expedite the repayment of our debt by special exports at times when normal demand was falling away" (Ibid., para. 25). This attempt to directly link employment to the sterling balances seems to have been favoured by the Board of Trade, but nothing seems to have come of it.

The great importance of the sterling balances for British policy was particularly in focussing so much attention on Britain's reserve position. The worries about Britain's short-term liabilities had been the reason for the Macmillan Committee's call for Britain to accumulate greater reserves. Willy nilly this had happened in the 1930s, with the inflows into sterling, and a year before the war these reserves had risen to a value in excess of £1,000m. Sterling came under pressure before the war began, and by September 1939 the figure was down to £620m. By April 1941 it was down to £66m. - or £3m.

if one subtracted £63m. of gold liabilities (Ibid., para. 29). Here, too, the position had only been saved by Lend-Lease, though the Americans did not like the growth of Britain's reserves which followed Lend-Lease, sometimes reducing the scale of that aid, when these accumulations were held to be excessive.

Whilst the U.S.A. tended to see the accumulation of reserves as a violation of the spirit of Lend-Lease, and as part of Britain's excessive zeal to preserve itself as a world power - part of the "Sterling Area, Imperial Preference and all that" (Sayers 1956, p.377) - the wartime Treasury was adamant on the need for such reserves. These were seen as an essential counterpart to the accumulation of the sterling balances, as well as for the purposes of reconstruction and multilateral trade.

The reserves were built up in the latter years of the war and in the post-war period, to reach over £1,000m. again by 1958 (Radcliffe Report, para. 613). However the reserve/liability ratio deteriorated from about 1:1 just before the war to about 1:4 in the 1950s. Whilst the sterling balances of India and Egypt proved perhaps less intractable than wartime discussions had implied, and were successfully run down in stages, those of other countries increased in the decade or so after the war, particularly during the primary commodity boom at the time of the Korean War.

Whilst the discussions of the post-war trading regime, the sterling balances, and Britain's reserves arose directly out of the predicament of Britain at the end of the Second World War, another central aspect of Britain's post-war balance of payments problem arose less directly, that of the export of capital.

Whilst Britain did of course sell off a large fraction of her foreign capital assets during the war, and so lost a traditional source of invisible income, this was far from being the main reason for so much attention being given to the promotion of capital export in the post-war period. This seems to have arisen from two other sources.

First there was the concern with 'economic development' in underdeveloped countries. This seems to have emerged as a concern for countries such as Britain in the 1930s, and was greatly strengthened during World War Two (see generally on this Rimmer 1979 and Arndt 1981). Development became associated especially[9] with <u>investment</u> in underdeveloped countries.

The Balance of Payments and the Exchange Rate

The other aspect of the concern with foreign investment was its relationship to domestic employment. Of course, this was not new in the 1940s; it had long been part of the defence of the scale of Britain's capital exports, and had found official expression in the Colonial Development Act of 1929 which had the "primary object of relieving unemployment in Great Britain (Ady in Worswick and Ady 1952, p.550). After the wartime commitment to full employment this linkage was again stressed and this went along with a general stress on other countries' prosperity as a condition for Britain's own (e.g. Henderson in Worswick and Ady 1952, p.71).

It is of great interest to note that Paish's well-known call for a higher level of unemployment in the 1950s was directly linked to the need to finance overseas investment. "It is urgently necessary that the U.K. should henceforward restrain its home demand sufficiently both to supply its share of the resources so urgently needed by the developing countries of the Commonwealth and at the same time to begin to restore the international financial position......" (Paish 1956, p.39).

Foreign investment (and therefore the current account surplus to finance it) could be amenable to all political opinions if presented as aid to poor countries, especially if those poor countries happened to be within the Commonwealth. However the post-war flow of capital were not in the main towards those countries which most urgently needed development resources. The largest recipients were South Africa, Australia and Canada.

The Exchange Rate

During the Second World War, as during the First, the question of the exchange rate was largely in abeyance. A rate of $4.03^{10} was fixed in 1939, and for most of the war this rate was taken for granted rather than actively pursued. However the accumulation of sterling balances ' solidified' the attachment to this exchange rate, and this was reinforced with the post-war commitment to a fixed exchange rate currency regime (Sayers 1956, p.461).

The pound was fixed at this level until after the fiasco of convertibility had passed, until 1949. In that year the pound was devalued by 30 per cent.

A striking feature of this decision was how untraumatic it was compared with that of 1967. (This seems the appropriate comparison, for 1931 was not in the same way a 'deliberate' decision but was

to a much greater extent forced on the authorities;
1949 was thus in a sense the first 'modern' devaluation). Whilst in 1967 the decision was accompanied
by much agonising by those responsible for the
decision and equally a great mass of non-governmen-
tal comment (see below Chapter 7) that of 1949
seems to have been largely unproblematic for those
who pursued it. The decision invited relatively
little comment by those concerned, and many of those
who have written on the period, Worswick and Ady
(1952) for example, only mention the event in
passing, and as much for its effects on Stafford
Cripps' wage freeze as for its international consequences. (However recently Cairncross and
Eichengreen have given the first extensive account,
1983, Ch. 4).

The rather low key way in which this decision
was, and has been, handled seems largely because the
devaluation can be seen as simply expressing the
acceptance of the reality of the greatly increased
relative strength of the dollar after World War Two,
a change not only vis-a-vis Britain but also the
other Sterling Area and Western European countries
who followed suit and devalued against the dollar
(unlike in 1967). As Cairncross and Eichengreen
(p.141) put it "what was in question was the value
of the dollar rather than the value of the pound".

However it is clear that the decision was
occasioned by two particular features of Britain's
position in 1949. First there was the slow down in
export growth which accompanied the relative mild
U.S. recession of 1949. Second there was the desire
to undercut the activities of the speculators once
and for all. These latter were active against
sterling in 1949, and the main reason for such a
large devaluation (30%) was in order to remove any
basis for speculation against a further devaluation.
One might also note that the decision was based on
balance of payments information which despite
official calls for change (e.g. CMND. 6527, para.
83) remained woefully inadequate, and which has
subsequently been suggested to have been grossly
inaccurate (Meyer, Corner and Parker 1970, p.546).

Subsequent critics of the scale of the devaluation have suggested that it was at best greatly
overdue. The undervaluation has been criticised for
its inflationary effects (Harrod 1963, pp.22-7) and
for its effects in slowing technological change and
growth in Britain (Meyer, Corner and Parker 1970,
pp.547-67). What is striking is that devaluation,
especially on such a scale ran counter to the well-

known wartime view of the Treasury (and others) that
devaluation was unlikely to help Britain's trade
problems because of the trade inelasticities. Thus
it may well be that, in 1949, the authorities were
panicked by short-term circumstances into a policy
which in retrospect appears curiously at odds with
the attachment to defending the role of sterling as
an international currency. (Cairncross and
Eichengreen argue that Britain's trade was "in
balance" at this time in any case (1983, Ch. 4).

Perceptions of the Balance of Payments Problem
During the war it became commonplace in official
circles that in the post-war period Britain would
face two pressing international economic problems.
One would be the problem of the sterling balances,
the other would be the problem of exports. In his
Memorandum The Problem of External Finance in
Transition (PRO CAB. 66 (52), 1944), Keynes had
stressed the problems of the sterling balances and
the need to build up British reserves, but this had
been the context of a stress (para. 5) that Britain
would need a 50 per cent increase in the volume of
exports over 1938 levels (5 x 1944 levels) in order
to cope with the effects of the war. This target
soon became a commonplace (Bloomfield 1945, p.13).
    In the 1947 Economic Survey the target was
raised to 75 per cent above the 1938 level to allow
for a greater volume of imports. This ambitious target was achieved by 1950. Black notes (Worswick and
Ady 1962, pp.115-6) that the British position was

Table 2.2: Volume of British Exports in 1950
(1938 = 100)

Raw Materials	52
Textiles and Clothing	108
Food, Drink and Tobacco	135
Metals and Engine Goods	264
All Manufacturing	200
All Exports	175

Source: G.D.N. Worswick and P. Ady (eds), The
British Economy in the 1950s, (Clarendon Press,
Oxford 1962), p.15.

not perhaps as strong as these figures suggest, because despite the weakness of German and Japan Britain's share of world trade was the same as 1938, at 28 per cent. Nevertheless, such data do suggest that Britain's balance of payments problem was not centrally that of the visible trade position. Through most of the fifties Britain financed most of its imports from exports of goods, and indeed whereas in 1938 goods exports paid for only 64 per cent of goods imported in 1950 to 1959 the figure was 94 per cent (calculated from the figures in Table 2.3).

Table 2.3: **Britain's Balance of Payments 1950-59** (£ millions)

	Imports	Exports	Net Invisibles	Current Balance	Net Long-Term Lending Abroad
1950	2390	2254	433	297	not known
1951	3501	2752	330	-419	not known
1952	2959	2831	335	227	-197
1953	2896	2677	298	179	-241
1954	3020	2825	406	211	-240
1955	3432	3076	283	- 73	-183
1956	3466	3402	219	155	-241
1957	3570	3543	219	192	-298
1958	3341	3432	254	345	-259
1959	3616	3556	199	139	-232

	Changes in Sterling Balances	Overall Surplus or Deficit
1950	341	519
1951	93	-676
1952	-357	-219
1953	274	287
1954	215	208
1955	-134	-230
1956	-156	-200
1957	-174	-129
1958	67	280
1959	137	86

Source: G.D.N. Worswick and P. Ady (eds), The British Economy in the Nineteen Fifties, (Clarendon Press, Oxford, 1962), p.214.

The Balance of Payments and the Exchange Rate

Such figures were the basis for the arguments, common in the period, that Britain's balance of payments problems were not largely due to a poor visible trade performance, but rather to objectives in balance of payments policies which could not be sustained. Above all, the arguments focussed on the role of government expenditure abroad, the scale of private foreign investment, the related attempt to keep the sterling area going, and the free movement of capital into and out of London (Strange 1971, esp. Ch. 4; Shonfield 1959, Chs. 4-6).

In this critical view the authorities attempts to run a large current account surplus were the consequence of an attempt to maintain an unsustainable world economic and political role. This involved making overseas defence commitments without regard to the economic aspects "a deliberate decision to live beyond one's means" (Shonfield 1959, p.91). Coupled with this was a commitment to sustain private foreign investment, mainly in the sterling area, on a scale disproportionate to Britain's resources (Strange 1971, Ch. 4). This basis of foreign investment towards the sterling area was based partly on policy, which since 1900, with the Colonial Stocks Act, had favoured Empire and Commonwealth investment. The logic of this was twofold. One was the general support for 'growth' in underdeveloped countries already mentioned. The other was the belief that British investment underpinned the sterling area and that the sterling area was a major benefit to Britain.

This view of the sterling area was contested. Writers like Conan and Shonfield criticised this view of the Sterling Area. They stressed that whilst the Area might augment Britain's gold reserves, it at the same time made her more prone to balance of payments problems as the imbalance between liabilities and reserves in London, the "overhang", could easily encourage speculative attacks on sterling. Thus such critics opposed the authorities policy of encouraging sterling transactions, and suggested that only a fraction of the City of London's earnings would be lost if the international role of sterling were to be abandoned.

The Treasury and Bank of England offered their most extended defence of their policies before the Radcliffe Committee in 1957 to 1959. The Treasury (Memorandum of Evidence, Section 12, para. 3) outlined their perception of British economic policies as relating to:

(a)   the status of the pound as an international currency;
(b)   long-term investment overseas;
(c)   the present relationship between our external monetary assets and liabilities.
All of these issues were tied up with the question of the sterling area. The status of the pound as an international currency largely rested upon its use within that area. This use was in turn seen as con-ferring advantages upon both Britain, the sterling area and the world economy (Ibid., Section 11, para. 8; Minutes of Evidence, Qs. 2510-2562). The sterling area was also in turn the area within which most British foreign investment took place. One of the reasons why external liabilities grew post-war was because of the existence of the sterling area and the availability of capital to countries within that area.

This matrix of policy concerns then defined the basic balance of payments objectives of the authori-ties; the commitment to a large (£400-450m.) current account surplus, providing for long-term investment abroad and reserve accumulation within the context of the fixed parity of the pound.

All the aspects of this policy set came into question in evidence to Radcliffe and elsewhere.

A.C.L. Day questioned the focus on foreign investment and particularly revived the old argument that this investment was at the expense of domestic investment (Memorandum of Evidence, pp.71-6; Minutes Qs. 9891-9918;   see also Shonfield 1959, Ch. 5). It was also pointed out that the sterling area in a curious way was a mechanism whereby Britain borrowed short-term in poor countries and lent-long in rich Commonwealth countries (Streeten in Worswick and Ady 1962, p.100), which hardly matched the rhetoric of the area as a way of aiding the development of poor countries. Day also questioned the utility of the sterling area (e.g. Minutes of Q. 9965; see more generally Day 1954). Balogh questioned the focus on the use of sterling as an international currency "the insensate and exclusive concentration on the restoration of the mercantile and banking functions of the City" (Memorandum of Evidence, para. 81; see also Strange 1971, Ch. 7).

We are not centrally concerned here with the correctness or otherwise of these arguments except insofar as they bear on the formulation of the objectives of policy. Clearly the authorities at the time of Radcliffe saw their international economic policies very much in terms of the value of the pound/capital flows couple, which had dominated policy so much in the gold standard era. In many ways the Sterling Area and sterling balances controversies were the particular colour in which very much longer term policies now came to be etched. Britain's international pretensions were now scaled down to fit into the sterling area. The sterling balances were seen as an uneasy corollary of this areas existence, and one whose dangers were recognised. "The use of sterling as an international currency makes it inevitable that we should have large overseas monetary liabilities. But it does not explain their present size, which derives from economic developments in the war and post-war years and has little to do with the normal requirements of a centre for international finance. The international strength of sterling would obviously be greater if the balances could be reduced without any corresponding reduction in the reserves" (Treasury Memorandum of Evidence to Radcliffe, Section 11, para. 9; Minutes of Evidence, Q. 2581).

However, this seemingly appropriate evaluation of the dangers of the accumulation of sterling balances for balance of payments policies were somewhat undercut by other aspects of the authorities' policies. On the one hand the strong encouragement offered to foreign investment in the sterling area, which encouraged the holding of sterling balances. On the other hand, the absence of any policy to "do something" to reduce those balances. For example Day (Memorandum, paras. 27-33), called for the funding of the balances or their being taken over by an international body. This was specifically rejected by the Radcliffe Committee (Report, para. 678), albeit with the caveat of the acceptance of Day's long-term proposal for reviving Keynes' original idea of the International Monetary Fund as an international central bank. In practice there was therefore strong resistance to measures which might be seen as downgrading sterling's international role.

In the face of these two aspects of the authorities' policies, the logical conclusion was that the sterling balances should be offset in their potential effects by an increase in reserves.

Of course it might well be said that this
success of British exports was highly contingent, on
both the particular fact of the post-war weakness of
major competitors like Germany and Japan and the
more general fact of the unprecedented expansion of
world trade. As Shonfield wrote (1959, p.85) "The
truth is that the 1950s have been a period in which
any moderately efficient industrial country had
golden opportunities......".

The general expansion of world trade which
occurred in this period was liked to a fundamental
problem of international economic policy. The expansion of world trade took place for a number of
reasons, the build up of investment opportunities in
the war, the industrialisation of new areas, the
pursuit of domestic full employment in many countries, but one major condition of its existence was
undoubtedly the movement towards freer trade and
freer exchange convertibility. These were both
policies to which the British government had form-
ally committed itself from the war period, and which
were pursued with increased enthusiasm once a
Conservative government was elected in 1951. But
there was in the long-run a fundamental contradiction between the defence of the role of sterling in
all its aspects, within the defended fortress of the
sterling area, and the movement towards global
multilateralism. This contradiction was pointed to
by Balogh "What was wrong with recent British policy
was to remove unilaterally the preferential treatment of British goods (within the Commonwealth), yet
continue to act as a banker of the sterling area
without being protected against sudden growth of
capital movements, and without getting counter-
valuing advantages in the commercial field"
(Memorandum to Radcliffe, para. 81). His solution
was to maintain the trading discrimination of the
sterling area.

Day offered in some respects a similar analysis.
He argued that the sterling area was a short-term
benefit in the early post-war years, on the basis of
a tight discriminatory system, but that once this
basis was removed the sterling area would be disad-
vantageous to Britain (Radcliffe, Minutes, Q.9965;
see also Day 1954).

The working out of this contradiction was to be
central to the development of British balance of
payments policies in the 1960s and 1970s.

Conclusions

In the first two sections of this chapter some aspects of the way the notion of the balance of payments developed as a policy problem prior to the Second World War were sketched. In the next two sections the subsequent evolution of that policy problem were outlined.

This latter evolution is remarkable in the sense that it saw in many ways a reassertion of the priorities which predated the break up of the gold standard system, which initially created the balance of payments as a problem. The policies of the late nineteen fifties had remarkably little to do directly with the management of the domestic economy, and hinged around the role of sterling and the export of capital in a very nineteenth century manner, albeit now largely on a limited sterling area, rather than world stage.

In part this evolution derived from the falling away of the international constraint problem, which during and at the end of the war was seen as most likely to directly impinge on domestic economic management, the ability to pay for a full employment level of imports. As already noted, Britain enjoyed a remarkable success in expanding its exports in the post-war years, a point which was most commonly made by the critics of post-war international economic policy. As Streeten wrote (in Worswick and Ady 1962, p.77) "Although Britain was not living above her income, she did not always live within her income plus her intended lending".

This difference marked a substantial change in focus in Britain's balance of payments policies, as J. Sargent graphically outlined (Memorandum to Radcliffe, pp.236-42).

"Difficulties with the balance of payments have recurred regularly in the U.K. since the war, but their nature has been gradually changing. When the war was over the dominant question was whether as a nation we could "pay our way" internationally in the circumstances to which we have been reduced. It is now quite evident that we can from our performance in the last six years, during which our current surplus has averaged £180m. This is not to say that the question whether we can pay our way is not still frequently asked; but the fact that it is no longer asked in the form "can we export enough to pay for our capital exports" is in itself an indication of the change for the better that has taken place".

NOTES

1.   In discussing the gold standard the Bank of
England's role seems to have been <u>so</u> pre-eminent,
and so autonomous from government <u>as</u> to justify
talking of it as the policy maker.
2.   Also obviously important was the commitment
to free trade, which coupled with the commitment to
gold governed Britain's insertion into the international economy.
3.   Simply put, the 'rules of the game' implied
that a country incurring a balance of payments
surplus and hence a gold inflow should allow that
gold influx to expand the domestic money supply and
hence domestic demand for imports, thus correcting
the balance of payments surplus.
4.   For example the Official Committee on
Overseas Loans of 1925 which recommended the end of
the embargo on foreign loans introduced at the time
of the return to gold. J. Atkin, "Official Regulation of British Overseas Investment 1914-31",
<u>Economic History Review</u>, 23, 2, (May 1970),
pp.330-1.
5.   R. Sayers, <u>The Bank of England</u>, Vol. 2,
(C.U.P., Cambridge, 1976), p.473.
6. Rather the inflow reflected the relative
economic and political stability of the U.K. in the
"devil's decade".
7.   That foreign trade impacts on domestic
employment is hardly a new discovery. As Viner
stresses the idea of manipulating the balance of
payments to aid employment was present in the
earliest mercantilist writings. J. Viner, <u>Studies
in the Theory of International Trade</u>, (Harper, New
York, 1937), p.51. Rather like the theory of the
multiplier the general idea was around a long time
before being formalised in economists' writings. If
Kahn was the person who made the decisive theoretical breakthrough on the multiplier, the nearest
approach to such a formalisation for the employment
effect of foreign trade was the work of Robinson.
In her <u>Essays in the Theory of Employment</u>,
(Macmillan, London, 1937) she explicitly set out to
apply the principles of Keynes' General Theory to
foreign trade. (A discussion of which had been self-
consciously excluded from the General Theory
itself). In particular she focussed on Beggar-My-
Neighbour remedies for unemployment as were commonly
practiced in the 1930s. Overall though it is clear
that Robinson's work in this respect is very much a
"first stab", mainly descriptive in content and not

bringing about any fundamental shift in economists perceptions of these problems. A crucial work on the balance of payments in the Keynesian framework was Harrod's 2nd Edition of his <u>International Economics</u>, (Macmillan, London, 1938) which for the first time clearly recognised imports as 'leakages' from the circular flow of income and exports as a source of injection into that flow.

8.   Note also that where a country's foreign transactions are conducted mainly in another country's currency (e.g. sterling) the distinction between reserves and non-reserves becomes unclear.

9.   Later of course this link was to be challenged for ignoring the 'quality' rather than the quantity of investment.

10. Largely it would seem because $4.00 would look too much like a settled rate, and therefore any deviation from this parity a major policy change. R. Sayers, <u>Financial Policy</u> 1939-45, (H.M.S.O., London, 1956).

Chapter Three

ANTI-INFLATION

Governments have almost always condemned inflation. Economists have been more equivocal, though almost none have been willing to commit themselves to unambiguously welcoming it.[1] In some views this concern expressed by governments is paradoxical, if not positively hypocritical. Historically governments have undoubtedly been the major gainers from inflation, in the sense of having been the main gainers from the income and wealth redistribution that usually follows inflation, leaving aside the question of whether they have been its main initiators. This issue, of government benefits from inflation, is taken up in Chapter 9 below, in the context of the debates in which the issue has been posed. However, in the more general context here, it is important to note that inflation policy, unlike policy in other areas dealt with in this book, has major direct distributive consequences. In discussing policy towards inflation therefore, the clear likelihood of both gainers and losers from inflationary movements should always be borne in mind.[2]

Politicians and Economists on Inflation
Expressions by government of dislike of inflation have clearly had origins other than economic, however that word is defined. Nowhere is this more apparent than in the career of Keynes' suggestion that "Lenin is said to have declared that the best way to destroy the capitalist system was to debauch the currency ..... Lenin was certainly right" (1971, p.148). In fact Lenin never said anything of the kind, and like almost every other head of government vigorously pronounced against the evils of inflation (Fetter 1977). Some Soviet leaders may later have

rationalised the hyper-inflation of post-revolution-
ary period as pressaging the demise of money and the
transition to full communism, but this was to make a
virtue of necessity; such views quickly became
labelled an "infantile disease of leftism" (Carr
1966, pp.261, 356).

The importance of this tale is that Keynes'
linking of revolutionary change and inflation was
widely echoed after it first appeared in 1920. It
became the motif of many a bankers or politicians
speech. Its widespread use was symptomatic of the
political fears raised by inflation.

So if we ask why have governments worried about
inflation, the answer has certainly not been because
economists have clearly demonstrated that its costs
outweigh its benefits. The fear that inflation
threatens not just economic problems but the whole
fabric of society has been widespread; and in any
case economists have had no unambiguous message to
give to governments on inflation.

Broadly speaking economists have had remarkably
little to say on the costs of inflation. Most con-
troversy has of course been about the causes of
inflation (Coats 1974, p.17), and its consequences
have been more regretted than analysed. If one may
take a typical and well-known economists' analysis
of inflation (Jackman, Mulvey and Trevithick 1981),
one out of ten chapters is devoted to the effects of
inflation, and of this only three pages are devoted
to unanticipated inflation, historically by far the
most important kind. This balance of attention is
not idiosyncratic, but reflects the way in which
discussion of inflation has generally been conducted
by economists.

Prior to World War One it would seem broadly
accurate to say that inflation was discussed by
economists largely in the context of monetary dis-
turbances, clasically the Napoleonic Wars with its
movement to inconvertible paper money. Most
theorising arose from controversies over particular
bouts of inflation, resulting either from non-
economic crises like wars, or economic cycles.[3] The
downward trend of prices in the last quarter of the
century engendered some discussion of the effects of
long-run movements of prices. Marshall endorsed the
"general opinion" that a "steady upward tendency in
general prices conduces a little more to the general
well-being than does a tendency downwards, because
it keeps industry somewhat better employed". But he
equally thought downward price trends, by inducing
feelings of being worse off, encouraged people

(especially the working class) to spend their money more carefully (cited in Friedman 1974, p.33).

Broadly speaking by the time of the First World War the almost unanimous view that inflation was caused by changes in the money supply was coupled with analysis of its effects which focussed on "lead-lag" propositions, especially that wages lag behind profits in inflation; and "debtor-creditor" propositions, that debtors gain at the expense of creditors (Bach and Ando 1957, p.1). The first proposition can be traced back to Hume (Laidler and Parkin 1975, p.787), whilst the latter seems to have emerged from the debates during and after the Napoleonic Wars, reflecting in part the enormous legacy of the debt left by the war (e.g. O'Brien 1970, pp.159-67).

Whilst these notions had become embedded in economics literature by the time of the 1914 war, their importance to policy was minimal. After the end of the Napoleonic Wars the general price trend was downwards, and in any case the gold standard provided a powerful discipline against inflationary tendencies. In the twentieth as in the nineteenth century, it was to take a wartime inflation to put the question of inflation back somewhere near the centre of policy concern.

The Legacy of War
It would be difficult to exaggerate the impact of the First War and its aftermath in shaping views on inflation, both of economists and politicians (Johnson 1968, pp.108-9). In the wake of the Great War the Empires of Eastern and Central Europe collapsed to the accompaniment of hyper-inflations.[4] In Britain the price increase was far less dramatic, of the order of 150 per cent between the summer of 1914 and its peak in the spring of 1920, but it encouraged fears that Britain, too, was heading down the road of social revolution.

The institutional basis of these fears was the departure from the gold standard. Convertibility was ended de facto in 1914, but in 1919 the standard was officially abandoned in the fact of politicians' unwillingness to face the political consequences of the deflation required to return at the pre-war parity (Howson 1975, Ch. 1).

Absence of inflation and adherence to the gold standard were each seen as the condition of the other. The Cunliffe Committee, in its panegyric upon the standard, wrote "Unless the machinery which long experience was shown to be the only effective remedy for an adverse balance of trade and an undue growth of credit is once more brought into play, there will be a very grave danger of credit expansion in this country and a foreign drain of gold which might jeopardise the convertibility of our note issue and the international trade position of the country" (para. 15). The authorities were convinced that inflation, reluctantly accepted in the absence of easily available alternatives during the war, was the major post-war problem. Its continuation threatened to "dislocate all economic relationships" (Howson 1975, p.12).

As the political dangers appeared to diminish, the politicians eventually allowed the weight of official and expert opinion to tell, and in April 1920 Bank Rate was raised sharply to 7 per cent as a way of bringing the post-war inflationary boom to a close. (It was in any case in retreat, as the restocking which largely initiated the boom came to a natural conclusion).

Keynes was far from the least vociferous opponent of this inflationary spiral. In a memorandum at the time he wrote:

> Very grave issues are at stake. A continuance of inflationism and high prices will not only depress the exchanges but by their effect on prices will strike at the whole basis of contact, of security, and of the capitalist system generally (quoted, Howson 1975, p.20).

The Treasury therefore pursued a policy which was clearly hostile to its interests as a debtor. Unlike most other belligerents, Britain endured neither a hyper-inflation nor a currency reform after World War One, and so the debt accumulated in the war (amounting to about two-thirds of war expenditures), hung-over Britain's policy thereafter. Indeed, rather than trying to reduce the real value of the debt the Treasury focussed its attention on funding it, and therefore reducing any potential inflationary repercussions from its financing.

For the Bank of England the emphasis was perhaps on the gold standard rather than inflation per se. Nevertheless, the post-war inflation was seen and used as an example of what allowing monetary management to be lost by the central bank to the politicians was likely to involve. It provided a handy stick to beat any proponents of managed money who might appear.

In 1923 Keynes published his <u>Tract on Monetary Reform</u>. This can best be seen not as a precursor to future work, but as a highly effective summary of what was said by most economists at the time about the effects of inflation, and which was often also reflected in the sayings and doings of politicians (cf. Harrod 1952, p.472).

At the centre of the argument was the view that deflation and inflation was asymmetrical in their effects. Deflation was said largely to effect the production of wealth, but inflation its distribution. The major losers from the redistributions caused by inflation are investors. "We conclude that inflation redistributes wealth in a manner very injurious to the investor, very beneficial to the businessman and, probably, in modern industrial conditions, beneficial to the wage earner. Its most striking consequence is its <u>injustice</u> to those who in good faith have committed their savings to money rather than to things" (Keynes 1971A, p.29). This point was made more explicit: "Throughout the continent the pre-war savings of the middle class, so far as they were invested in bonds, mortgages or bank deposits, have been largely or entirely wiped out" (Ibid., p.16).

This striking attack on the evils of inflation catches the mood of much of the 1920s, and perhaps helps to explain why deflationary policies could be so strongly adhered to.

The alleged stimulus given to economic activity by upward movement in the price level was registered in the <u>Tract</u> (p.17) as "long recognised" but did not form a central part of the argument. It was however a central part of the <u>Treatise on Money</u>. Whilst stressing that "The experience of the post-war period led many of us to advocate stability of the price level as the best possible objective of practical policy" (1971B, Vol. I, p.263). However Chapter 30 of volume two of the Treatise was wholly given over to the illustration of the beneficial effects for growth of the profit inflation thesis, especially focussing on the expansion engendered by influx of Spanish bullion into Western Europe in the sixteenth century and the depressing effects of the shortage of bullion in the 1890s.

In the context of the policies then being pursued in Britain, and Keynes' view of these, this focus on the benefits of mild inflations was explicable. However whilst the hostility to inflation evident in the Tract may have reflected, and also perhaps helped mould, common perceptions in the early 1920s, the Treatise, in any case a very much less "popular" book, did not.

This is perhaps most evident in the discussions surrounding the demise of the gold standard in 1931, where fear of inflation if the standard were to collapse was a potent source of support for its defence. Whilst Snowden cannot be regarded as in all respects typical, his horror of inflation (e.g. Skidelsky 1970, pp.59-60) survived the deflation after 1929, and his fears were echoed by Macdonald in the famous flourishing of inflated German bank notes in the General Election after the creation of the National Government in 1931 (e.g. Taylor 1970, p.405).

These grave but ill-focussed fears of inflation were not without their counterparts in economic writing. Robbins in 1934 published a book entitled the Great Depression which focussed on the dangers of inflation. A year earlier Hayek had published his Prices and Production which offered a theoretical account of inflation which stressed not its effects on the distribution of wealth but its ill effects on production (see also Hayek 1960). Whilst the latter was perhaps most significant in heralding the beginnings of a half century long critique of inflationary policies, the former caught the mood of current British 'respectable' opinion, though it probably no longer reflected the consensus amongst economists.

In the evolution of British policy towards inflation the publication of Keynes' General Theory in 1936 occupies a somewhat paradoxical place. On the one hand it marked Keynes' transition in concern from the stability of prices (as in the Treatise) to the stability of employment. On the other hand, insofar as its ideas were to be an element in the growth of management of the economy, it had much of its impact rather paradoxically through the re-inforcement of concern with inflation which came with the war in 1939.

War, Inflation and Full Employment
"Thus it was that when, from the outbreak of the war onwards, we were once more confronted with the problems of inflation, there was very little disposition to consider them in terms of the influence of the quantity of money; there was a consistent habit to approach them with the presumptions of the expenditure theories which had been developed in the previous period" (Robbins 1971, p.76).

The Second World War and the perceived problem
of inflation it raised provided a major port of
entry for Keynesian formulations into the government's calculations. Opposition to inflation could
bring Keynes' support from those who had never
accepted the 'New Economics' (e.g. Hayek) as well as
linking the new theories to the concerns of the
authorities, in a way in which those advocating
these new techniques to aid unemployment had never
quite managed.

The newspaper articles which were eventually
brought together to form How to Pay for the War
(Keynes 1972) provided of course not only a schema
for reducing inflation but reasons as to why that
was important. This was well summarised by a Memorandum written by Keynes in late 1940 (Keynes 1978,
p.218) "The importance of a war budget is not
because it will 'finance' the war. The goods ordered
by the supply department will be financed anyway.
Its importance is social; to prevent the social
evils of inflation now and later; to do this in a
way which satisfies the popular sense of social
justice; whilst maintaining adequate incentives to
work and economy".

The traditional opposition of the authorities
to inflation, stressed by Montagu Norman in a rare
written memorandum to the Chancellor of the
Exchequer in September 1939 (Sayers 1956, p.25), was
greatly increased by the war. There were powerful
memories of the First War, when inflation had been a
major stimulant to unrest.

Keynes argued not only that inflation would
cause unrest if allowed on the scale of the First
World War, but it would also be ineffective as a way
of diverting resources to the government. He argued
that inflation had worked to raise revenue in the
First War by the lag (of about a year) between the
rise in prices and the subsequent rise in wages.
This gave higher profits to entrepreneurs who would
either save more voluntarily than workers out of an
equivalent income, or be taxed upon these profits.
However in World War Two, Keynes suggested, such a
mechanism was no longer available, due to the extent
of de facto indexation of wages (Trevithick 1975).
Inflation would thus serve no positive purpose, but
merely fuel discontent, stimulate attacks on "prof-
iteering", and create pressures for the maximum
rather than minimum interference with the market
mechanism.

The schema of How to Pay for the War were not
comprehensively adopted by the wartime government.

In particular, the stress laid on deferred pay found only a pale shadow in the scheme of Post-War Credits (Harrod 1952, pp.492-4). Equally, price controls and rationing were used on a scale which Keynes had hoped would be avoided. But the important point in the current context is that the convergence of Keynes' and the authorities' concerns on inflation was crucial to the acceptance of the income-expenditure analysis of the government budget. Inflation was, if not the Trojan Horse of Keynesian economics, a powerful battering ram in the hands of those wishing to storm the Treasury's temple.[5] To further extend the metaphor, we might also say that rearmament had acted as an advance guard in changing Treasury perceptions and policies (Peden 1979 and 1980).

The pre-occupation with inflation at the beginning of the war soon gave way to other concerns, either directly related to the war effort or to what was to follow the ending of the war. As is suggested in Chapter 1 above, this latter occurred remarkably early in the war, though this is not meant to imply that most economists in the civil service in the war spent most of their time on post-war plans. When these plans, dominated on internal matters by the question of employment, did come up for serious attention in the later years of the war, the question of inflation seems to have been drastically relegated.

When the Economic Section of the War Cabinet Secretariat put up its draft proposals for post-war employment policy this evinced an extremely hostile response from the Treasury (PRO CAB 87 63 EC 43 (6), 16 October 1943). However the focus of the attack on the document was not its possible inflationary consequences. Rather the emphasis was on the idea that unemployment was largely caused by a deficiency of aggregate demand rather than structural factors; the expression of scepticism on the capacity of governments to control aggregate investment; the neglect of the structure as opposed to the aggregate level of investment; and wariness about "long-continued" budget deficits. The latter of course might be considered a concern with inflation, but insofar as it was, it was at most an indirect concern. The central concern was with international confidence, to which an unbalanced budget was seen as a threat, and which would arguably operate independently of any direct inflationary consequences.

As is well-known the document which eventually emerged in 1944 as the White Paper on Employment Policy was something of a compromise between these

diverse views, especially on the question of budgetary policy. The White Paper did refer to inflation,
in two quite separate contexts. One discussion was
in the context of the post-war transition period,
when under conditions of demand generally out-
running supply. "This would mean an inflationary
boom - bringing with it the social injustice and
economic disturbance which incidentally accompany
inflation" (CMD. 6527, para. 16). The longer-term
policy of maintaining full employment was argued to
have as a <u>condition</u> that "The level of prices and
wages must be kept reasonably stable" (para. 39(b)).
More extensive discussion was given (in paras. 49-
54) in a section headed "The stability of prices and
wages". It was not stated explicitly here what the
effects of pursuit of full employment might have on
the price level, though it was implicit that the
scope for price and wage increases would be enhanced
under such conditions.

Two important points emerge from this section.
One is that there was no suggestion that full employment could or should imply any changes in the traditional mechanisms of price and wage setting. Merely
there was an admonition to good behaviour "it must
be regarded as the duty of both sides of industry to
consider together all possible means of preventing a
rise in the costs of production and distribution and
so avoiding a rise in prices which is the initial
step in the inflationary process" (para. 53).
Secondly, the White Paper argued that the dangers of
inflation under the new policy regime would be that
the increased expenditures would go into prices
rather than an increase in employment. This is
important because it suggested that the government
would aim at a given level of <u>expenditure</u> not
employment, leaving the effects of this level of
expenditure on employment to be determined by the
wage and price behaviour of the economic agents
concerned. This conception has much more in common
with the arguments of the 1970s and 1980s, (especially Meade 1982), than what evolved as policy in the
immediate post-war period. In that period the
target was directly one of <u>employment</u>, which had the
important though no doubt unintended consequence of
absolving other economic agents (especially trades
unions) of any responsibility for the level of
employment in their own practices. (This point will
be returned to below, Section IV).

Beveridge's <u>Full Employment in a Free Society</u>
was more overtly sensitive to the likely effects of
full employment on collective bargaining and hence

on inflation. "There is a real danger that sectional wage bargaining, pursued without regard to its effects upon prices, may lead to a vicious spiral of inflation, with money wages chasing prices and without any gain in real wages for the working class as a whole" (para. 284). Within this context the Report stressed that the responsibility for preventing a wage/prices spiral will fall on collective bargainers (p.288), though the government should provide an appropriate framework of stable prices within which collective bargaining could take place (para. 290). No changes in the mechanisms of collective bargaining were suggested.

In 1945 Keynes wrote "One is also, simply because one knows no solution, inclined to turn a blind eye to the wages problem in a full employment economy" (1980, p.385). This attitude permeated much of the policy pursued in the next decade and a half. Whilst a wages policy was briefly, albeit successfully, pursued under Cripps following devaluation in 1949, systematic policy on wage bargaining did not accompany full employment policy. Economists might lament what was occurring, but recognised that "the strength of the sentiment in favour of avoiding unemployment at all hazards is likely to bring it about that most deviations or mistakes will be on the side of making the stream of monetary demand excessive" (Robertson 1956, p.118).

Governments in the immediate post-war period did not of course advocate inflation, but they did little to construct a long-term policy to avoid it.[6] No doubt partly this was because for some years after 1945 inflationary pressures could be seen as temporary, the result of short-run circumstances of post-war reconstruction, devaluation in 1949, and then the Korean War. Writers such as Brown (1955) reflected this uncertainty as to the contribution of these factors to inflation, compared with the long-term effects of the full employment policies.

By the early 1950s economists had come to focus a great deal of attention on the problem (see below) but it was still the case, certainly until the mid-1950s that governments took little action to prevent it. The attitude prevalent is well illustrated in the evidence given by Sir Robert Hall, Economic Adviser to the Government, to the Radcliffe Committee (Minutes of Evidence, para. 1376).

> I think the government's position has always been that sound money is a desirable objective and continually rising prices are a most unfor-

tunate thing. But since, by and large, they have taken the view that conditions of full employment allowed the situation to be exploited by movements on prices, the stress has been on trying to persuade people not to take advantage of the situation, rather than trying, as might have been argued in days when full employment was not an objective of policy, to say that the way to deal with it was through monetary actions.

The Inflationary Economy

As the quotation at the end of the previous section suggests the revival of concern with inflation as a serious, rather than merely a rhetorical, concern of policy was tied up with the revival of monetary policy. It would seem fair to say that the revival of such policies largely pre-dated and provided a basis for renewed policy on inflation rather than the other way round.

In the late 1940s the overriding short-term aims of policy was reconstruction, full employment being assumed. For a variety of reasons this reconstruction was linked to a rejection of monetary policy, and reliance on fiscal and direct controls. On the one hand "Alike as a selector of the most urgent capital works and a deterrent of expenditure, when everyone has money to spend, the rate of interest was thought an unsuitable weapon" (Radcliffe Report, para. 400). Equally post-war Chancellors had continued the wartime policy of low interest rates, seeing this as an important part of minimising the costs of the National Debt accumulated in war time.

There was also the doctrinal adherence to 'fiscalism' and direct controls. However perhaps these should not be overstated in their significance. Particularly in the latter case, the destruction of such controls was well under way before the Labour Government lost office in 1951, though this was a trend reinforced by the incoming Conservative Government. In the case of fiscal policy, the perceived problems of this after 1951 were not so much doctrinal (i.e. views as to its effectiveness), but an unwillingness to see the rising taxes, even in the short-run, that attachment to such policies was taken to imply (Kennedy in Worswick and Ady 1962, pp.301-2).

Central though to the renewed concern within monetary measures was the balance of payments position. "It was, however, the foreign exchange situation rather than internal pressures that occasioned the swing towards monetary measures, although the background of internal inflation, - and, more directly, overseas opinion on this - was part of the story" (Radcliffe Report, para. 402).

Up until the mid-1950s this renewed emphasis on monetary policy did not make much difference to policies, which, while recognising in a general way that full employment tends to be inflationary (e.g. Treasury Evidence to Radcliffe, Minutes, paras. 1364-7), focussed directly on the balance of payments and employment, with monetary policy aimed at those objectives. The following question and answer by Sir Robert Hall before the Radcliffe Committee summarise the position very aptly: "Have not successive governments taken the view that the objectives of full employment, no slumps and growth in the economy, are King, and that monetary policy is employed and its effects are to be judged in a particular context in which there are dominant aims of policy? Yes. Whether these points were made or explicit, I think they were implicit in what was done......".

Of course under a regime of fixed exchange rates concern with the balance of payments is de facto a concern with relative, if not absolute, levels of inflation. But in terms of how economic policy objectives are perceived and pursued it obviously does matter whether inflation is seen as a problem in its own right, or a problem because of possible constraints imposed by its continuation on the pursuit of other objectives. Up until the mid-1950s it was the latter that predominated.

What occurred in 1956 and 1957 was a shift in emphasis rather than a sharp break. In his budget speech of 1957, which announced the setting up of the Radcliffe Committee, the Chancellor of the Exchequer argued that there was general agreement on the objectives of monetary policy. "This country stands determined to maintain a fixed and stable exchange rate. The preliminary requisite for this is that we shall be able and determined to avoid inflation at home. Equally it is also agreed policy to avoid slumps and severe unemployment" (Hansard, Commons, Vol. 568, Col. 985, 9 April 1957; see also Radcliffe Report, para. 5).

This implies little difference from the position outlined above as to the 'indirect' objective of counter inflation. However it fitted into a shift of focus taking place among the authorities. Else-

where the new emphasis on inflation was more
explicit. For example, it had pride of place as a
problem in the Government document The Economic
Implications of Full Employment (CMD. 9725, 1956).
Here the emphasis was not just on the problems
caused for the balance of payments by inflation, but
also the problems caused for growth (this might
operate simultaneously by balance of payments constraints inhibiting the realisation of growth potential). Thus the document reflected the new found
(see Chapter 4) explicit commitment to economic
growth as a policy objective "rising prices endanger
the full realisation of the possibilities of
economic progress, and it must be one of our major
objectives to maintain in future a much greater
degree of price stability than has been achieved in
the past 10 years" (para. 6).

This elevation in the significance of inflation
was reflected in a speech by the Governor of the
Bank of England in July 1956 which emphasised that
the control of inflation was an "essential condition
of success in dealing with all other economic
problems" (Bank of England Memorandum to Radcliffe
Committee, Memorandum of Evidence, Vol. I, Section
9, para. 114).

The deflationary measures introduced in 1957
may have been symptomatic of new perceptions of the
inflation problem amongst policy makers, but they
were also linked to more immediate concerns. Above
all, they reflected a speculative run on the pound
which saw the Bank Rate raised sharply to 7 per
·cent. Domestically there was also evidence of weakness in the gilt market, which was perceived as
showing that investors' inflationary expectations
were beginning to adjust to the reality of inflation
(e.g. Robbins Evidence to Radcliffe, Minutes of
Evidence, para. 10199; Cohen, 1st Report, para. 96).

In addition to these immediate conditions one
should also note that the Chancellor in 1957 was
Thorneycroft, perhaps the Chancellor in the post-war
period who up until that date most distrusted the
post-war consensus. However, the Treasury failed to
carry their continuing deflationary policies through
the Cabinet, and in early 1958 Thorneycroft and two
other Treasury ministers resigned (see for example
Shonfield 1958, pp. 248-50).

Shonfield is probably right to suppose that to
a degree these three were the political sacrificial
lambs to policies which had strong support in the
upper echelons of the Treasury. Whilst inflation had
achieved a new place in government objectives, there

were few who were willing to sacrifice other goals
to reduce inflation, and no-one at that time argued
that in the short-run at least, such a sacrifice
would not be necessary. This was especially so when
policy had strongly attached itself not only to full
employment, but also to growth. Both attachments
inhibited anti-inflationary policies (Cairncross
1975, pp.71-5).

Thus the events of 1956-7 did mark a break with
previous policies, but they were soon reversed.
However they did mark a new awareness of inflation,
and an awareness which was albeit gradually, to have
its impact on policy. The events of 1957 also lead
to the creation of two important committees. One was
of course Radcliffe, which will be returned to in a
moment. The other was the 'Cohen' Council (after its
first chairman), The Council on Productivity Prices
and Incomes. This was established in August 1957.
Its terms of reference were "Having regard to the
desirability of full employment and increasing
standards of life and expanding production and
reasonable stability of prices, to keep under review
changes in prices, productivity and the level of
income (including wages, salaries and profits) and
to report thereon from time to time" (Cohen, 1st
Report, para. 1).

This rather ambiguous remit did not prevent the
Committee in its reports focussing primarily on
prices, the "one big failure" of post-war economic
policy (Ibid., para. 16). It did not engage in the
Gotterdammerung kind of discussion of inflation
which some were subject to (see e.g. Evidence of
W.H. Salomon to the Radcliffe Committee, Memoranda
of Evidence, Vol. III). Instead it focussed on the
redistributive and balance of payments consequences
of inflation. In particular, it argued against the
view that the effects of inflation in reducing the
value of debts was to be in any way welcomed "In the
present state of our social arrangements it seems to
us clear that the arbitrary redistribution resulting
from a steady rise in prices, even if slow, is very
unjust" (para. 98).

This focus on the redistributive and balance of
payments consequences of inflation is predominant
also in the evidence to Radcliffe. However the
positions taken by economists on inflation before
this Committee were extremely varied, and some discussion of these differences will help explain the
intellectual context of policy debates at the time,
without implying that policy was the translation of
any one of those views into practice.

Broadly speaking, we can divide attitudes to inflation exhibited at the Radcliffe Committee into three; it is a positively good thing under certain circumstances; it doesn't matter much; it matters a great deal. Within the latter two groups there was also a distinction, which was to be of growing importance, on what should be done about inflation.

The view that inflation is, under definite circumstances, a good thing was expressed largely by Kaldor. His argument (Memoranda, Vol. III), was based on the view that in inflation prices would run ahead of wages and provide the profits and low real interest rates necessary to encourage investment. This led him to argue that "the objective of stable or falling prices may well be regarded as a luxury which only fast growing economies can afford" (para. 12).

Pressed on this by the Committee, Kaldor refused to endorse inflation without qualification, but did argue that "given the present dynamism of the British economy, to keep the ship on an even keel and prevent it from foundering may require doping it with inflation because its dynamism is low" (Minutes, para. 10668; for a formal statement see Kaldor 1959).

This position clearly built upon, though gave a specific twist to, the profit inflation position endorsed by Keynes in the Treatise. In some quarters they came to be regarded as typically Keynesian, though they clearly owed little to the polemics of Keynes against inflation noted above (see also Hayek 1973, p.103).

A more common view expressed before the Committee was that inflation, whilst not desirable, was not something to be too worried about. Day for example assumed "that some degree of price inflation is inevitable in a fully employed economy in the U.K., and that this should not be regarded too tragically. Price inflation, kept to a moderately slow and if possible intermittent rate is by no means the worst economic evil" (Memoranda, Vol. III, para. 1). This view was not very commonly expressed by economists, (though see Worswick in Worswick and Ady 1962, pp.4-5; Reddaway 1966, p.9). But it probably reflects the implied consensus of policy making for much of the 1950s and 1960s.

Thirdly, there were those economists who took inflation very seriously. Some did thus in terms which whilst suggesting that inflation was a profound problem provided little evidence of why. For example Gregory argued that the provision of a legal

system and sound money were the two fundamental responsibilities of government, the latter having been
neglected in Britain to an appalling extent (Minutes
of Evidence, paras. 10860-64). Others commented upon
the effects of inflation in rather less grandilo-
quent terms. Firstly there was a stress on the point
that inflation as an inducement to growth, via
profit inflation or low real interest rates, could
work only as long as the losers from such processes
were willing to accede in their loss. If the process
were to be continued under those conditions the
inflation would have to accelerate (Hicks, Evidence,
10911; Robbins, Memoranda, para. 14). More positively,
such economists pointed to the balance of payments
consequences of inflation, with the assumption that
any attempt to resolve this by devaluation was
likely to bring an upward spiral of prices (Robbins,
Memoranda, para. 53). In addition the redistributive
consequences were stressed. Finally there was a
strong albeit general view that inflation would
eventually have the effect of undermining the
"efficiency and stability of the capital market"
(Ibid., para. 30).

In addition to these differences on the significance of inflation there was a considerable difference of view on what should be done about it.
Partly this was expressed as a theoretical dispute -
was inflation largely of a 'cost push' or 'demand
pull' kind? But this theoretical view went along
with, and probably can only be understood, in the
light of its perceived implications. Adherents of
the 'cost push' view broadly speaking were also
adherents of the view that the appropriate policy to
deal with inflation were some kind of reform of
collective bargaining (e.g. Little, Nield and Ross,
Memoranda, para. 2). On the other hand those who
stressed the 'demand pull' aspect logically enough
proposed measures to lower the level of demand as
the appropriate remedy (e.g. Paish, Memoranda).

Inflation as Unfortunate Side Effect
In the longer run it was probably these latter differences which mattered. For they pointed to the
horns of the dilemma. If governments were committed
to full employment, and this led to inflation with
the existing institutions of the labour market, what
were they to do? They could drop the commitment to
full employment per se. This they were not yet
willing to do. Or they could attempt to change the
process of collective bargaining - thus in a variety

of ways they were to try to do, albeit largely unsuccessfully (Chapter 9 below).

One way out of this dilemma was to let the
government aim at a level of aggregate expenditure
compatible with full employment, but allow the
process of collective bargaining to determine the
actual level. This, as noted above, was suggested in
the White Paper on Employment Policy of 1944. It was
also suggested by Robbins to the Radcliffe Committee
(Memoranda, para. 32). This was not pursued. Why is
not clear. Perhaps it was the belief that the government should be directly responsible for such
objectives as full employment, and that to farm out
this responsibility was either a dereliction of duty
or perhaps an infringement of governmental sovereignty.

Insofar as policy was concerned with inflation
in the 1950s and 1960s it focussed on remedies which
did not question the priority of full employment.
Increasingly this was to be the debate of the 1960s.
But the position at the end of the 1950s especially
up to 1957 is well summarised by Cairncross (1975,
p.71):

> So long as inflation was thought to be no more
> than the consequence of excess demand it could
> be dismissed as an error on the right side,
> obviously to be preferred to a deficiency of
> demand and the unemployment accompanying it....
> The change in the value of money from year to
> year was treated as a somewhat accidental by-
> product of a system governed by other consid-
> erations; and so long as it remained almost
> within the limits of errors of estimation it
> could be regarded as publicly acceptable.

NOTES

1.   P. Streeten, "The Objectives of Economic
Policy" in P.D. Henderson (ed), Economic Growth in
Britain, (Weidenfeld and Nicolson, London, 1966),
pp.39-40), has expressed economists scepticism
strongly: "But it is not equally clear why inflation
is bad. Bankers assure us that it is an evil, and
the electorate seems to share their view..... But
since public opinion and other authors in this book
consider the avoidance of domestic inflation as an
important objective, we shall accept this here". See
also M. Artis, Economists and Inflation, (The
University, Swansea, 1973), esp. pp.16-21.

2.   Keynes suggested that the frequent recurrence of inflation in history "is not an accident and has behind it two great driving forces - the unpecuniosity of governments and the superior political influence of the debtor class". Keynes, <u>Collected Writings</u>, Vol. IV. The Tract on Monetary Reform, (Macmillan, London, 1971), p.8.

3. There is a good brief account of this episode, and inflation in history more generally, in P. Deane, "Inflation in History", in D. Heathfield (ed), <u>Perspectives on Inflation</u>, (Longmans, London, 1979), pp.1-36.

4.   In Cagan's account five of the twentieth century's hyper-inflations occurred in the early 1920s - in Austria, Germany, Hungary, Poland and Russia. P. Cagan, "The Monetary Dynamics of Hyper-Inflation", in M. Friedman (ed), <u>Studies in the Quantity Theory of Money</u>, (Chicago U.P., Chicago, 1956), pp.25-117.

5.   A. Booth, ("The 'Keynesian Revolution' in Economic Policy Making", <u>Economic History Review</u>, <u>36</u>, 1, (February 1983), pp.103-23), argues that the final conversion of the Treasury to Keynesian policy came only in 1947, but he emphasises that it was concern with inflation that gave the initial impetus to this conversion in 1940-41 and its consummation after the war.

6.   Though the retention of physical controls into the 1950s was predominantly a means of restraining inflation, and inflation was a concern very much to the fore at the Treasury (see footnote 5).

Chapter Four

GROWTH

All four objectives of economic policy discussed in
this book have always been much more than economic
objectives narrowly defined. To varying degrees they
have been invested with political, social and moral
significance as well. For example, inflation has
commonly not been seen as a specific, narrowly
defined, economic problem but as involving broad
political and social dangers, and its existence has
also functioned as a sign of moral decline.[1]
Equally, hostility to unemployment has involved not
only notions of the economic consequences of such
unemployment, but also the idea that its existence
has political and social implications, which in the
broadest view act as an indictment of the economic
system as a whole. Economic growth has also been
invested with a much broader significance than
simply a rise in the level of Gross National
Product. As we shall see below the presence or
absence of such growth have been viewed amongst
other things as an index of the moral status of the
country's inhabitants, slow growth being something
equivalent to "lack of moral fibre" in military
jargon.
    A second general point which is applicable to
economic growth is that its pursuit cannot be understood separately from the means perceived as functional to that pursuit. In the period focussed on in
this chapter, the 1960s, we cannot understand the
status of growth as an objective without considerable attention also to planning as the means to that
end. A similar argument may also be applied to the
later episode of "dashing for growth" in the 1970s
(see Chapter 9 below).
    Finally, as a general point, the specific pur-
suit of growth has been episodic. That is to say
that since the middle 1950s growth has been an

agreed objective of British policy in some vague sense, but its active pursuit has been largely confined to the early 1960s and the early 1970s. In this chapter we will be concerned with the initial creation of growth as an objective in the 1950s as well as the episode of the 1960s. Chapter 9 will look at the 1970s episode.

Worrying About Growth

In 1959 the Radcliffe Report (para. 58) suggested that "During recent years there has been an increasing mention, both in public discussion and in Government pronouncements, of the need to foster economic growth and the general raising of standards of living". It cited as an explicit example of this the 1956 White Paper on the Economic Implications of Full Employment, which included the pronouncement that (para. 25):

> This government is pledged to foster conditions in which the nation, if it so wills, realise its full potentialities for growth in terms of production and living standards.

Whilst the Radcliffe Report is undoubtedly right in pointing to this new explicitness in the desire for economic growth, first becoming clear in the mid-1950s, it is also the case that as far as policy measures are concerned little happened before 1960 (Hopkin in Cairncross (ed) 1981, p.36). Only from about that date did economic growth move to the centre of economic policy-making and become actively pursued.

As the quote from the 1956 White Paper suggests, the interest in economic growth at that time focussed on conditions for facilitating rather than causing growth. The government would remove the obstacles which prevented market forces from achieving faster growth, rather than developing new policies of its own. Nevertheless, this limited commitment to growth needs to be understood as "setting the stage" for the later more positive approach.

As far as professional economists were concerned the Second World War ended a long period of lack of explicit discussion of economic growth. The classical economists had of course had this, "the wealth of nations", at the centre of their concerns, and much of their policy writing was clearly concerned with clearing the obstacles to such growth.

However, even the classical economists normally
assumed rather than argued the case for such growth
(Arndt 1978, p.7), and as something approaching
"laisser-faire" was achieved in the mid-nineteenth
century the discussion of growth faded. Particularly
after the rise of neo-classical economics from the
late nineteenth century the neglect of growth by
economists is striking; "it is remarkable how little
thought was given for well over a century to economic growth as opposed to such matters as tariffs,
monopoly, taxation, imperialism, unemployment and
financial crises" (Cairncross 1975, p.46).

This unconcern vanished in the 1940s and 1950s.
Part of the reason for this was internal to economics as a discipline, especially the attempts to
"dynamise" the Keynesian system, work in Britain
notably carried out by Harrod (see Jones 1975,
Ch. 3). Also important, though less detached perhaps
from wider issues, was the increased concern with
the development of "underdeveloped" countries, whose
development became for a time seen as synonymous
with growth (Arndt 1981). This in turn was partly
predicated on the development of national income
statistics, pioneered by writers such as Colin Clark
before the Second War and powerfully developed by
writers such as Kuznets in the 1940s and 1950s, now
backed by substantial resources from such bodies as
the U.N. and the O.E.E.C. By the early and mid-
fifties "league tables" of economic growth were
beginning to appear (Hutchinson 1968, p.125-6).

Whilst theoretical work on economic growth pre-
dates its status as an explicit policy objective,[2]
such work was given an enormous stimulus by that new
explicitness. But the reasons for this new explicitness do not seem to any great extent to have depended on economists' theories. Economic growth theory
has, almost from its inception, been a butt of
economists' jokes, as the area of economic theory
most removed from any "practical application".

As Arndt's book clearly shows, the new focus on
growth in the mid-fifties was international in
character, and the reasons for this focus included
both elements common to different countries and
others more specific. For example in the U.S.A. the
focus on growth as a means to full employment and as
a necessary response to the Soviet challenge were
more important than in the U.K. (Arndt 1978, p.58).
In Britain there was at this stage a much greater
commitment to macro-economic, rather than growth-
based, solutions to unemployment than in the U.S.A.,
and the Cold War did not generate quite the same

hysteria. (Though see for example Shanks 1961, Ch.
1, where competition with the Communist bloc is
given pride of place as a reason for pursuing
growth).

In Britain, more important than employment or
the Cold War was the idea of growth as a solution to
other problems, notably those of the balance of payments and of inflation. Now this was an extremely
contentious matter; the relationship between these
problems was an area of great dispute. Some saw
these problems as soluble by growth; others saw
growth as desirable on other grounds but hindered by
possible inflationary and balance of payments constraints. (These issues are thoroughly discussed in
Henderson (ed), 1966). Initially it seems to have
been the idea that economic growth was a way of solving other problems that made it so attractive
"economic growth came to be regarded as a prophylac-
tic or remedy for all the major current ailments of
western economies - balance of payments difficulties
and especially dollar shortage, underemployment, and
inflation whether due to excess demand or competing
income claims" (Arndt 1978, p.43).

But economic growth was not only a solution to
the standard macro-economic problems, it was also a
means to reconciling the competing claims on
resources. One of these claims was the development
of other poorer countries; in a context where development of such countries was seen as almost synonymous with higher investment, any commitment to helping them was seen as conditional on higher domestic
growth to finance aid and private investment, as
well as requiring a balance of payments surplus to
enable such resources to be transferred (see for
example Radcliffe Report, para. 59; Crosland 1956,
p.377). Growth was also seen as a means to defusing
domestic social tensions by reconciling competing
domestic claims on resources both between public and
private sectors and especially claims from different
social classes. Crosland (1962, pp.97-8) cited
Galbraith to argue that the growth of incomes of
American workers had lessened social tensions.
Growth was thus central to Crosland's focus on
equality as the touchstone of socialist politics,
albeit in a specific way "... the higher the average
level of real income, whatever its distribution, the
greater the subjective sense of social equality"
(Ibid., p.97).[3]

Overall, across the political spectrum in the
late 1950s growth came to have something of the panacea about it. Few registered dissent, because

everyones' objectives could seemingly be achieved by growth. Herbivore attitudes to growth had hardly yet been born, and only the determinedly heterodox questioned its desirability. When Joan Robinson wrote "The ideology of growth is designed to prevent us from asking what we want to do with it" (1966, p.51) she had a point. Growth was a way of putting off "the unpleasant choice at the margin between different priorities among policy aims, and between groups differentially affected by different policy combinations" (Winch 1972, p.329).

Growth and Planning

Section I was something of a <u>Tour d'horizon</u> in the rise in concern for economic growth of the 1950s. It was very much in line with Arndt's excellent (1978) account of the general forces at work in propelling economic growth to the forefront in this period. If Arndt's work is open to criticism, it is that in making his work international in scope and focussing on economists writings he underanalyses the specific British context of the pursuit of growth, especially its attachment to the notion of planning. In this section the argument will be made that the sudden burst of activity on growth policy from about 1960 can only be understood in relation to this notion of planning, with all its diverse ideological and institutional connotations.

Prior to this it is worth pointing out that something very akin to growth - productivity - had been the object of policy in the 1940s. In 1952 Leyland (in Worswick and Ady 1952, p.381) had noted that:

> Before the war the word productivity was largely confined to academic discussion. Today it is common currency. In higher production is seen the easiest solution to our problems, and, in a state of full employment, total output of any given composition can only expand if the productivity of individual workers increases.

Such a focus derived a great deal from the adverse productivity comparisons made with the U.S.A. during the period of wartime partnership, and which found its most famous academic expression in the work of Rostas (1948). It found its general policy application in the Anglo-American Productivity Council (founded by Cripps), which attempted to spread American practice to the U.K., though there had been many more particular attempts both in the war and early post-war years.

However whilst reflecting some of the same concerns as growth was later to do - above all that the scale of claims on a fully employed and almost stationary labour force was impossible to fulfil - concern with productivity was not really a precursor of later growth policy. Above all because raising productivity was seen not in dynamic but in "comparative static" terms (Arndt 1978, pp.31-2) i.e. as a way of attaining a new plateau of output, not as a means to an infinite process of expansion.

As already noted, the idea of growth as an explicit object of policy was initially associated with removing constraints rather than positive policies. When in 1954 the Conservative Chancellor of the Exchequer talked of doubling the standard of living in 25 years this was more an application of the slogan "Tory Freedom Works", and the anti-planning rhetoric of the late 1940s and early 1950s, than a call to change the direction of economic policy (Budd 1978, pp.83-4). Butler's talk in this vein was "rather a happy aspiration than a serious statement of purpose or a promise" (Harris 1972, p.239).

The commitment to growth policies from 1960 resulted from the erosion of this free market rhetoric on the Conservative side, and a degree of revisionism in the Labour Party. These forces meant that there was a convergence of ideologies between the parties, which is apparent in the continuity of rhetoric and policy between the last years of Conservative rule and the first few years of Labour after 1964.

Across the political spectrum this convergence was in part the result of a decline in belief in the post-war pattern of economic management, especially with its stop-go character. On the Conservative side this disillusion was partly because of the growing worries about inflation (Ch. 3). This led both to the creation of the Cohen Council in 1957 and the Radcliffe Committee in 1958. The Reports of the former body show a clear transition from an 'orthodox' deflationary response to inflation in the first Report, to a much more <u>dirigiste</u> approach involving incomes policy in the Fourth. Whilst the primary focus remained on inflation, a wider disillusion with traditional macro policies is apparent. This then fed into the growing concern with growth,

Britain's performance being compared unfavourably with that of the other major countries of Western Europe.

The discontent with existing policy was brought to something of a head by the deflationary measures of 1961 in response to the traditional sterling crisis. "The simple principle which had governed demand management since the war - of reducing demand when it was excessive and increasing it when it was inadequate - began to appear more and more threadbare, so that moves were made to evolve longer term policies - medium term planning and new institutions for an incomes policy" (Blackaby 1978, pp.16-7; see also Catherwood 1966, p.13).

Whilst the events of 1961 were important in this way, they came in a context of already rising discontent with Britain's economic performance. For example this had been signalled in the widely read book by Shonfield (1959), which argued for the importance of increasing growth, and saw as a precondition for this a reduction in Britain's political pretensions, as exampled by the scale of its overseas military expenditure and commitments to foreign investment and the sterling area.[4]

A similar questioning of accepted policies was apparent in Shanks' (1961) book whose title "The Stagnant Society: A Warning" both encapsulated and served to develop a popular mood. Indeed towards the end of this book (p.232), Shanks wrote a passage whose rhetoric might serve as a Leitmotif for this period, and is therefore worth quoting in full.

> What sort of an island do we want to be? This is the question to which we come back in the end. A lotus island of easy, tolerant ways, bathed in the golden glow of an imperial sunset, shielded from discontent by a threadbare welfare state and an acceptance of genteel poverty? Or the tough dynamic race we have been in the past, striving always to better ourselves, seeking new worlds to conquer in place of those we have lost, ready to accept growing pains as the price of growth.

Whilst it was right-wing Labour writers, like Shonfield and Shanks, who crystallised common perceptions of the time, it was the Conservative government which took the initiative in the movement towards "planning". "Planning" seemed to summon up the effort of will which the Conservative Government felt it lacked - indeed planning as a concept could be very widely acceded to precisely because it had little meaning except as a sign of a new sense of purpose.

What may seem a slightly perverse affiliation between Conservatism and planning was explicable partly because of the vacuity of the term. But it also depended on a vague notion that there existed a kind of planning consistent with the Conservative commitment to free enterprise, that in existence in France. The traditional Francophilia of the British middle class found its expression most vividly at this time in an appreciation and attempt to ape the seeming successes of French indicative planning (e.g. P.E.P. 1960, pp.220-2, pp.234-5; see also Leruez 1975, pp.86-9). What exactly this consisted of was rarely spelt out, but in a negative way it made most of the Conservative party swallow planning, as offering no threat to their traditional ideological positions.

Not only did the Conservative party readily swallow "planning", but a large part of the initiative to turn the slogan into a policy came from the rather surprising quarter, the Federation of British Industry (as it then was). At the November 1960 meeting of the F.B.I. open disagreement was expressed with the remarks of the current Chancellor of the Exchequer (Amory) who had opened the conference. Stop-go was severely attacked, growth proposed as a way of breaking out of this vicious circle, and the view expressed that this would be facilitated by government and industry getting together to consider "whether it would be possible to argue on an assessment of expectations and intentions which should be before the country for the next five years". Such vague suggestions of indicative planning soon became F.B.I. policy (Leruez 1975, pp.85-7).

Whilst the Conservatives and their natural allies took the lead in the movement towards planning, there was movement in a convergent direction on the Labour side. There also the French example was used to urge a change of position, this time away from detailed central planning towards "indicative". In a 1958 document Plan for Progress, the Labour Party spoke of a planning system in which:- "day-to-day decisions can be left to industry and the customer.... The object of planning will be to provide a broad framework within which the creation of new wealth can go smoothly and rapidly ahead whilst the detailed decisions of industry do not come into conflict with national objectives" (cited in Polanyi 1967, p.22). When the Conservatives moved

towards an endorsement of planning the Labour Party
was wary in its response. It was still somewhat
afraid of the word's associations with die-hard
socialism and post-war austerity, especially in face
of its third election defeat in a row in 1959,
despite such pronouncements as the one cited above.
Eventually of course the rhetoric of planning was to
be enthusiastically endorsed by Labour, and to find
its peak around and after the election of a Labour
Government in 1964.

Commitment to growth in Britain can then only
be fully understood in the context of the rhetoric
of planning, a word which evoked a sense of purpose
and urgency but had little obvious institutional
implications. It could in substance mean almost all
things to all people. However what planning did
serve to crystallise, and what did serve to give it
an institutional framework, was hostility to the
Treasury.

The Treasury had regained its primary role in
the management of the national economy when Cripps
became Chancellor in 1947. It had become in the age
of demand management the agency primarily responsible for that management, especially as the "bonfire
of controls" had undercut the role of ministries
such as the Board of Trade. When therefore the
pattern of demand management, stop-go, came under
attack it was natural that this should focus on the
Treasury. Criticism of the Treasury had always been
a staple of political argument on the Left, but in
the early 1960s the sources of criticism went much
wider. In Harrod's (1963) presentation of the
British economy to an American audience, the
Treasury was pilloried as the "enemy of growth".
This view seems to have been shared by many indus-
trialists, for whom the Treasury was the body primarily responsible for the pursuit of stop-go.
"Rightly or wrongly the Treasury was considered as a
stronghold of conservatism and caution which was
happier as watchdog of the public purse at home and
guardian of the pound abroad than acting as the
spearhead of modernisation" (Leruez 1975, p.104).

When the discontents outlined above came into
focus in 1961 it was unsurprising that some politicians thought it important to create a planning body
outside the Treasury. Selwyn Lloyd, as Chancellor of
the Exchequer, at the very least wanted a source of
advice separate from the Treasury. "The constitution
of the National Economic Development Council (and
that of the Department of Economic Affairs afterwards), cannot be understood in isolation from the

mood of profound distrust which had gathered round
the Treasury by the time of the 1961 sterling
crisis" (Brittan 1971, pp.243-4).

In this way the comment by Brittan (Ibid.,
p.234) that Lloyd, with the N.E.D.C. encouraged the
notion that "new organisations and procedures could
be a substitute for difficult policy choices"
ignores the point that the Treasury seemed at least
to make policy choices that all went in one direction. Whilst the Treasury initially opposed N.E.D.C.
as a derogation from its role, some at the Treasury
saw the new body as a useful means of getting better
contact with industry, and also as a means to
achieving an incomes policy - almost always a policy
popular with the Treasury.

Thus, N.E.D.C. itself, like the slogan of
"planning" which surrounded its creation, was deeply
ambivalent in its significance. Some have seen it as
a 'corporatist' body drawing the trade unions almost
unwittingly into management of the economy (Harris
1972, pp.237-8; Middlemas 1978, Ch. 14). Equally the
dirigiste aspect of the N.E.D.C. was attractive to
the trade unions as a general principle in microeconomic policy, but feared as a stalking horse for
an incomes policy, which they were wholly unwilling
to countenance. This fear was certainly not entirely
misplaced, because not only was the Treasury looking
for policies in that direction, but for many of the
publicists of the "new thinking" at this time an
incomes policy was to be part of the break with
traditional policies. (Both Shanks and Shonfield
were advocates of incomes policies). Indeed the
government used the occasion of the sterling crisis
of the summer of 1961 to introduce a 'pay pause'.
This did not secure union co-operation, and it
delayed T.U.C. agreement to participate in the
N.E.D.C. But it is probably right to treat the
almost continuous search for incomes policies in
Britain thereafter as in part the consequence of the
same mood that initiated the 'planning' of growth
part of a new purposive policy regime. (N.E.D.C.
itself advocated incomes policy, albeit saying that
it was only acceptable as "part of a wider programme
for growth of real incomes", N.E.D.C. 1963A, para.
215).

As already noted, a condition for the widespread support for planning was its vague status.
Apart from being something different to the wartime
(or Soviet) variant, perhaps akin to the French
experiment, and separate from the Treasury, planning
was generally most significant as a sign of a change

of will and purpose than for any particular proposals. Thus in introducing the idea of the N.E.D.C. to
the House of Commons Selwyn Lloyd said:

> I say frankly that I want something more power-
> ful.... I envisage a joint examination of the
> economic prospects of the country stretching
> five or more years into the future. It would
> cover the growth of national production and
> distribution of our resources between the main
> uses, consumption, Government expenditure and
> so on. Above all, it would try to establish
> what are the essential conditions for realis-
> ing potential growth (Hansard, Vol. 645,
> 25 July 1961, Col. 439).

N.E.D.C. activities broadly followed these
ideas. It thus did not have much to do with planning
in any sense recognisable in the great theoretical
debates over planning and the market in the
1930s and 1940s, nor the practices of planning in
wartime and early post-war Britain. Thus the 4 per
cent growth "target" which eventually emerged from
the N.E.D.C.'s deliberations was nothing to do with
the kind of plan targets a Soviet planner might
recognise, but rather 'an experimental hypothesis
adopted for this "trial run" in seeking to estimate
the implications of faster growth in individual
sectors of the economy' (Polanyi 1967, p.31). The
4 per cent figure was highly contingent - (Ibid.,
pp.31-2). Of course for an Institute of Economic
Affairs writer like Polanyi all planning is futile,[5]
and indicative planning could provide no viable
halfway house between the free market and Soviet-
style planning. French planning was therefore in no
meaningful sense planning at all (Ibid., p.100).
This is not the place to pursue the question of the
nature of French planning at this time and how it
differed from what occurred in Britain. Suffice to
say that French planning never depended almost
entirely on "moral suasion" as it did with the
N.E.D.C.; it also brought into play public power in
a way far distant from anything conceived by
Selwyn Lloyd (see Shonfield 1965, esp. Ch. VIII and
Estrin and Holmes 1983).

New Frontiers
The pursuit of economic growth arose partly from a
dissatisfaction with existing policies which was
based on doubts about the highly particular form of

demand management practiced in Britain in the 1950s. For some commentators this dissatisfaction "unfortunately" became focussed on "planning" as a solution (Brittan 1967, p.23). Unfortunate or not, it is clear that this linkage was highly contingent, the attempt to break out of the existing policy framework was capable of going in various ways as the 1970s and early 1980s were to show.

Like many public policy debates, that leading up to the creation of N.E.D.C. focussed on highly dubious dichotomies. Two of these which overlaid each other were physical versus financial and long-term versus short-term. Essentially these involved picturing the Treasury as obsessively concerned with the short-run and financial problems, thus being willing always to deflate in order to fend off sterling crises and thus sacrificing long-term growth. Growth advocates tended to view 'planning' as making possible the avoidance of short-term hindrances to output expansion, but given the vagueness of the notion of planning involved this did not provide any specific policy proposals, notably for the balance of payments. Without such proposals the Treasury could sensibly remain sceptical of the N.E.D.C. growth targets, especially as they implied a 5 per cent per annum growth in exports compared with an existing level of around 3 per cent (Brittan 1971, p.278).

N.E.D.C.'s targets were not realised. The 22 per cent growth target for 1961 to 1966 (N.E.D.C. 1963A) was matched by an outturn of 16 per cent. Investment rose by 24 per cent rather than a forecast 30 per cent (Polanyi 1967, p.60, Table 2). Whilst the "little Neddies" were planned for particular industries, the central focus of N.E.D.C. on national output targets receded into the background after 1962. From 1963 the economy rapidly expanded, but this was an expansion of capacity utilisation not capacity, fuelled not by planning, but by an "old-fashioned" pre-election fiscal expansion, albeit with a hope of this being accompanied by an incomes policy (Blackaby 1978, p.25).

The rhetoric of new frontiers' was of course central to the election of 1964, but it was of course a rhetoric which was central to the Labour Party's programme. The general election brought to power a government committed to growth as an objective to an even greater extent (at least rhetorically) than that of the period 1960 to 1962.

The Labour Party had been somewhat taken aback by the Conservatives' enthusiasm for planning at the beginning of the 1960s; this they not unreasonably felt, was their natural prerogative. In fact as already noted the evolution of Labour Party doctrine in the late 1950s had made their meaning of planning little different from that of the Conservatives. However elections are about stressing differences not similarities, and so in the run up to 1964 Labour leaders focussed on how <u>their</u> planning would differ from that of the Conservatives. Above all this meant stressing that Labour planning unlike Conservative would have "teeth", would not be "Planning in a Vacuum". There was something of a shift back in Labour doctrine to the older ideas of planning with some element of compulsion (Polanyi 1967, pp.49-50). This reflected perhaps not only electoral considerations but also the belief that N.E.D.C. style planning had shown its ineffectiveness, and required some toughening up.

The wider rhetoric of Labour's economic policy prior to the 1964 election was a similarity parallel but 'stiffened' version of the themes of the earlier period outlined above. The predominant theme was that of needing to break-out of the stop-go cycle, above all by more interventionist policies. These included a commitment to incomes policy and a whole series of variegated interventions in industry. Thus the priority was to be medium and long-term policy and a break with the short-term obsessions of the past. This was accompanied by the same hostility to the role of the Treasury, and this led eventually to the creation of two new Ministries, the Department of Economic Affairs and the Ministry of Technology.

If the rhetoric of the Labour government was like a variation on an existing theme, much the same can also be said for the policies substance. The new Department of Economic Affairs eventually produced a National Plan, but despite its title this was little more of a plan than the N.E.D.C.s' projections. Despite all the talk of "planning with teeth", the D.E.A. remained largely toothless - no mechanisms of enforcement were tried out.

The division of authority between the new D.E.A. and the Treasury was unclear.[6] George Brown, the first Minister at this new Department, saw its role as overload of the Treasury and the other economic departments. Wilson saw it more as a division of responsibilities amongst equals between "monetary responsibilities on the one hand, which must come under the Treasury, and, on the other, the co-ordinating responsibilities for industry and everything to do with the mobilisation of real resources for productivity and exports" (Wilson 1971, p.5). This dichotomy was a bizarre one in principle, but especially so when so much of the problems of exports related to a highly 'monetary' phenomenon, the exchange rate.

The National Plan, with its projection of 25 per cent growth between 1964-70 was aborted much like its N.E.D.C. predecessor. A whole series of deflationary measures to defend the pound culminated in the "July measures" of 1966. The sharp stop-go pattern of earlier years was replaced by a more pro-longed stop "the defence of the pound was put before expansion; in other words short-term management of the economy was not a means of implementing the Plan, as it should have been if the Plan had indeed been the "central strategy" for the nation that Mr. Wilson had said it was" (Leruez 1975, pp.179-80).

Something Completely Different

A commitment to growth in some general sense was part of policy assumptions in Britain from the mid-1950s through all the fluctuations of subsequent events. This general commitment reflected the features outlined in Section II above; it promised a solution to all other economic problems and in a way which would lessen rather than heighten social and political tensions. This view is well summarised by the report from a sub-group at the 1961 F.B.I. Conference:

> In our priorities growth comes first, because given growth all else can follow - stable prices, high unemployment, exports and a secure balance of payments (cited in Brittan 1967, p.25).

Equally planning promised to resolve all the painful dilemmas of policy - in an equally unspecific way. Growth and planning became more or less synonymous (e.g. Lipton 1968, pp.46-51), and both remained equally vague. Who (then at least) could dissent from the view that more would be better, and that to get more one should have the will ("plan") to attain it?

The strength of this growth/planning couple cannot be understood separately from the character of macro-policy at that time. By the late 1950s British policy had become one of "Pavlovian reactions" to either the balance of payments or sterling crises on one hand, or the level of unemployment on the other. In a context where government policy was ascribed enormous capacities, it was assumed that any failings of the economy - such as slow growth - must be accounted for by policy failings. Stop-go thus became the focus of discontent. Of course demand management does not have to take the form of short cycles of sto-go as it did in Britain; this was the consequence of peculiar features of the British policy regime to be discussed in Chapter 5. But the equation of demand management and stop-go meant that those who wished to break with the latter tended to consider the former equally condemned. Therefore policy alternatives focussed on something "completely different" (at least in rhetoric).

This is most striking in relation to the balance of payments, where suggestions to change the parameters within which policy operated - by devaluation, reductions in foreign investment and military expenditure, or import controls - were not taken up. There was, in Brittan's (1972, p.42) word, a lack of balance of payments strategy. Rather policy, at least up to 1967, consisted of a series of ad hoc responses to particular crises. Any longer time horizons were displaced on to an essentially empty rhetoric of planning for growth.[7]

This short-term/long-term dichotomy probably served to exacerbate the a-strategic nature of macro-policy. The long-term was the responsibility of some other kind of policy. But whilst this dichotomy may have certain uses in the narrow context of economic theory it was unhelpful in economic policy. Macro-management could not be separated off from questions about the long-term development of the productive forces of the economy.

NOTES

1. e.g. Clark, "Anyone who knowingly promotes or condones a policy that leads to persistently rising prices is morally responsible for plundering the savings of the poor and of other groups who cannot help themselves......". C. Clark, Growthmanship, (I.E.A., London, 1961), p.8.
2. A good index of economists concerns is Samuelson's famous textbook. Economic growth first had a chapter devoted to it in the 3rd, 1955, edition. H.W. Arndt, The Rise and Fall of Economic Growth, (Longman, Cheshire, Melbourne, 1978), p.42.
3. Crosland was hostile to Crossman's focus on Soviet growth as a reason for trying to accelerate

British growth. A. Crosland, <u>The Future of Social-</u><u>ism</u>, (Cape, London, 1956), p.381.

4. Interestingly, in the light of its role in the planning arguments, France was cited as a warning of a country which "tries to support a bigger political burden than its economy will readily bear" (pp.11-2).

5. It is striking that Polanyi, who gives a very interesting account of planning in Britain in the 1960s, couples this not only with a wholesale offhand dismissal of French planning but also the wholly ludicrous suggestion that the fall in production in Russia between 1913 and 1921 of between 2/3rds and ¾ was due solely to "central planning" (p.88). Apparently in comparison with this evil, national war, revolution and civil war and foreign intervention were without effects. Such are the effects of I.E.A. rhetoric. G. Polanyi, <u>Planning in Britain; the Experience of the 1960s</u>, (I.E.A., London, 1967).

6. For a detailed account of the D.E.A. see J. Mitchell, <u>The Groundwork to Economic Planning</u>, (Secker and Warburg, London, 1966), esp. Ch. VI; J. Leruez, <u>Economic Planning and Politics in Britain</u>, (Martin Robertson, Oxford, 1975), Ch. 6.

7. This is not, of course, to imply that planning is always an empty rhetoric; only that it was such in Britain.

Chapter Five

THE NEW REGIME

This chapter is concerned with trying to understand
the central features of the policy regime which
emerged after the Second World War, and whose
objectives have been discussed in the previous chapters. In such a task there would seem to be two
crucial elements. First, if (following Matthews
1968) the period of the 1950s and 1960s is not to be
seen as one when budget deficits generated full
employment, how far is the epithet "Keynesian"
appropriate for describing policies in this period?
The point is not to engage in a semantic dispute
about the meaning of "Keynesian", but to suggest
that the use of this term may mislead us about the
type of policies pursued in this period, and in
doing so exaggerate the role of changes in economic
theory in bringing about the undoubtedly radical
changes in policies since pre-1939. Secondly, and
following from this, the chapter attempts to outline
the main elements which sustained this policy
regime, the elements whose "withering away" help us
to understand the crisis of policy from the late
1960s onwards.

What is a Keynesian Policy?
In discussing the first of these elements the appropriateness of Matthews discussion of fiscal policy
in the post-war period is taken for granted, though
it should be pointed out that, as always, calculations of such policy depend upon the conceptual
framework which is brought to bear. If a different
framework is used then the record of fiscal policy
looks rather different (Neild and Ward 1978, p.39).
Here, however, we are concerned with the more general question of whether, even if budgetary policy

is defined in Matthews way, this radically affects
our understanding of the post-war policy regime.

The argument that budgetary deficits are
central to Keynesian policy depends partly on the
view that a central feature of what the Keynesian
revolution was about for economics was the legitimation of such deficits. Whilst that revolution
involved proposing the use of the budget per se in a
new way, as a means of managing the economy, surpluses and deficits are not symmetrical. Deficits
raise the spectre of government freeing itself from
the political constraints of having to finance
itself by the method of taxation. Deficits thus
potentially threatened the notion of "sound
finance", which functioned, as Kalecki pointed out
(1943, p.325), to "make the level of employment
dependent on the state of confidence".

Now it may be objected that the focus on budget
deficits as crucial to Keynesianism cannot be
derived from the Keynesian classics, as Dow (1964,
p.179) points out "It may nowadays be forgotten that
the use of budgetary policy had practically no place
among the proposal for action suggested in the
General Theory". This point seems to me however misleading if taken to imply that the question of
budgetary policy and budgetary deficits has no place
in the pre-1939 disputes over Keynesian policy. If
one looks back to, for example, Keynes and
Henderson's "Can Lloyd George Do it?" of 1929, it is
clear that whilst in supporting proposals for public
works they do not thereby propose budget deficits,
they are extremely sensitive to the accusation that
this will be the consequence of such a policy. In
the section on What Will it Cost? (pp.110-2) they
stress the small scale of the expenditure involved
in the Liberal programme, the benefit to the
Unemployment Fund, and mention though do not calculate the savings on the Poor Law. In addition
(Section IX) they stress the possibility of financing the government deficit without inflation, and
without diverting funds from private enterprise by
reducing foreign lending.

So I do not think it justified to suggest that
concern with budgetary policy was only a later
addition to the Keynesian project. Nevertheless Dow
is clearly right to suggest that the identification
of Keynesianism with budgetary policy tout court
is by no means inherent in pre-World War Two
Keynesian theory or policy proposals.

This identification arose from a series of both
constraints on alternatives to budgetary policy, and

conditions which made its use relatively unproblematic. One of the primary focusses of inter-war Keynesianism was on the rate of interest, and the attempt to use reductions in this as a means of stimulating recovery. But as Keynes himself argued, such a policy would be central to a reflationary policy in a country like the U.S.A. because of a high degree of insulation from international economic events. In Britain by contrast such a policy was much more difficult because of the openness of the economy, thus leading to an emphasis on public works as an alternative reflationary mechanism.

In the post-war world the degree of openness of the economy was increased, and coupled with (eventually), free movement of capital and a fixed exchange rate, the possibility of using the interest rate in this manner was extremely limited. This might have implied therefore a focus on public works (or more generally public investment) as the major weapon, but there were a number of reasons why this was not so. First, and most obviously, the advocacy of public works in the 1930s was linked to a policy of recovery from a severe depression. This meant attempting to pump in large sums of purchasing power into the economy to deal with a large gap in aggregate demand. This was definitely not the problem of the 1950s and 1960s, though this was not clear in the late 1940s (Blackaby 1978, p.77). Rather the role of economic management in those decades was to "fine tune" the economy. As Dow stresses (1964, Ch. VIII) variations in public investment are very ill adapted to such a purpose. The time scale of the planning and implementation of public investment is not readily compatible with adjustment for short-run variations in aggregate demand, especially when these adjustments are made within the periodic framework set by annual budgets. (Problems of timing exist of course for any type of budgetary policy, but not as seriously for other items in the budget as investment. On this see further below).

Now as already suggested the Keynesian battle required both a legitimation of budgetary policy per se, and a legitimation of budget deficits. In fact in the peculiar circumstance of World War Two one got the former but in a sense not the latter. In other words budgetary policy was legitimised by its use to contain inflation in the war economy (though physical controls played a large part in this also).[1] The wartime budget used for this purpose did of course involve substantial deficits, but fighting wars had always been accepted as justifying public borrowing. So the acceptance of budgetary policy in the context of the Second World War did not involve a breach in the tradition of sound finance, did not represent a victory for the subordination of budgetary policy to economic management in normal peacetime conditions.

In the post-1945 period budgetary policy then became central to Keynesianism, but in conditions where this did not involve large public deficits. The P.S.B.R. figures are a bone of contention, but certainly on any reading were far lower than in the 1970s (see below, Section II).

Thus the limits of the Keynesian victory were not exposed. Even when governments did borrow, this was not done in a manner which threatened sound finance. The fears that once government borrowing was legitimised governments would be unconstrained was clearly unfounded. As the government's debts were financed largely by private sector financial institutions, these institutions maintained a scrutiny over public borrowing, both of its scale and character. Thus in the post-war decades sound finance was threatened neither by the scale nor manner of public borrowing.

Keynesian policy in the post-war period thus came to be identified with budgetary policy within the context of fine tuning around a high level of economic activity, that level of activity itself primarily the consequence of the high level of private investment, both in the U.K. and abroad (Matthews 1968). This fine tuning was spatchcocked onto the pre-existing annual budgetary process (more frequent budgets did not become common until the late 1960s). There is clearly no a priori logic in this, no reason to suppose that the rhythms of whatever private sector forces determined fluctuations in aggregate demand would match the rhythms of annual budgets.

Another aspect of this coupling of the budget as a traditional device linked to the political and administrative cycles of Westminster and Whitehall, with its new role as a weapon of economic management, was that expenditure decisions were made prior to revenue decisions. This meant that, certainly as far as the annual cycle of budget making was concerned, it was taxation which was adjusted for purposes of management, not expenditure. Whilst periodic proposals were made for changes in public expenditure, these were not easily assimilated to the annual budgetary process.

Thus the short-term focus on demand management in the post-war years was not some kind of ideologically based short sightedness on the part of governments, an unconcern with the day after tomorrow. It resulted from the focus of demand management on budgetary policy, and the lack of any attempt to adjust the time scale of budgetary policy to accord with its new task of economic management.

Smith (1982) has argued that it is wrong to reduce Keynesian policy to the existence of budget deficits, or indeed to the use of the budget as a means of economic management. He writes (p.227):

> What is "Keynesian", it seems to me it is not necessarily any particular policy instrument, but rather the specification which involves a set of legitimations and exclusions for the field of state economic activity. The legitimated area includes the whole realm of demand management (which may extend further than the budgetary aggregates), and the policy instruments pertinent thereto, whilst the exclusions concern any process of direct intervention, either through public ownership via a planned system of state corporations, or by less overt forms of state direction through financial institutions, or by indicative planning. In the light of this structure of approved and proscribed instruments of intervention it seems to me that British economic policy can be seen as quite definitely Keynesian, compared to the more directly interventionist administrations of Japan, Germany or Scandinavia.

Now it should be clear from what has been said already in this chapter that my characterisation of Keynesianism involves more stress on the role of budget deficits than does Smith's position. As already argued the Keynesian revolution was in large part a battle to legitimise budget deficits, a battle which existed because of the asymmetry of surpluses and deficits. Secondly I want to argue that the failure of Keynesianism to fully legitimise budget deficits is very important. It is important because most generally it helps us to see the Utopianism of the Keynesian project in the sense that the project suggested that the budgetary process could be subordinated in the needs of demand management, and that in such a subordination the major obstacles were "ideological" i.e. required only that agents in the economy see that economy in a new light.

The failure of legitimisation is also important in helping to explain events since the 1950s and 1960s. The constraint on fiscal policy imposed by the manner of financing deficits was not a problem in these early post-war years. Because of the buoyancy of the private sector, demand management to obtain full employment required no or only small deficits. Only when this buoyancy evaporated was the very partial success of these efforts at legitimation apparent.

Nevertheless, it is clear that Smith's more general characterisation of Keynesianism provides a great deal of insight into the character of the post-war policy regime.

First it is clearly the case in such a view that, insofar as British Keynesianism involved a stress on budgetary policy, this was highly contingent, and should not be seen as in any sense the 'essence' of Keynesianism. This indeed is borne out by the points made above about how the focus on budgetary policy was particularly the consequence of the wartime context in which Keynesianism first made its impact.

Secondly such a view highlights the possibility of alternative Keynesian policies to those actually pursued in Britain. As Smith (p.226) points out Kaldor, a Keynesian par excellence, proposed a Keynesian policy for Britain which was primarily orientated around exchange rate policy, and in which budgetary policy would be subordinated to achieving growth objectives, both of output and exports, coupled with a target surplus in the balance of payments (Kaldor 1971, p.12).

Now this policy proposal differed strongly from those made by Kaldor in earlier years, when he like most Keynesians had focussed on the budgetary process as crucial - indeed Kaldor provided pioneering estimates of the scale of the budgetary adjustment required for full employment in the Beveridge Report (Beveridge 1944, Appendix C; reprinted in Kaldor 1964).

Also it is clear that Kaldor's policy proposals of 1971 reflect the concern with growth as an objective of policy, something which as already suggested (Chapter 4), is not an important policy objective until the mid-1950s. It is not clear how far Kaldor's change of position is a consequence of this change in emphasis in objectives, though certainly central to his critique of existing policy

was its failure to deliver growth (1971, pp.15-9),
though Kaldor of course retained full employment as
a central aim.

Despite these caveats, the general point that
Smith makes that Keynesianism can take many different forms than that of the 1950s and 1960s, is
clearly both right and important. Clearly the
Cambridge Economic Policy Group's arguments could be
cited as a more recent example of the wide possibilities of Keynesian argument on the economy. In
looking at the 'decline' of Keynesianism in Britain
it is important to bear in mind that what is usually
attacked under that label is often the fine tuning
fiscalism of the 1950s and 1960s. Whilst economic
theory has attacked Keynesianism more generally,
much of the policy related attack appears to play
off this highly particular and idiosyncratic form of
Keynesian policy.

Thirdly Smith's argument is valuable for opening up the question of the exclusions from policy
made by Keynesianism. One might say that Keynesianism is most strikingly unified precisely by what it
rules out of the policy repertoire.

Keynesianism is of course above all concerned
with the management of macro-economic aggregates and
not with the decisions of any particular economic
agents (except governments). This rules out a whole
series of possible policy mechanisms outlined by
Smith in the quotation given above, and which have
been generally adopted in other advanced capitalist
countries.

It is not relevant here to examine in detail
why this pattern of exclusions arose in Britain. In
part no doubt it arises from a certain theoretical
heritage in which Keynesians were keen to assert the
acceptability of traditional (micro) economic
doctrines about the market allocation of resources,
and to confine their critique to the level of aggregate activity. Possibly more powerful was the
consonance of a macro-economic emphasis with a
certain politics, which wanted to render the traditional political concern with private or public
ownership irrelevant (see above, Chapter 1).

Whatever the reasons for this pattern of exclusions, it had serious implications for policy making. First of all, it meant that economic policy's
capacity to deliver full employment, and especially
full employment without rapid inflation was highly
constrained. It was able to deliver this objective
only in the transient circumstances of the 1950s

and 1960s. This point is returned to in Section II of this chapter.

In addition, when policy was addressed to other objectives - most notably economic growth - it was clearly inadequate (cf. Cairncross 1971, p.33). Now this point was commonly registered from the late 1950s when growth first came on to the agenda. As pointed out in Chapter 4, once growth became important to policy then there was a search for policies which went beyond the norms of macro management at that time, most especially a concern with planning.

One of the difficulties of the way the problem of growth was perceived in these debates was through a dichotomy of macro policy versus planning, in which the former was portrayed as inherently short-run in character and more generally inherently concerned with budgetary adjustment to attain full employment. From this developed the tremendous focus on "stop-go" as an inhibition to growth. But the evidence seems to suggest both that the amplitudes of fluctuations in output were not particularly large in Britain at this time, and that other countries grew much faster than Britain with either similar or greater fluctuations of output (Whiting 1976).

The implication of this is not that macro policy in general is unimportant to growth. Rather it is that the macro policy of the 1950s and 1960s was ill designed to make growth more likely and that other macro policies might have helped achieved this objective.

This argument is perhaps best illustrated by Kaldor. He argues that in this post-war pattern of macro policy, it was consumption that was the autonomous factor in regulating the growth of the economy. The scale and pattern of investment was thus by and large determined by the scale and pattern of domestic consumption, not world demand. This "consumption-led growth" he argues had a number of disadvantages in an open economy. First it induced caution in the management of consumer demand because any induced investment demand would rapidly spill over into a trade deficit. Second this meant the incentive to invest was weak. For a full employment level of output therefore consumption will be larger and investment smaller than might otherwise be the case. Because investment is tied to domestic demand it has been difficult to shift resources from consumption to investment, unlike with export-led growth where domestic consumption can be restrained whilst investment increases in response to export demand.

Thirdly the focus on domestic demand will reduce the possibility of gaining fast manufacturing growth and the productivity increasing potential this would release. Finally with the growth of exports following rather than leading the growth of productive capacity, but imports growth simultaneous with growth of domestic consumption and investment, there will be a constant danger of balance of payments problems (Kaldor 1971, pp.14-7).

It is for these reasons that Kaldor advocated the kind of exchange rate based policy already mentioned above. Now my point here is not to pronounce on whether such a policy would have been feasible to desirable. Indeed Kaldor himself stresses the difficulties of such a policy in the early post-war years, especially given the problems if Britain had not adhered to the new international regime of fixed exchange rates (Ibid., pp.12-3). Rather the point is that such a policy was just as much a Keynesian one, and just as plausible in the light of current objectives, as the predominant fiscalism. More importantly it was a policy which might have increased the level of investment, which was one, though far from the only, aspect of Britain's slow growth in this period. More generally such a policy would have cut across the dichotomy between short-run macro policy and long-term planning which rendered so much of the early growth arguments rather beside the point.

Overall we may describe the post-war policy regime as Keynesian in Smith's sense, whilst also emphasising that the limits of the success of the attempt to legitimise budget deficits was a crucial element in determining the fate of Keynesianism in the long-run, when the advantageous circumstances of the 1950s and early 1960s began to evaporate. Such a failure of legitimation would have been much less significant if Keynesian policies in Britain had not been so budgetary in character - for example if they had taken a Kaldorean form. But they didn't. Such a result was not inherent in theoretical Keynesianism, but the outcome produced was centrally important for British policy in the post-war period.

The Keynesian Achievement?

In this section the basis of the full employment
with relatively low inflation and relatively good
balance of payments attainment is examined. Now
clearly in doing this it is a danger that the argument will be overly schematic and in particular will
divide up policy and its conditions into two neatly
divided time periods. So it should be borne in mind
that what is attempted here is a general picture of
the period roughly from 1945 to the mid-1960s, but
where no one aspect will conform exactly to that
periodisation.

In Section I the broad appropriateness of
Matthews' characterisation of the post-war period
was taken for granted. Here that characterisation is
much crucial, for if Matthews is wrong then this
section's purpose is beside the point. If fiscal
policy explains the post-war period of full employment by itself there is no need to seek for further
explanation.

If one takes Neild and Ward's (1979, p.39) data
on the budget for this period this shows a different
pattern to that of Matthews. This data is based on a
framework which calculates the deficit as approximately equivalent to modern measurements of the
P.S.B.R.[2] The result is that whilst Matthews shows a
persistent budget surplus, Neild and Ward show a
persistent public deficit every year between 1949
and 1964 except 1950.

The main reason for this divergence is that
Matthews uses an orthodox Keynesian framework where
$Y = C + G + I + X - M$, within which G relates only
to current public sector expenditure. The basis of
this seems to be first of all a traditional focus on
real magnitudes, and not therefore on the question
of financing public expenditure. Secondly it relies
on a view that the determinants of investment,
private and public, are in principle different from
the determinants of current expenditure, and that
therefore they are not to be treated as part of a
strict fiscal policy. Thus Matthews (1970, pp.174-5,
footnote) "The overall surplus is indeed what is
relevant for financial purposes or flow-of-funds
analysis. But within the present framework it seems
most appropriate to treat public investment not as
part of the budget but as part of investment".

On the other hand Neild and Ward are more concerned with the financial position of the government. Their measurement is further discussed below.

What is interesting however is that if one
makes the comparison, as Matthews does, between 1937

and this post-war period and asks how far the rise
in employment between these dates was due to fiscal
policy, it is far from clear that Ward and Neild's
data yield a substantially different answer. In
other words, whilst the latter authors show a budget
deficit, this is not, given plausible estimates of
the multipliers involved, sufficient to explain much
of the difference in employment levels between 1937
and the 1950s and 1960s. In other words Matthews'
result does not seem to be so sensitive to the
calculation of budgetary posture as the contrast
with Ward and Neild might initially suggest.

One of the central problems in assessing
Matthews' argument is the question of confidence. If
one stresses the demand side and confidence aspects
of investment decisions, it is plausible that the
simple commitment of government to stimulate a full
employment level of demand will induce employment-
creating investment independently of the means,
budgetary or otherwise, used to sustain this commitment. In the nature of things such an argument is
difficult to assess, confidence is an intangible
factor more or less impossible to measure. One can
perhaps make two points. First as Matthews stresses
(1968, pp.560-3) there were lots of other good
reasons for high investment in this period apart
from any confidence imparted by government commitment.

Secondly, one might turn this argument on its
head and say that the governmental commitment to
full employment might inhibit confidence and investment if investors feared the consequences, either
consequences for labour discipline and hence productivity and profits, or consequences for inflation
and general economic stability (see Kalecki 1943).
Only with the demonstration that this commitment did
not necessarily involve these consequences might its
effects on the demand side outweigh its possible
inhibitory consequences.

Finally on the plausibility of Matthews' argument, there is the question of the effects of fiscal
policy in stabilising the economy. If policy in this
period was such as to actually destabilise the
economy then it would seem logical to say that the
fiscal policy can hardly have been crucial to the
full employment of the period. If in year X there
are both autonomous deflationary forces and the
government's policies also act to depress demand,
and yet unemployment is say only 500,000, it does
seem unlikely that fiscal policy is central to the
level of demand. And there is good (though

disputed[3]) evidence that demand management was pro
rather than counter cyclical. In particular Dow
(1964, p.384) argues that "As far as internal conditions are concerned then, budgetary and monetary
policy failed to be stabilising, and must on the
contrary be regarded as having been positively
destabilising".

This kind of conclusion is surely not surprising. Fine tuning an open economy (unlike attempting
to stimulate a secularly depressed closed economy),
requires techniques of forecasting, policy instruments of high calibration, and impeccable timing to
secure an 'ideal' pattern of stabilisation. Indeed,
the more one thinks of what is involved in such a
programme perhaps the less one is surprised by the
failures incurred and the more impressed that such a
task should be attempted at all.

The clear implication of all the above is that
fine tuning policy period in the British economy in
the post-war economy was remarkably successful only
because of a series of highly favourable factors.

First of all, as already noted, there was the
high level of investment which whether measured
gross or net rose steadily up until 1973 (Wright
1979, pp.24-6). Now as Matthews notes (1968, p.560)
"Economists have been so pre-occupied with explaining why investment in this country has been low compared with other countries that they have devoted
little attention to considering why investment has
been so much higher relatively to national income
than it has ever been before in this country".
Matthews himself offers no clear conclusion on this,
but the balance of his argument would seem to be
that there was an upward shift in the investment
demand function largely for reasons similar to those
which caused previous cyclical booms. In particular,
an increased pace of technological change, perhaps
partly induced by the war, adding to an accumulation
of back-logs of investment opportunities resulting
from a low level of investment in the U.K. throughout almost all of the first half of the twentieth
century. There was, in addition, the increasingly
generous tax treatment of investment which acted to
at least offset the decline in profitability which
(arguably[4]) affected British industry in this
period.

The general nature of this investment boom and
hence its concurrent occurrence in other advanced
countries meant that trade also boomed, which added
to the difference in "autonomous" demand between the
1950s and 1960s and 1937.

As already argued, this period did not "require" a large budget deficit to maintain full employment. The government ran a constant current account surplus, offset by a public investment programme.

The position regarding P.S.B.R. is more complex, as definitional problems are more acute (see Alexander and Toland 1980). Ward and Neild use the definition common in Britain before 1976. In that year the borrowing requirements of publicly owned industries were excluded, which obviously reduced the figure. Neild and Ward justify continuing to use the old measure because "the receipts and expenditure of nationalised industries are in large measure under direct government influence. Not only do the respective corporations have to obtain government sanction for all planned investment and borrow via the government, but the prices charged for goods and services they produce have in a number of cases been partly determined by general economic policy considerations since 1971" (1970, p.8).

Table 5.1: Budgets 1952-68

	Budget current account surplus (£m.)	Public investment (£m.)
1952	604	1168
1953	507	1445
1954	549	1232
1955	777	1475
1956	743	1541
1957	854	1667
1958	935	1632
1959	874	1768
1960	745	1863
1961	905	2152
1962	1272	2222
1963	1079	2366
1964	1444	2944
1965	1834	3296
1966	2103	3621
1967	2148	4353
1968	2891	4736

Source: National Income and Expenditure of the U.K., (H.M.S.O., London, Various dates).

Clearly the latter point is irrelevant to the period under consideration here and may be disregarded. Also it may be noted that the 1976 change in definition brought Britain broadly into line with other countries. As Pliatzky (1982, pp.162-3) points

Table 5.2:|P.S.B.R. 1952-68

	(A) Neild and Ward's definition (% of GNP)	(B) Absolute Figure (£m.)
1952	-4.9	771
1953	-5.6	591
1954	-3.7	367
1955	-3.2	469
1956	-3.7	564
1957	-3.4	486
1958	-2.9	491
1959	-3.4	571
1960	-3.9	710
1961	-3.9	704
1962	-2.8	546
1963	-3.8	842
1964	-3.9	989
1965	-3.1	1205
1966	-3.3	961
1967	-5.3	1863

Sources: (A) R. Neild and T. Ward, The Measurement and Reform of Budgetary Policy, (Heinemann, London, 1979), Tables 4.1 and 4.2.
(B) J. Buchanan, J. Burton and R. Wagner, The Consequences of Mr. Keynes, (I.E.A., London, 1978), p.34.

out, it made little sense to treat the whole of the nationalised industries capital expenditure as public expenditure if some proportion of this is raised from the internal resources of the industries, as was done up to 1976. More complex was how to treat money raised by the government. The ideal solution would seem to be to treat Public Dividend Capital "a form of pseudo-equity" (Pliatzky, p.162), as part of the public sector expenditure, but that moneys borrowed from the National Loans Fund and lent - on to the industries at market interest rates and repayment of capital expected should not be so treated. This solution was not agreed to in 1976 because some sections of the Treasury wanted to continue to treat public dividend capital as if it were

real, not "pseudo-equity". Therefore, as there
seemed to be a strong case for common treatment,
National Loans Fund finance was also included in the
public expenditure total. Only borrowing direct from
the market and overseas was excluded.

Therefore, there seems to be a good case for
saying that at a minimum pre-1976 figure as used by
Neild and Ward exaggerate the size of public borrowing by including all nationalised industry investment expenditure. This is to leave on one side the
rather peculiar fact that moneys raised via the
National Loans Fund at full commercial rates should
be treated as part of public sector borrowing.

In one respect, certainly, the P.S.B.R. was not
a problem - there was no occasion in this period
when the scale of government borrowing was affected
by a loss of confidence by either domestic or
foreign lenders. The government had no problem in
selling its debt, and its size did not act as an
index of foreign confidence as it did in 1931 or was
to again in the 1970s.

The latter point was of course only partly the
consequence of the scale of government borrowing. In
1931 this role for public borrowing reflected a
world-wide financial crisis, the existence of a
Labour government, and the scale of expenditure by
that government on unemployment assistance. The
more relevant comparison for the 1950s and 1960s is
the mid-1970s. What made a substantial difference
between these periods was not only the scale of
government borrowing, but the extent to which this
was linked to flows of short-term capital funds.
These showed a sharp change in their volatility from
the late 1960s onwards and especially in the oil-
crisis years of the 1970s (Lamfalussy in Cairncross
1981, pp.203-7). This meant an increasing sensitivity, and increasingly violent response, to whatever
factors affected confidence in a country. Whilst the
scale of public borrowing was not the only one of
such factors it was an important one.

Finally on the public sector deficit it should
be noted that there was no interruption to the operation of fiscal policy brought about by the absolute
levels of public expenditure and taxation. (Unlike
the 1970s - see Chapter 6 below). In particular the
operation of a fiscal policy primarily based on
variations in tax levels was around a trend reduction in tax rates, especially because of the growth
of private savings (Dow 1964, pp.263-4).

The 1950s and 1960s were remarkable not only
for the maintenance of full employment without

fiscal problems, they also saw relatively little in the way of problems on the balance of payments (certainly until the mid-1960s) or inflation (until right at the end of the 1960s).

The balance of payments did not figure very largely in wartime discussions of post-war full employment policies, mainly because the potential problems were seen to be ones of deflation not inflation. Nevertheless in the early post-war years Britain did remarkably well in increasing its exports to try and compensate for the loss of overseas assets incurred in the war (Chapter 2).

The effect of this exporting success was however partly offset by a decline in the terms of trade (ratio of export to import prices). "The net result was that by 1950 the balance on current account, with imports severely controlled to 70 per cent of their 1938 volume, required 175 per cent of the 1938 volume of exports" (Wright 1979, pp.147-8). But from 1951 the balance of payments Wright estimates[5] (p.148) gained to the extent of £100m. a year from the reversal of this trend, and the slow down of the improvement from the mid-1960s undoubtedly added to balance of payments problems from that year, especially as the export drive could not be maintained against reviving continental competition from 1950 onwards.

Probably more important than this external factor in reducing the balance of payments constraint (under a fixed exchange rate system) was the slow pace of inflation. Whilst the danger of inflation under conditions of full employment was recognised from the earliest wartime days of discussion of this objective, its recognition did not lead to any systematic policy response. In particular it did not lead to any systematic attempt to change the pattern and organisations for wage and salary bargaining in the economy (Kaldor 1971, p.3).

The often rather vague notion of expectations has some substance here. As suggested in Chapter 3, it was not until the mid-1950s that it came to be generally accepted even amongst economists that inflation was not contingent upon a series of specific events, but a correlate of the new full employment policy regime. But the pace and scale of adjustment to this new era was undoubtedly slow. For example, it was not until the mid-1960s that the annual wage increase became an accepted part of the collective bargaining scene (see for the position at the end of the 1950s Knowles in Worswick and Ady (1962), pp.519-22). Other evidence of the slow

adaptation of expectations to inflation is given by
Wright (1979, pp.175-6). For example commercial
rents traditionally fixed for at least twenty one
years became commonly reviewable after 7 years in
the 1960s. Equally the boom in owner-occupation owed
a lot to the belief that house ownership offered a
hedge against inflation. All this meant that the
potential of full employment, coupled with a fundamentally unchanged collective bargaining system, for
creating inflation was long delayed in realisation,
but could not be for ever denied.

Finally, one must mention the "revolution of
rising expectations". Again such a term may appear
gross and unhelpful if not treated with care. But
equally to ignore the climate of expectations about
living standards would be as foolish as to ignore
that about inflation (which in any case cannot be
neatly separated off).

From the mid-1950s, as pointed out in Chapter
4, the objective of economic growth became an
explicit part of the policy agenda in Britain.
Expectations of economic growth, of a general pattern of lifetime rises in earnings, rapidly became
institutionalised. When in 1954 Butler as Chancellor
of the Exchequer argued .... "I see no reason why,
in the next quarter of a century, if we run our
policy properly and soundly, we should not double
our standard of living in this country" (quoted in
Worswick and Ady 1962, p.32) he put into words a
belief that was soon to extend far beyond the makers
of government policy.

Expectations of future growth became built into
public expenditure plans very explicitly - but also
if less measurably into the pattern of domestic,
educational and political life. The promise of
growth offered a solution to all manner of problems,
and there was a common slippage from arguing its
desirability to assuming its attainability by
government policy.

One does not have to accept the Whiggism of
1979 style conservatism to accept that the capacity
of government to deliver economic growth, especially
in an open economy like the U.K. is highly constrained. There is no good reason to suppose that
the historically high and sustained level of growth
of the post-war period owed much directly to government policy, and therefore it is unsurprising if
this growth could no longer be delivered in the much
less favourable circumstances of the late 1970s and
early 1980s.

Yet the expectation of growth, and the belief that governments could deliver that growth was established in the early post-war decades. When governments revealed their impotence then another plank of the policy regime of those years was undermined.

Conclusion

The objective of this chapter has not been to argue that government policy in the period under discussion did nothing to maintain full employment in the economy. At the very least the political commitment to this goal prevented more deflationary responses to the periodic and increasingly severe balance of payments crises.

But it is to argue that the highly fortunate conjecture of circumstances of the 1950s and 1960s led to exaggeration of the capacities of governments in capitalist countries to deliver policy objectives. In that sense, the disillusionments of the 1970s were based on misunderstandings of the conditions of success in the 1950s and 1960s, as much as if not more than on the counter-revolutions in economic theory or retrogressions in political ideology and rhetoric.

NOTES

1. See Chapter 3.
2. For the differences see R. Neild and T. Ward, The Measurement and Reform of Budgetary Policy, (Heinemann, London, 1979), p.8.
3. e.g. G.D.N. Worswick, "Trade and Payments" in A. Cairncross (ed), Britain's Economic Prospects Reconsidered, (Allen and Unwin, London, 1971), pp.36-60.
4. For a close analysis of the declining profitability argument, see M. King, "The United Kingdom Profits Crisis: Myth or Reality?", Economic Journal, 85, 1, (March 1975), pp.33-47.
5. Though his calculation would seem to ignore the effects of the lower prices for exports on primary producers on their purchases of British exports. Primary producers at this time purchased about 70 per cent of all British exports. P. Ady, "The Terms of Trade" in G. Worswick and P. Ady (eds), The British Economy in the 1950s, (Clarendon Press, Oxford, 1962), pp.147-72. See also J. Wright, "Comment" in F. Cairncross (ed), Changing Percep-

tions of the British Economy, (Methuen, London, 1981), pp.22-5.

PART TWO

THE NEW REGIME IN DECLINE

Chapter Six

FULL EMPLOYMENT

By the mid-1970s the commitment to full employment,
which had seemed the cornerstone of post-war policy
in the 1950s and 1960s, looked to be dead. In the
budget of 1975, for example, for the first time in
the post-war period, unemployment was increased as a
deliberate, rather than a 'side-effect', of macro-
economic policy. Where in 1974 Healey as Chancellor
of the Exchequer had argued that "Deliberately to
adopt a strategy which requires mass unemployment
would be no less an economic than a moral crime"
(Hansard, 12 November 1974, Col. 253), by 1975 he
could reject advice that unemployment was the main
problem "I do not believe it would be wise to follow
this advice today.... I cannot afford to increase
demand further today when 5p. in every £ we spend at
home has been provided by our creditors abroad and
inflation is running at its current rate" (Hansard,
15 April 1975, Col. 282). In 1976 Callaghan made his
(in)famous speech at the Labour Party Conference,
asserting that the option of spending our way out of
recession "no longer exists, and that insofar as it
ever did exist it only worked on each occasion since
the war by injecting a bigger dose of inflation
into the economy" (Labour Party 1976, p.188).
      Whilst too much of long-term significance
should not perhaps be read into these two highly
political events by themselves, (see Section
"Fiscal Ambiguity" below), they did signal a shift
in policy perceptions which this chapter will
attempt to analyse. The first part deals with some
of the characteristics of the full employment regime
of the 1950s and 1960s which provided the context
for the attack on the employment goal in the 1970s.
The second part will look in some detail at the
crisis of the 1970s which was of central importance
in the eventual jetissoning of the full employment

commitment. (Table 6.1 gives the unemployment figures as a background to the discussion).

Table 6.1:   Percentage Unemployment 1956-1980

(Total unemployed, excluding school leavers, as proportion of total employees)

Year	%	Year	%
1956	1.0	1969	2.3
1957	1.0	1970	2.5
1958	1.8	1971	3.3
1959	1.7	1972	3.6
1960	1.5	1973	2.6
1961	1.3	1974	2.5
1962	1.8	1975	3.9
1963	2.2	1976	5.3
1964	1.6	1977	5.7
1965	1.3	1978	5.5
1966	1.4	1979	5.1
1967	2.2	1980	6.4
1968	2.3		

Source: Economic Trends, (H.M.S.O., London, Various Dates).

The Context of Full Employment Policy
In Chapter 5, above following Matthews (1968) it has been argued that the post-war period of 'full' employment in the 1950s and 1960s was not largely the consequence of a 'Keynesian' policy. That is to say that 'full' employment was mainly the consequence of factors not directly responsive to government measures - private investment and exports - rather than government budgetary policy. Fiscal policy was central to macro-economic policy in this period, but it was a policy pursued around a level of activity largely determined by the private sector, and its capacity to deal with a substantial depression was never put to the test. The Keynesian revolution had altered both the rhetoric and substance of policy: but it is important to note what that substance was. That substance was definitely not one where the government was continuously intervening to drag the economy out of deep recession and back to full employment.
    One curiosity of the development of macro-economic policy in Britain was its emphasis on fiscal policy. The analytically separate issues of whether a capitalist economy needed and should be stabilised, and the means to be used to effect such

stabilisation were in large measure conflated. Keynesianism became largely associated with fiscal policy, with monetary policy at most used to rein- force fiscal policy in the restrictionary phase of the policy cycle. As Dow (1964) and Worswick (1976) suggest this is explicable "as a reflection of British institutions and practical experience" (Worswick, p.3), especially the constitutional and political abilities of the executive in the area of budget making, which make a striking contrast with the position in the U.S.A., where the executive has never had such quick acting and extensive powers over the means of economic management via fiscal policy changes.

Given the centrality attached to fiscal policy in macro-economic management in the 1950s and 1960s, it is important to look at the character of that policy. First of all fiscal policy in the 1950s and 1960s meant constant current account surpluses (Table 6.1). This surplus is of course the basic data upon which Matthews based his argument. In a simple Keynesian framework it is this current balance which is the appropriate measure of fiscal stance because the forces which determine the levels of investment (public or private) are thought to be wholly different from the determinants of current expenditures. Matthews (1970, pp.174-5, footnote) defended his position thus: "The overall surplus is indeed what is relevant for financial purposes or for flow-of-funds analysis. But within the present framework it seems most appropriate to treat public investment not as part of the budget but as part of investment".

The "present framework" refers to a simple Keynesian expenditure model of National Income, $Y = C + G + I + X - M$, within which G relates only to current public sector expenditure. The focus is on real rather than nominal expenditures, so the model is not concerned with questions concerning the financing of public expenditure. This focus was also consistent with the practice, which was quickly established after the war, of <u>not</u> using public investment as a stabilisation weapon (Dow 1964, p.186 and Ch. 8).

One might also note that what later became a much more popular measure of the public sector's position - the Public Sector Borrowing Requirement - was not in common use in Britain until the mid-1970s. Whilst the idea of overall public sector borrowing was mentioned in the Radcliffe Report (e.g. para. 123), its use in the 1960s was mainly

confined to the Bank of England's analyses of inter-
sectoral financial flows. Only with the coming of
money supply targets (D.C.E.) at the end of the
nineteen sixties did the P.S.B.R. enter the mainstream of debates on the economy (Alexander and
Toland 1980).

Table 6.2: Government Finance 1952-70

Public sector balance
as percentage of GNP

	(a)	(b)	(c)	(d)
	Actual basis	Constant employment basis	Budget current account surplus (£m.)	Public investment (£m.)
1952	-4.9	-5.6	604	1168
1953	-5.6	-6.8	507	1445
1954	-3.7	-4.7	549	1232
1955	-3.2	-4.9	777	1475
1956	-3.7	-5.1	743	1541
1957	-3.4	-4.7	854	1667
1958	-2.9	-3.2	935	1632
1959	-3.4	-3.9	874	1768
1960	-3.9	-4.7	745	1863
1961	-3.9	-4.9	905	2152
1962	-2.8	-3.4	1272	2222
1963	-3.8	-4.6	1079	2366
1964	-3.9	-5.9	1444	2944
1965	-3.1	-4.4	1834	3296
1966	-3.3	-4.5	2103	3261
1967	-5.1	-5.5	2148	4353
1968	-3.7	-4.2	2891	4736
1969	-0.3	+0.1	4214	4704
1970	+0.6	+1.4	5007	5216

Note: the figures in columns (a) and (b) are not exactly
equivalent to the current definition of the P.S.B.R. - on the
small differences see R. Neild and T. Ward, The Measurement
and Reform of Budgetary Policy, (Heinemann, London, 1979),
pp.8-9.

Sources: (a) and (b) from R. Neild and T. Ward, Ibid.,
Tables 4.1 and 4.2.
          (c) and (d): 1952-67 from National Income and
Expenditure of the U.K., (H.M.S.O., London, various dates);
1960 onwards from Financial Statistics, (H.M.S.O., London,
various dates).

Secondly because the scale of public investment did not fluctuate violently in this period, and <u>very approximately</u> the P.S.B.R. = public investment minus the current account surplus (see Table 6.1), the pattern of change of the P.S.B.R. over time was similar to that of the budget surplus. Of course the P.S.B.R. was positive (except in 1970) because public investment was greater than the budget surplus, but whichever is used as a measure of fiscal stance shows a similar picture. Above all, both figures show that full employment was sustained without recourse to bigger and bigger budget stimuli. Whatever may have been maintained in subsequent literature (e.g. Buchanan and Wagner 1977; Buchanan et al. 1979), it was <u>not</u> the case that the 1950s and 1960s were characterised by increasingly profligate spending and borrowing by governments as a consequence of the Keynesian endorsement of budget deficits. As a cursory inspection of the (actual) public sector balance or current account figures in Table 6.1 will show, neither showed any strong secular trend.

The nominal National Debt rose slowly from £25,899m. in 1950 to £33,079m. in 1970, falling as a ratio to GNP from almost 3:1 in 1945 to 0.7:1 in 1970 (Reid 1977). Most of this deficit seems to have been incurred for income generating purposes, fully in accord with 'classical' budgetary precepts.

The very strong linkage between demand management and fiscal policy had very important consequences for the debate on and conduct of policy in Britain. Commitment to full employment became strongly linked to <u>short-term</u> stabilisation policies, and in particular to fiscal policy. This in turn meant that public expenditure and its financing and control became intertwined with the question of policy on full employment (and inflation) in a way which analytically appears 'unnecessary' but in British practice has been very important. The question of stabilisation policy and the question of the size of government expenditure have never been separated in British debates in the way monetarists would have wished (Laidler 1975; Friedman 1980; see also Chapter 10 below). Again it is useful to note what was happening to public expenditure in this period given the way in which the debate over fiscal policy became intertwined with that of the absolute size and trend of public expenditure.

Public sector expenditure rose on trend as a proportion of national output in Britain in the period 1950 to 1970, though the precise figures depend on the conventions used in making the measurement.[1] Figures for total government expenditure as a proportion of National Income are given in Table 6.3.

Table 6.3:   U.K. Government Total Expenditure as a Percentage of National Income

	Total	Defence	Domestic Transfers
1950	39.1	7.6	6.5
1951	42.6	9.1	6.1
1952	45.3	11.3	6.6
1953	43.9	11.1	6.7
1954	41.0	10.4	6.5
1955	39.6	9.4	6.7
1956	39.5	9.2	6.6
1957	38.8	8.5	6.5
1958	39.2	7.9	7.5
1959	39.7	7.7	7.9
1960	39.4	7.7	7.6
1961	41.4	7.6	8.7
1962	42.5	7.8	9.2
1963	42.5	7.5	9.7
1964	42.1	7.2	9.5
1965	43.4	7.2	10.1
1966	44.8	7.1	10.5
1967	47.9	7.4	11.2
1968	49.2	7.0	12.0
1969	49.1	6.3	12.3
1970	49.3	6.3	12.3

Source: W. Nutter, Growth of Government in the West, (American Enterprise Institute, Washington, 1978), Table B-3.

Two points are worth making about such figures. First, they reflect a pattern common to the advanced capitalist world. Indeed Britain ranks around the average both for the proportion of government expenditure to National Income in this period in the O.E.C.D. area, and for the rate of growth of such expenditure (Nutter 1978). Secondly, much of this increase was due to a sharp rise in transfer payments rather than public consumption, so the figures greatly exaggerate the 'control of resources' by government as opposed to the resources they take from one set of households and give to others. As with the data on public sector deficit, these figures should be borne in mind when looking at the debates of the 1970s.

For most of the 1950s and 1960s demand management consisted of periodic 'stops' and 'gos' largely determined with reference to balance of payments figures and unemployment, and with the timing of policy decisions linked, albeit not always straightforwardly, to electoral considerations. But if this is what the 'Keynesian revolution' consisted of it was pretty small beer on any account. It arguably made the cycles of the economic system greater (Dow 1965, esp. p.384; Godley 1974), though this has been contested (Little 1966; Worswick 1971). But whatever the case the actual amplitudes of fluctuation suffered were mild both in historical and comparative perspective (N.E.D.O. 1976; Whiting 1976). Fluctuations in both GDP and industrial production were low compared with other advanced capitalist countries. Cycles have shortened to 4 or 5 years as compared with the historic 'trade cycle' of 7 to 11 years, but the amplitude of the fluctuations has been very much less than before the Second World War (Matthews 1969).

Stop-go may not be evidence of a particularly successful policy, but its importance has probably been greatly exaggerated, certainly regarding its direct economic effects. Economic growth has been comparatively slow in Britain in the post-war period, but there seems little evidence that this was to any substantial extent the consequence of demand management. Nevertheless the equation of demand management and commitment to full employment with these sharp reversals of policy, did not help the proponents of full employment when the underlying position of the economy deteriorated from the early 1970s.

During the "long boom" unemployment largely disappeared from public view for almost 25 years, even the 'rediscovery' of poverty in the early 1960s not being linked with unemployment (Sinfield 1981, pp.127-32). Thus there was an absence of argument about the effects of unemployment. "It tended to be widely assumed that the problem of unemployment did not exist and therefore there was nothing to study" (Blackaby in Worswick 1976, p.296). Opposition to unemployment was largely based on a vague "folk memory" of the 1930s by the public and fears of its electoral consequences on the part of government. In a variety of ways both these were eroded in the 1970s.

The Crisis of the mid-1970s

The growing rejection of full employment as the pre-
dominent objective of government policy in the 1970s
may be seen as a consequence of the combination of a
change in the constraints on the pursuit of such a
policy and a parallel shift in perceptions of policy
makers. However I want to argue in this section that
this shift in perception was not simply a reflection
of this change in "reality" - we do not know reality
separate from the perceptions we bring to bear on
it. So whilst the discussion of policy in the period
fed upon the non-discursive, i.e. changes in constraints, it cannot be reduced to those changes.

As stressed in Section I above the pursuit of
full employment in the 1950s and 1960s did not
involve any radical departure from pre-Keynesian
fiscal norms. It was sustained by 'mild' policies
largely revolving around adjustments to tax levels.
In the 1970s the slow drift upwards in the unemployment level evident from the late 1960s was coupled
with major exogenous shocks to the economy,
especially the oil price rise and the break up of
the international monetary system, which put the
question of the policies necessary for full employment 'on the agenda' in a way never true in the
previous decades. That the debate was resolved in a
manner largely unfavourable to full employment seems
to have depended upon two major factors. These were
the strong linkage of employment policy to fiscal
policy and hence to the 'crisis of public expenditure' which occurred in the 1970s. Secondly the
'moral panic' over inflation, which is looked at in
Chapter 9.

As shown in Tables 6.1 and 6.2 below the 1950s
and 1960s were characterised by no pronounced
increase in fiscal stimulus to the economy measured
by fiscal deficits, but a general upward drift in
the level of public expenditure. In the 1970s the
former pattern was radically altered and the latter
accelerated to produce a 'fiscal crisis'.

The crisis of the mid-1970s was composed of
both a rapid rise in public expenditure and a rapid
rise in the proportion of this expenditure not
financed by taxation (Table 6.4). These elements can
to some extent be treated separately.

From 1970/1 to 1975/6 public expenditure in
real terms rose from £40bn. to £49bn. Godley in a
famous piece of evidence to the House of Commons
Expenditure Committee (Godley, Memorandum to House
of Commons 1975/6) argued that at least £5bn. of
this could not be accounted for by announced public

Table 6.4: The Public Sector in the 1970s

| | Public Sector Share in GNP | Public Sector Financial Balance | |
| | (a) | (b) | (c) |
		Actual	Constant employment
1970	39.3	0.6	+1.4
1971	38.4	-1.7	0
1972	40.0	-4.3	-2.2
1973	41.1	-4.8	-4.0
1974	45.2	-6.7	-5.1
1975	46.9	-8.6	-5.7
1976	46.1	-9.0	-3.8
1977	44.1	-5.1	+1.1

Sources: (a) D. Heald, Public Expenditure, Its Defence and Reform, (Martin Robertson, Oxford, 1983), Table 2.3, pp.30-1. These are O.E.C.D. figures, called "total outlays of government".

(b) and (c) R. Neild and T. Ward, The Measurement and Reform of Budgetary Policy, (Heinemann, London, 1979), Table 4.2 (Note Tables (b) and (c) obviously diverge much more than the comparable tables in Table 6.2 because of the growing level of unemployment).

policy changes. The Treasury responded to Godley's arguments and criticised them, but even by their account there was a major problem. The Treasury (House of Commons 1975/6, Minutes, Qs. 852-854) argued that 'only' £3½bn. came from unannounced changes - £1¾bn. from the effects of relative price changes, £¾bn. from an increase in debt interest, and £1bn. from 'implicit' policy changes.

This 'loss of control' of the public sector focussed attention on the existing control procedures. Under the prevailing P.E.S.C. system, control was exercised largely in volume terms, plans being made in relation to the expected growth of real output, with largely automatic adjustment for inflation. This system, introduced in 1961, did not generate great problems in the 1960s because the relatively low inflation did not entail great disparities between real and nominal magnitudes. In the rapid inflation of the 1970s this changed. Partly this was because of the traditional 'catching up' (Dean 1975) of public sector pay with that in the private sector, but especially because of the faster-than-average rise in the price of land and buildings.

A considerable part of the growth of the public sector in the early 1970s can then be linked to the existing mode of control. This mode of control was based on the conception that government expenditure could not and should not be varied year by year, and was in a sense the other side of the emphasis on stabilisation taking place through short-term changes in tax. This system meant that government expenditure was planned in relation to (hypothetical) real resources rather than government revenue. This system had a powerful rationale, given the waste involved in for example varying the number of schools built for short-term stabilisation purposes (Dow 1965, Ch. 8, on the growing realisation of this in the years prior to P.E.S.C.). However it did involve effectively ignoring the constraints on governments in raising the revenues to make these real resources available to the public sector, a problem enormously exacerbated by the rise in inflation.

Much of this expenditure growth, as already suggested, did not reflect deliberate policy on the part of the government, something to be explained as the effects of rational calculations by bureaucrats and politicians in the 'economics of politics' framework. Apart from the contingent effects of the early 1970s inflation on the relative price of public sector inputs, the rise in expenditure resulted from the continuation of the demographic shift - more and more old people of pensionable age, and more and more unemployed in receipt of unemployment or social security benefit. Increased payments on such accounts were largely the consequence of 'exogenous' factors, i.e. demographic shifts and the rise in the number of unemployed rather than factors controlled by governments, including the level of benefits (see Tomlinson 1981C). Wright (1977, p.146) calculates that between 1955/9 and 1975/6 transfers plus loans accounted for 80 per cent of the total increase in public consumption. It did not involve an enormous increase in the public sector 'engrossing' of public sector resources.

The scale of public spending became a focus of attention in its own right in the 1970s, with for example Roy Jenkins claiming that society as we know it would be threatened by public expenditure reaching 60 per cent of National Income. (As this figure includes transfer payments in the numerator but not in the denominator it is highly misleading in this

context, because the maximum such a figure can
attain is in principle infinity, not 100 per cent).
On such problems of definition see Heald (1983),
pp.12-8.

That such a panic impacted on the full employment debate resulted from the focus of British
demand management on fiscal policy. The analytically
separate issues of the size of the public sector and
the character of stabilisation policies tended to be
run together, as the increase in size of the public
sector was presented as the consequence of post-war
fiscal policy.

In fact the fiscal policy of the mid-1970s i.e.
the growing P.S.B.R. was not largely the consequence
of deliberate demand management aimed at reducing
the level of unemployment. That is to say, whilst it
is true that the expenditure increase of the period
was not matched by a parallel increase in tax, this
was not because of the attachment of the authorities
to deficit-financing as a principle, but because of
the substantial constraints under the prevailing
conditions, of raising taxes in line with expenditure:

Part of the problem was the failure of successive governments to adjust many indirect taxes to
inflation, so that an increasing proportion of taxes
fell on personal incomes. This is shown by the ratio
of income tax to GNP, which rose much faster than
the ratio of total taxation to GNP, rising from
8.8 per cent in 1950 to 15.8 per cent by 1975. At
the same time taxes on drink and tobacco, for
example, fell from 8.6 per cent to 3.8 per cent.
Taxes on company incomes fell from 6.7 per cent to
1.2 per cent of GNP over the same period. The consequence of all this was that the burden of income tax
greatly increased, partly via high marginal rates on
high incomes, but especially by shifting the payment
of income tax down radically at the lower levels of
income (Field, Meacher, Pond 1977).

This shift reflected constraints on government
on raising taxes in other ways. It was largely the
consequence of, on one hand, continuing government
commitment to incomes policies, which meant failure
to raise indirect tax levels because such rises fed
directly into the Retail Price Index and hence into
wage bargaining. On the other hand, the decline of
company taxation was mainly the consequence of
government attempts to offset the fall in pre-tax
profits. The tax base was being narrowed (Kay and
King 1978, e.g. p.243), boxing in governments.

The 'crisis of public expenditure' in the mid-1970s was not then the culmination of a long period of fiscal 'degeneration'. Whilst the problems of erosion of the tax base had developed over a long period, the rise in expenditure was a considerable acceleration of what had been previously a slow creep upwards. All this was of course compounded by the exogenous shock from the oil price rise. This was clearly deflationary in its implications for the world economy, because it meant a sharp upward movement in the world 'propensity to save' as the oil producers increased their incomes much faster than their expenditures. Most oil importing countries responded to the crisis by deflating domestically, in order to offset the balance of payments consequences of the sharp rise in import prices. In Britain this reaction was delayed, partly as a deliberate attempt to limit world deflation, partly as a consequence of the specific political context of the 1974 crisis culminating in the miners' strike and the 3-day week. The two budgets of 1974 were argued in the form of 'why Britain should not deflate', not in the form of 'why Britain should reflate to offset deflation elsewhere'. And by spring 1975 the argument was specifically 'why Britain should not reflate to offset the effects of deflation elsewhere'.

In other words, on the first occasion that full employment in the post-war period seemed to require a substantial Keynesian response, such a policy was not forthcoming. Part of the reason was, as already suggested, the general opposition to the public sector per se which existed in Britain at this period. Part of course was due to the fear of inflation (Chapter 9). But it is also clear that events of the mid-seventies demonstrated the constraints on such 'Keynesian' policies under the institutional arrangements then in force.

First in looking at the events of 1975/76 the rapidity of change in the fiscal position should be stressed. P.S.B.R. increased by 250 per cent in 2 years (1974 to 1976). In consequence, the government enormously increased the amount of debt it was trying to sell in a very short period. The stress was on selling long-term debt to avoid the perceived inflationary consequences of sales of shorter debt. This was a cleft stick for government policy, because emphasising long-term debt sales meant a commitment to long-term high interest rates which had to be offered to sell the debt. This was then an intensification of the contradictory demands imposed on debt policy by the debt's dual role as both source of revenue and credit base.

But more than simply an intensification of a problem that both economists and the monetary authorities had long since recognised to exist, 1975/6 revealed much greater constraints on government borrowing. In a system where government borrowing is financed by selling financial assets to private institutions, these institutions have a very substantial leverage over policy - they can, at the limit, refuse to buy unless policy reflects their desires. In 1975/6 this meant that the 'ideology' prevalent amongst potential purchases of government debt was crucially important. This provided a major entry point for monetarist ideology. Central to the public case for monetarism in the U.K. were the writings of financial journalists - Brittan, Jay, Cairncross - in the columns of the 'serious' press. By changing market sentiment in this direction monetarism was able to impose itself, not by the intellectual conversion of policy makers but by force majeure under prevailing modes of government finance. (For some possible implications of the form of expectations in the financial sector, see Boltho 1983).

A constant theme of journalistic accounts of the period is the sudden importance accorded by policy makers to market conditions (Keegan and Pennant-Rea 1979, pp.30-1, 94-5, 131-7). This was summarised by the Permanent Secretary to the Treasury (Wass 1978, p.99):

> If markets take the view that the policies pursued by a particular country are likely to damage assets held in that country or in the country's currency, they are likely to behave in ways which can actually enforce a policy change. Market behaviour has become a significant input in policy making.

Under conditions such as those of 1976 this dependence on market sentiment is central to policy - whatever governments may feel is appropriate policy. As Neild and Ward (1979, Appendix B) point out government expenditure in Britain at this time was not out of line with other European countries. Equally the P.S.B.R. of 1975 was not out of line with other industrialised countries such as West Germany and Japan (Economic Trends 1976). But such 'rational' measures of policy are beside the point insofar as markets are not concerned with/do not believe such arguments.

In 1975 and 1976 the markets seemed strongly to believe that government expenditure and government borrowing was far too high. Their response was to stop buying long-term debt for a substantial period - a "gilt strike" (Keegan and Pennant Rea, p.133), which lasted for practically the whole of the May to September period in 1976, and forced the authorities to flood the market with short-term debt. This was not just a case of purchasers demanding higher interest rates, because higher interest rates them-selves functioned as an index of the failure of government policy on public expenditure (Economist, 25 December 1976, p.73).

A consequence of this squeeze on government policy was of course a series of public expenditure cuts (February, July, November 1976) which were largely aimed at placating the markets. "A few young men in stockbrokers' offices are now virtually in charge of economic policy" allegedly became a popu-lar refrain in ministerial circles (Keegan and Pennant-Rea, p.132).

This perception of the constraints on govern-ment policy was articulated by the Permanent Secretary to the Treasury in 1978 (see quote above). He argued that this represented not a short-term problem, soon to go away, but a long-term change in the constraints on national economic policy, because it represented "an internationalisation of economic activity which is in my view the single most import-ant structural change in the world economy in the second half of the twentieth century. Its implica-tions for the independence of national economic management are still not fully guaged" (Wass 1978, p.98).

This emphasises the important point that the sales of government debt have increasingly been to foreign purchasers, so that any loss of confidence in budgetary policy is likely to be strongly reflec-ted in the foreign exchange market, i.e. not only will domestic investors possibly turn abroad to invest, but foreign investors may sell sterling. In 1976 therefore there was a clear parallel to 1931 - loss of faith in British budgetary policy was reflected in a foreign exchange crisis, which com-bined with domestic pressures led to a reversal of budgetary policy.

Of course in 1976 it was not just private markets which put pressure on the government but also the I.M.F., which post-war had become

establised as <u>the</u> international agency for borrowing
(compared with the informal inter-central bank lending which pre-dominated in the inter-war period).
The I.M.F. also acted as an agency of 'monetarist
ideas', though this too may be seen as reflecting
that agencies' perception of what private international lenders would stomach.

Thus the capacity of private lenders to con-
strain government policy, linked in part to the
scale of internationalisation of the British economy, which had been reduced markedly after the
demise of the gold standard in 1931, but revived
afterwards. It depended also on the manner of raising finance in the British system - for example the
absence of government borrowing directly from the
central bank, or the relatively small weight of
contractual savings in financing public debt. So the
constraints on budget deficits in 1976 were conditional on definite institutional arrangements. But
they were no less powerful for that.

So the panic over public sector deficits in
1975/6 was effective in bringing about a reversal of
fiscal policy which was afterwards sustained (Table
6.5). A similar panic was apparent in the U.S.A.
following the deficits of 1975 and 1976 (Tobin 1977,
p.463).

Table 6.5:   Public Sector Budget Balance (percentage
of GNP)

	(a)	(b)
	Actual	Constant employment basis
1975	-8.3	-8.2
1976	-7.8	-7.8
1977	-5.2	-4.6
1978	-6.2	-5.7
1979	-5.8	-4.5
1980-81	-5.9	-0.8

Source: K. Coutts, R. Tarling, T. Ward and
F. Wilkinson, "The Economic Consequences of
Mrs. Thatcher", Cambridge Journal of Economics, 5,
1, (March 1981), p.89. (Note the definitions used
here are the same as Neild and Ward 1979, see Table
6.4, but the base year against which constant
employment is measured is 1976).

Many of the arguments raised to support this panic - for example the suggestion that the public sector was crowding out the private - appear extremely weak. Some economists have forcefully pointed this out - for example Jackson (1980), Blackaby (1979). But unfortunately or otherwise, policy is not decided by rational debate amongst economists. Nevertheless politicians do like to argue their policies in a rational manner, and there were not of course lacking economists willing to endorse and extend the panic about the public sector. For example Bacon and Eltis (1976) seems to have been very influential despite its poor reception by economists. More specifically, there were economists who were willing to supply arguments that if full employment could no longer be achieved, it was in any case not a problem because either unemployment more or less didn't exist, and where it did was mainly the consequence of choice.

A pioneer in this respect was Wood (1972). He argued that "Unemployment today is quite different from what it was not only before the last war, but even as recently as five years ago" adding that "Inflation has arguably become by far the greater social evil" (p.12). The more specific thrust of his argument was that many of those included in the Department of Employment's unemployed figure should be excluded as not indicating any real general shortage of demand for labour. On this basis he argued for the exclusion of the temporarily stopped, school leavers, those unemployed for less than 8 weeks, and the disabled. The first category was in fact soon after dropped by the Department of Employment, but the other suggested amendments were rejected by an official committee (CMND. 5157, 1972). The grounds for so doing are powerful. The numbers of school leavers, those employed for short periods, the numbers of disabled out of work all tend to move very strongly with the unemployment rate. This is very clear in the case of the disabled (Blackaby 1976, p.297). It is also important to note that whilst short-term unemployment can easily be re-labelled redeployment (Wood, p.18; see also Deacon 1981, p.71) it is far from painless, because often part of a long-term pattern of short spells in and out of employment (Sinfield 1976).

In historical perspective a striking feature of Wood's argument and others of similar kind was to try and recreate a category of the 'unemployables' - a category commonly in use before the First World War, but discredited entirely by that war in which

unemployment virtually disappeared. The Webb's were
one of those who used this category but at least had
the grace to admit its inapplicability when they
came to write in the 1920s. The crucial point is of
course that unemployability is just one end of a
continuum of desirability to employers "One can
certainly agree that the long-term unemployed are
those whom employers will reject if they get the
chance; most employers would probably like, if they
could, to employ exclusively able bodied persons
between the ages of 25 and 40". Normally of course
they cannot - because of the pressure of demand and
therefore their own demand for labour.

Wood repeated his arguments in 1975, albeit
more agressively (e.g. pp.32, 45) in keeping with
the tone of the times. His arguments were taken up
and endorsed by Brittan (1975) and Joseph (1978).
Some impetus was given to the popularity of such
arguments by the suggestion that the shortages of
labour encountered in the 1973 boom had demonstrated
the unreliability of unemployment figures as indices
of the general state of demand, and the capacity of
macro policy to reduce unemployment. Such views seem
to have been important in Brittan, and partly seem
to explain Joseph's "conversion" (Deacon 1981,
pp.75-7). But as Blackaby (1976, p.285) has argued
the shortages of labour of that period may be
explained not as a consequence of the level of
demand but as a consequence of the rapidity of the
expansion following a long period of stagnation
(dating back some five years). In other words the
period did not show that there was no 'slack' in the
labour movement, but only that it had to be taken up
slowly.

We may find the attempt to disguise the scale
and consequences of involuntary unemployment unconvincing, and see them as in effect, if not in
intent, as rationalisation of policy made on other
grounds. Nevertheless they both reflected and reinforced a public mood of hostility towards the
unemployed amongst the employed which politicians
have slowly come to appreciate offers some insulation from the previously perceived electoral consequences of mass unemployment. One piece of evidence
of this hostility and misunderstanding is given by
a survey of estimates of the exchequer costs of
unemployment, which showed that the average inter-
viewee thought that unemployment cost £20 in every
£100 spent on seven items of government expenditure,
rather than the £2 it actually cost (Harris and
Seldom 1979, pp.123-6).

Fiscal Ambiguity

In 1976 Blackaby (p.303) wrote that "There is a risk that politicians will discover that they can run the country with one million unemployed without committing electoral suicide". This soon became not a future risk but a current reality - and the one million mark was soon surpassed. But in the late 1970s it is also true to say that the conversion of the authorities to the 'new orthodoxy' in which full employment could be jetissoned was as yet partial.[3]

For example whilst fiscal policy has tended in a general deflationary direction after 1975, the rejection of fiscal policy per se was not final. In the 1978 budget Healey argued that "It is the first purpose of this budget to encourage a level of economic activity to get unemployment moving significantly down" and "our main objective in the coming years, like that of other countries, must be to reduce the intolerable level of unemployment by stimulating demand in ways which create jobs at home without refuelling inflation" (Hansard, 11 April 1978, Cols. 1184, 1187). Whilst it was still asserted that "inflation is the main enemy of full employment" (Col. 1189) the context of a balance of payments surplus, a falling inflation rate, and the money supply being under control was said to allow a fiscal stimulus.

In some ways this episode supports the suspicions of some monetarists that the policy changes of 1975/6 rested not on an intellectual conversion but on force of circumstance. Walters suggested in 1978 that "The most obvious and apparently far-reaching development - the adoption of monetary targets - is largely cosmetic and probably for foreign consumption only" (p.29). Whilst this may exaggerate, monetary targets being also important in relation to domestic financial markets and not simply cosmetic, it does accurately reflect one important part of the adoption of monetarist rhetoric in the mid-1970s. It is also the case that the presentation of the crisis by the authorities as if they fully accepted the monetarist arguments was in part a tactical weapon in the internal labour movement battle over policy, especially in the struggle by the government to make the Social Contract an effective anti-inflationary device.

The size of the shift in policy perceptions by the late 1970s is probably well measured by Wass' (1978) statement. He noted the "mood of almost Victorian optimism about demand management in his predecessors' statement in 1968, and stressed the

current constraints on such policy arising from the
international environment, rapid inflation, the
"basic inertia" of the economy and the level of
international economic integration. Nevertheless he
stressed the continuing role of demand management,
as well as "measures to influence the price level"
(p.99) and action to improve the potential growth
rate of output. He accepted the desirability of a
money supply target, but wanted this to be consistent with other policies (p.100). He also remained
fairly sympathetic to incomes policies (p.101). All
this suggests an 'electic' view of the economy, a
continuing attachment to demand management albeit
with strong qualifications, and a sympathy with non-
market policies like incomes policies wholly out of
line with monetarist ideology.

However this statement may be seen as reflecting the 'calm between the storms'. The short-term
crisis of 1975/6 had gone away. But none of the
other circumstances outlined above had changed, and
if a new external crisis were to arise a similar set
of policy consequences to those of 1975/6 might be
expected, but possibly with a new ideological
virulence.

NOTES

1.   The public sector may be defined in a
variety of ways. Since 1977 the measure used in
public expenditure White Papers has been revised,
mainly relating to the treatment of nationalised
industries. This both reduced the level of public
expenditure substantially (thus the alleged '60 per
cent' levels of the mid-1970s around which so much
hysteria was generated disappeared) and brought
British practice more in line with international
conventions. The current figure is defined as total
general government expenditure as a proportion of
GDP at market prices.

2.   The debate over macro policy in 1975 was
much affected by the 'New Cambridge School' who
asserted a direct relation between the Public Sector
Deficit and the Balance of Payments Deficit. This of
course implied a radical criticism of using the
former to 'fine tune' the economy. The Report of the
Expenditure Committee (9th Report from the Expenditure Committee, House of Commons Paper HC328,
1975/6, H.M.S.O.) was largely built around an
assessment of Godley's assertion that "The record of
demand management during the last 20 years has been
extremely poor. Throughout this period fiscal policy

has operated in alternating directions to provide periods of strong demand expansion, followed by reversals of policy in crisis conditions" (Ibid., para. 5), based on New Cambridge arguments. Mosley has argued that the New Cambridge School was like a Trojan horse for monetarism's entry into policy-making because it was Labour Party oriented, and hence viewed sympathetically by the Labour Party, but had policy conclusions on the non-use of public expenditure to stabilise the economy similar to monetarism. P. Mosley, <u>The Making of Economic Policy</u>, (Wheatsheaf, Brighton, 1984), p.155, foot-note 12.

    3.   See also Mosley, Ibid., pp.123-31.

Chapter Seven

THE BALANCE OF PAYMENTS AND THE EXCHANGE RATE

Of the four objectives of policy focussed upon in
this book the status of the balance of payments as
one of this "magic quadrilateral" has probably been
most open to challenge. This challenge is on the
grounds of the undesirability of any particular
state of the balance of payments, except in relation
to other objectives, the implication being that the
balance of payments should be seen as a constraint
on attaining other objectives, rather than an
objective in its own right. Such a view can rightly
be objected to on the grounds that the same point
can be applied to the other objectives, e.g. growth,
which could be said to be desirable only insofar as
it increased consumption over some time horizon.
This is something of a reductio ad absurdum - everything is lost in some vague pursuit of an 'ultimate
goal'. However this view does rightly emphasise the
inter-connectedness between external objectives
(balance of payments or exchange rate) and domestic
ones.
      In relation to British policy it is clear that
the balance of payments has generally been perceived
as an objective (or rather series of changing
objectives) in its own right.[1] This was challenged
in the 1970s with the demise of fixed exchange rates,
but to a considerable extent this brought into play
an additional variable, the exchange rate, rather
than abolishing external objectives as some proponents of floating seem to have hoped. "The whole
balance of payments problem is an artificially created one due to the co-existence of different
national currencies....if this artificial rigidity
were removed, governments would be free to concen-
trate on their real economic problem...." (Brittan
1971, p.415).

139

The Balance of Payments and the Exchange Rate

As stressed in Chapter 2, in the 1950s British balance of payments policy was dominated by a desire to defend the "strength of sterling" in all its ramifications, which meant the defence of the sterling area, a fixed parity of the pound coupled with movement towards free transactions on current account and, to a more limited extent, on capital account. Pursuit of these objectives met with considerable success in the 1950s, not least because of the very favourable international environment.

That those objectives might have unfavourable domestic repercussions was certainly suggested in the 1950s - for example by Shonfield in 1959. But the evidence to Radcliffe shows little support for such views in official circles. Of those giving evidence only Kahn (Memoranda of Evidence, pp.138-46) focussed on the domestic impact of current international objectives. The Treasury indeed saw the problem as the other way around - the pound was said to be weak because of the conduct of domestic policy, not because of the external objectives being pursued (Q.2594). This was also the traditional Bank of England view (Hirsch 1965, p.147).

What was to alter the whole manner of discussion of balance of payments objectives in the 1960s was the new focus on domestic economic growth as an objective, coupled with radical changes in the international economy, especially impinging on the sterling area. The former forced discussion much more on to the plane of conflicts between domestic and balance of payments objectives, which was the staple of balance of payments policy in the 1960s. The latter undercut the previous orientation of policy towards sterling and the sterling area. This is discussed in the first section of this chapter. The second section looks at the further re-orientation of policy which came with the floating of the currency in the 1970s, arguing that this reflected a combination of changing priorities accorded to other policy objectives, especially inflation, coupled with the increasing difficulties of pursuing any external policy because of the changing structure of the world economy.

Growth and the Sterling Area
Chapters 4 and 9 look in some detail at the development of economic growth as an objective in Britain and these points will not be repeated here. Obviously growth did not emerge overnight as an objective and equally its emergence did not impact on balance

of payments policy in one fell swoop. The objective
of growth was fully explicit in government pronouncement by the mid-1950s (e.g. CMD. 9725, para. 25),
but whilst this was recognised by the Radcliffe
Report (para. 58) the rest of that report summarised
the "orthodoxy of the fifties", in giving defence of
sterling priority as an international economic
objective.

Yet even by the time the Radcliffe Report was
being written the conditions for the continued
survival of sterling's international role in general
and the Sterling Area in particular were being
undercut.

The Sterling Area was in the 1950s essentially
a club for discriminating against the dollar. The
Commonwealth[2] countries and Britain shared a common
problem of 'dollar shortage' which gave incentives
for holding reserves in common and for controlling
transactions which would incur dollar liabilities.
However this sterling area should not be seen as
simply reinforcing other strong ties between the
countries involved. Rather the opposite was true.
The Commonwealth was subject in the 1950s to very
strong centrifugal forces which, once the immediate
problems of the post-war years were solved, were to
undercut the organisation of British policy around
the presumption of such strong ties. As Strange
emphasises (1971, p.67) there was "not much in the
field of foreign or defence policy even in the 1950s
that the independent Commonwealth could find to
agree about". Thus the Sterling Area "helped to
arrest the process of imperial disintegration"
(Ibid.).

Part of the reason for this disintegration was
of course the growth of multilateralism in trade and
payments. By the mid-1950s the European Payments
Union and the Sterling Area meant there was already
more or less complete multilateralism outside the
dollar area (Tew 1982, pp.41-3), and in 1958 general
convertibility of currencies for current account
transactions ended the dollar discrimination basis
of the sterling area.

Even in the fifties the trade links between the
Sterling Area countries were being weakened. In 1950
the Overseas Sterling Area took 51 per cent of its
imports from Britain, in 1965 the figure was 38 per
cent. For Britain's imports the proportion from the
O.S.A. was 40 per cent in 1950 and 31 per cent in
1965 (Cooper in Caves (1968), p.183). See also
Table 7.1.

The Balance of Payments and the Exchange Rate

Table 7.1: **Geographical Composition of British Trade 1955-67**

	Imports		Exports		
1955	1967	1955	1967	
39.4	27.4	47.0	30.4	Sterling Area
19.5	19.7	11.8	16.5	North America
(10.7)	(12.6)	(7.0)	(12.2)	(U.S.A.)
6.1	4.5	3.8	3.3	Latin America
25.7	36.4	28.1	38.0	Western Europe
(12.6)	(19.6)	(14.0)	(19.2)	(E.E.C.)
2.7	3.9	1.2	3.3	Soviet Union and Eastern Europe
6.6	8.1	8.1	8.5	Rest of World

Source: A.R. Prest (ed), The U.K. Economy: A Manual of Applied Economics, (Weidenfeld and Nicolson, London, 1968), 2nd edition, p.109.

More slowly there was also a shift in the geographical distribution of British overseas investment. This was only just perceptible by the late 1960s (see Strange 1971, p.145), but thereafter became increasingly marked. Broadly speaking foreign investment followed trade in being more and more directed to other advanced capitalist countries, in both Western Europe and the United States (Dunning 1979).

Thus the commitment to multilateralism in British policy was bound to undercut the conditions of existence of the Sterling Area as a discriminatory trading zone. Under conditions of rapid expansion in manufacturing trade, Britain's traditional links with the Commonwealth as buyers of their primary products was bound to decline, so the change in commodity composition of Britain's trade had as its natural correlate a change in its geographical composition (Table 7.2).

The decline of the Sterling Area as a discriminatory trading and investment unit greatly reduced the incentives for members to hold sterling as a reserve asset (as well as reducing the supply of that sterling). The maintenance of such reserves by Sterling Area countries in the early part of the 1960s owed little to sentimental attachment to the pound, but reflected the fear of capital loss if liquidation were to force a devaluation coupled with the returns from the high interest rates London

Table 7.2: Import Composition of British Trade 1951-66
(% of G.D.P. at market prices)

1951	1956	1961	1966	
8.9	6.9	5.5	4.5	Food
10.5	5.3	3.7	2.8	Materials
4.4	3.2	3.6	3.9	Semi-manufactures
1.0	1.1	2.0	2.6	Finished Manufactures
2.2	2.0	1.8	1.6	Mineral Fuels

Source: J.F. Wright, Britain in the Age of Economic Management, (Oxford University Press, Oxford, 1979), p.10.

offered. In any case there was a creeping diversification of reserves from the mid-1960s before the scramble out in 1968. Australia for example held 90 per cent of its reserves in sterling in 1951, 60 per cent by 1966 (Conan 1968, p.431).

This movement towards a less economically integrated Commonwealth was signalled by the first (abortive) attempt by the British authorities to enter the E.E.C. in 1962. Whatever else might be said about this episode, it did coincide with increasing economic ties with the E.E.C. countries.

In the 1950s the defence by the authorities of the Sterling Area and the international role of sterling had partly been based on the belief that the role of the City of London as an international financial centre depended upon the role of sterling in the world economy. However after 1958, when convertibility of sterling was restored, there grew up in London a financial market which was increasingly a dollar market, encouraged by the controls exercised over interest rates payable on dollar deposits in the United States. In this way was formed the Euro-dollar market, which was to grow so rapidly in the 1960s and 1970s. One significance of the growth of this market was to detach concern for the role of the City's earnings in the balance of payments from concern for the international role of sterling. That such a separation was possible was seemingly only reluctantly accepted by the City. Whilst the Clarke Report of 1967 recognised that the reserve role of sterling was not important to the City's invisible earnings (Clarke 1967, para. 494), this distinction could still be treated as innovatory by the Governor of the Bank of England in 1971

(BEQB, March 1972, pp.84-5). The further distinction between the international financial role of the City and the role of sterling implied by the rise of the Euro-dollar markets was slower of realisation.

This weakening of the position of sterling coupled with the emergence of growth as a domestic policy objective were the basis of the creation of the famous "stop-go" cycle. This was characterised by the lurching of policy from "stop" when there was a balance of payments problem (or more exactly a run on the reserves), to "go" when unemployment was believed to be approaching unacceptable levels.

The first of such cycles was really that of 1957 - previous runs on sterling in 1951/2 and 1955 had engendered little in the way of domestic deflation. The Radcliffe Committee saw the solution to such crises as the accumulation of more reserves, as the problem was seen largely as a consequence of the volatility of certain elements in the balance of payments rather than any 'underlying' problems (Report, para. 633). This position may have had plausibility in the 1950s, when indeed the underlying balance of payments however measured was better than the 1960s (Table 7.3). It was also understandable that the focus of the Radcliffe Committee should be on reserve accumulation rather than on the conflict of domestic with international objectives, because as already noted this latter conflict does not clearly emerge until 1957. Indeed "stop-go" was a remarkably short lived policy as it did not really start until 1957 and can at most be said to have lasted until balance of payments pressures from 1965 onwards inaugurated an unprecedented "stop".

The conflict between domestic and international objectives in the 1960s was not normally seen in the way stressed by Shonfield in his 1959 book. There he was above all concerned to argue for less foreign investment on the basis that this reduced domestic investment and therefore growth. Whilst there was extraordinarily little official appraisal of Britain's foreign investment role until the Reddaway Report of 1968, the effect of this investment was decreasingly felt on the balance of payments, as it was increasingly financed abroad, on a self-financing basis akin to that of the nineteenth century. The possibility of direct conflict between home and foreign private investment was little more than a footnote to discussions in the 1960s.

Rather the conflict was one concerning the pressure of demand appropriate for domestic growth

Table 7.3: British Balance of Payments in the 1950s and 1960s (£m.)

	Visible Trade Balance	Current Balance	Total Currency Flow[1]
1951	−689	−369	− 334
1952	−279	+163	− 175
1953	−244	+145	+ 296
1954	−204	+117	+ 126
1955	−313	−155	− 229
1956	+ 53	+208	− 159
1957	− 29	+233	+ 13
1958	+ 29	+344	+ 290
1959	−117	+152	+ 18
1960	−406	−255	+ 325
1961	−152	+ 6	− 339
1962	−102	+122	+ 192
1963	− 80	+124	− 58
1964	−519	−382	− 695
1965	−237	− 49	− 353
1966	− 73	+ 84	− 547
1967	−557	−316	− 671
1968	−659	−284	−1410
1969	−143	+445	+ 743
1970	− 9	+692	+1287

Source: United Kingdom Balance of Payments (The Pink Book), (H.M.S.O., London, various dates)

[1]Total Currency Flow comprises the current balance, the net balance of investment and other capital flows and the net total of unidentified transactions. Before 1970 the official accounts used the "basic balance", the sum of the current balance and the long-term capital position. This was discontinued because it was no longer possible to sensibly separate long-term capital flows from monetary movements.

and that appropriate for external balance. Whilst the level of unemployment was normally the trigger for measures to initiate the "go" part of the cycle, it was the effects of the "stop" on the long-term growth of the economy which seem to have dominated official concerns. Thus it was in the context of preventing "stop-go" inhibiting growth that devaluation was first discussed in the early 1960s (Hutchinson 1977, p.102), as in the early 1970s it was the desire to maintain the 'dash for growth' that led to the floating of the pound (see further below).

The sixties in balance of payments policy may be seen as the period when reluctantly and hesitantly the pretensions of the 1950s were abandoned by the authorities. Britain became the centre of a 'decaying currency area; and had not the necessary funds available in a sufficiently liquid form to wind up the business and repay all the depositors' (Strange 1971, p.74).

Recognition of this necessarily came unevenly. Strange (p.75) suggests that it was only after the devaluation of 1967 that the role of sterling was properly re-appraised in official circles. But it would be wrong to imply that the defence of the sterling parity in the 1960s was only the result of some historical backwardness, an overhang attachment to past glories. For as is clear from Wilson's memoirs in particular, there was a <u>political</u> commitment to the sterling parity which owed <u>little</u> to any economic ideology, except perhaps the belief that Britain's economic problems could be solved by ill-specified "structural" reforms rather than by traditional macro-economic management (see Brittan 1971, Ch. 10).

And recognition of the insupportability of previous policies on sterling was not of course the same as the provision of solutions to the problems of sterling's role. We may say that in the 1960s British balance of payments policy was made in the context of both a residual attachment to the policies of the 1950s, but <u>without</u> the underlying strength in the balance of <u>payments</u> that the 1950s maintained. For it is important to stress that the British balance of payments since 1945 should <u>not</u> be seen in terms of a linear 'decline'. The position for most of the 1950s was entirely satisfactory by any but the most ambitious criteria concerning the level of reserves and foreign investment that could be financed. It was only in the 1960s that the 'decline' set in.

But that 'decline' in turn was to a large extent the result of attempting to expand the growth of the economy above the levels achieved in the fifties. Thus the enormous visible trade deficit of 1964 (Table 7.3) was not the result of a sudden lurch into "uncompetitiveness" but the consequence of attempts to expand the economy <u>very quickly</u>, both because of the fashionable focus on growth and of course the political considerations arising from the General Election of 1964 (Thirlwall 1980, pp.148-50 and Appendix 7.1).[3] As authors like Thirlwall have stressed, it is important in understanding Britain's renown propensity to suck in imports to distinguish between the level of demand and the rate of expansion of that demand. If the central problem of the balance of payments is a supply constraint, then the latter is the crucial measure, as it is the inability of supply to respond quickly to a rapid expansion of demand that leads to a rapid rise in imports.

The new domestic orientation of policy ran up against the still continuing legacy of the policies of the fifties. For example whilst the private sector invisible balance increased between the mid-1950s and mid-1960s the government's invisible deficit increased roughly in line because of increased payments for defence and aid. Now part of these payments were no doubt difficult to avoid, "a temporary reflection of the difficult post-imperial adjustment process" (Strange 1971, p.200). But they were payments largely made within the Sterling Area, and which still seemed to appear to have a privileged place in the calculations of officials in London.

Governments of both parties accepted the need for cuts in overseas government expenditure, and it was noticeable in particular that the defence estimates had a new sensitivity to the balance of payments consequences of defence expenditure. As Tew (in Blackaby 1978) stresses, it was in the area of government expenditure overseas, and that of controls on private overseas investment that long-term policies were pursued in the 1960s to reduce balance of payments difficulties. In both these areas policy was not directly very successful. In this case both of these areas of expenditure balance of payments 'relief' came more through offsetting flows - the returns to previous private investment financing new asset acquisitions, and an increasing proportion of government overseas military expenditure being offset by cash contributions or purchases of British military equipment (see Fry 1968).

The most signal failure of re-orientation away from 'past glories' was however in the area of short term capital flows. Clearly British policy faced a general problem of increased short-term capital mobility, which put constraints on possible policy (a theme returned to below). But even allowing for this, there was a failure of policy to deal with the problem of the sterling balances which played a crucial, if mainly indirect part, in the crises of 1960, 1964 and 1967, in the last case of course precipitating devaluation. Their role may have been most important indirectly; the problem arising being not so much their withdrawal at the time of lack of confidence in the pound but that they have "induced or aggravated speculative movements of other funds, since the presence of large liabilities makes Britain's liquidity position look precarious" (Cooper in Caves (1968), p.186).

Only with the Basle Group Arrangements of 1966, and then again in 1968, did the British authorities gain international support for the sterling balances, though the first occasion did not prevent the devaluation of 1967 (see CMND. 3787, 1968). After 1968 the problem declined in importance. In 1972 exchange controls were extended to the Sterling Area and this was coupled with the float of sterling. Most of the Sterling countries abandoned the peg to the pound and diversified their reserves. After 1974 no guarantees on the value of sterling balances were offered (Tew 1982, pp.79, 123-5). However in 1976 the problem re-emerged, official sterling balances falling by almost 40 per cent in 7 months. From 1977 the trend was reversed as the attempt to attract oil-producers funds, coupled with the new attractiveness of an "oil backed" sterling led to very large inflows, such that by the end of 1971 sterling balances were around three times their 1975 level.

The devaluation of 1967 can best be linked to the way in which the Labour government of 1964-70 saw its objectives. At the centre of these was the desire to secure a higher rate of economic growth, based above all on institutional reforms (many of which, if not the rhetoric which accompanied them, were in fact inherited from the previous Conservative government - see Brittan 1971). The attachment to institutional reform was seen as an alternative to macro policies to reconcile domestic growth and the balance of payments. In this way Wilson reflected views common on the social democratic Left at the time - for example the views expressed by Balogh before the Radcliffe Committee (Memoranda of Evidence, Vol. 3, pp.31-47).

This position saw devaluation as unnecessary (as well as politically undesirable) as structural reforms would deliver a satisfactory balance of payments at the existing parity. The short-run problems of the balance of payments could be dealt with by whatever expedient lay at hand, including import controls, but especially borrowing aided by support from the U.S.A. which saw the defence of sterling as the first line of defence of the dollar.

The Bank of England seems to have maintained a parallel anti-devaluation stance but for entirely different reasons. The Bank saw the defence of sterling at $2.80 as necessary for the international role of the pound, and it supported sharply deflationary measures in order to achieve this. (It was strongly attached both to cuts in government expenditure and incomes policies).

Economists, it may be noted, were far from unanimous on the issue, though for differing reasons. Some like Ball (1967) opposed it on grounds of the inflationary consequences, others because of pessimism about the relevant elasticities (Hutchinson 1977, Ch. 5). However, as always, it is important not to exaggerate the role of economics and economists in such decisions. For example the failure to deflate immediately after 1967 in order to make devaluation effective does not seem to have been due to economic ignorance, as alleged by, for example, Harry Johnson, but for political reasons (Higham 1981, pp.75-6).

The devaluation of the pound itself owed little to economists' discussions of the desirability or otherwise of more flexible (i.e. in Britain's case, lower) exchange rates and much more to the conditions demanded by the I.M.F. in return for further loans - conditions which the Wilson government was unwilling to agree to (Wilson 1971, p.453). However the devaluation did not bring an end to pressure on the pound, and further I.M.F. loans were necessary. These loans not only put a further nail in the coffin of the Sterling Area, but were also of course the conduit for the transmission of the I.M.F. attachment to monetary targets into British economic policy, in the form of Domestic Credit Expansion targets. A less formal undertaking on the money supply was given in the first Letter of Intent to the I.M.F. in November 1967; D.C.E. followed in 1969. This episode demonstrated clearly enough the capacity of lenders to enforce on borrowers certain conditions in return for obtaining loans. But whilst the Bank of England and Treasury did at the behest of the I.M.F. introduce D.C.E. targets, these institutions were unwilling adherents to such policies, and the targets ceased to have any significance after the end of April 1971 when the I.M.F. loan conditions expired (Cobham 1982, p.444).

Through the 1950s and 1960s there was a whole series of writings on British balance of payments problems which saw these as centrally about a lag in British policy adjusting to a new second rank status. Continued attachment to past glories was seen as generating excessive external commitments which in turn inhibited domestic expansion. The fountain head of much of this was Shonfield (1959). Probably its best exponent is Strange (1971). Whilst this 'lag' theory has something to commend it, it does not of itself tell us much about the institutional conditions which kept in place those 'outmoded' objectives for so long.

Probably central to this was the role of the Bank of England. Part (but only part) of the problem was that the Bank always saw one aspect of its role as a 'second chamber' (Hirsch 1965, p.149), as responsible for deflecting governments from the unwise courses they were inherently bound to pursue. Traditionally such a role had been played in relation to government's tendency to inflation. But in the 1950s and 1960s it was played particularly in relation to government's propensity to advocate or at least raise for discussion, policies - exchange control, devaluation - which cut across the Bank's view of the proper role of sterling in the world economy.

Again part of this was due to the Bank of England's relations to the City of London, for which it has always, nationalisation notwithstanding, acted as a kind of lobbyist. To a degree this is inescapeable, part of the necessary function of the Bank being to represent City's responses to the Treasury and the government. But the role played by the Bank often seemed to go beyond this, with the Bank seeming to give the concerns of the City a central role in its policy proposals (Hirsch, Ibid., pp.150-4).

This is not to say that the Bank was simply a proponent of all the policies that the economic radicals of the 1950s and 1960s abused. It is striking for example that one of the central planks of the Governor of the Bank, Lord Cromer, attacks on current policies in 1965 was the excessive scale of military expenditure overseas, because of the effect of this in weakening the balance of payments and thereby sterling's role. This indeed seems to have been a general bankers' complaint. For example the Banker, in its postmortem on the 1967 devaluation, cites excessive government overseas spending as one of the major reasons for this event, and carried two articles critical of this expenditure (Banker, June 1968).

Equally these points about the role of the Bank of England are not intended to support the view that governments were powerless in the face of the machinations of the Bankers. What is striking in particular is how timid governments of the 1960s were (perhaps especially the 1964 Labour government) in the face of the Bank of England's positions. Allegations of "Banker's ramps" seem to have served not only as a convenient scapegoating, but also as an alibi for not developing the alternative <u>policies</u> which could be posed against those of the Bank.

A Floating Exchange Rate

The devaluation of the pound was, as the Americans rightly feared, a prologue to pressure on the dollar and ultimately on the Bretton Woods system in its entirety. The collapse of that system inaugurated a new era in British balance of payments policy, the central new element being the floating of the pound, initially to allow growth to continue unimpeded, but later becoming intertwined with a new emphasis on inflation as a problem for policy. Eventually, by the end of the 1970s, exchange rate policy was transformed from the centre piece of balance of payments policy to another weapon, albeit an unreliable one, in the battle against inflation.

There were three elements in the breakdown of Bretton Woods and the eventual emergence of a floating currency regime which are of significance in the context of British balance of payments objectives in the 1970s.

The Bretton Woods system has been called a system of "reluctant adjustment" of exchange rates. This reluctance was partly the result of the political investment in particular parities especially in Britain (which saw a change as a threat to its international role of the pound) and on the other side of the account, for surplus countries like Germany, who believed that the primary source of adjustment should be by deficit countries (Scammell 1980, p.111).[4] Politically it was much easier to 'sit tight' than to adjust the parity. The delays thereby engendered in the adjustment of parities provided a source of disruption to the international monetary system, as the scale of adjustment tended to be magnified by the delay. Such traumatic and drawn out adjustment processes in turn created profitable opportunities for large scale speculation. The direction of exchange rate changes were almost always wholly predictable and therefore provided little danger to those gambling on future changes (Scammell 1980, p.103).

The Bretton Woods conference was certainly well aware of the dangers of destabilising short-term capital movements, conscious as they were of trying to avoid the dangers of the inter-war period which included such movements, as spelt out in Nurske's famous book (1944). However they seem to have believed that adequate controls could be exerted by national governments over such capital movements, an assumption that was increasingly belied once free capital movements were largely restored in 1959. (Whilst the Bretton Woods agreement was de jure concerned only with free transactions on <u>current</u> account, most countries accepted to a greater or lesser extent that this put great <u>de facto</u> limits on their ability to control capital transactions (Tew 1982, pp.77-8).

Apart from the fixity of exchange rates it was the growth in the volume and mobility of short-term funds which undercut the Bretton Woods system. (Of course fixity of exchange rates was seen in some cases as a <u>defence</u> against the effects of short-term flows - but this could only be so if these rates could be held permanently - an impossible objective). By the 1960s "the volume of mobile funds in the international monetary system was now so large that in a speculative confrontation no central bank, no accumulation of exchange reserves could defend an exchange rate for long if the international financial community considered it to be too high" (Scammell 1980, p.103).

These movements of short-term funds were not wholly or even mainly 'speculative' in the sense that exchange transactions took place solely for expected gains on parity changes. Rather holdings of foreign currencies became increasingly part of the everyday business of more and more economic agents, not least multinational corporations (see Fishman 1980). In this way they reflected not the rather ephemeral machinations of the few gnomes in Zurich (or the City of London), but rather were an integral aspect of the enormous leap in the scale of international economic integration which increasingly constrained the objectives and actions of national governments in the post-war period.

The second aspect of the break up of Bretton Woods and the movement to floating rates is the way in which it was seen as a solution to the contradiction, so often alleged in the sixties, between the balance of payments equilibrium and domestic

economic growth. It is important to distinguish here
between writers like Meade (1966) who were calling
in pragmatic manner for more flexibility in exchange
rates, and those advocates of floating rates who saw
them as just another aspect of free market principles (notably Friedman (1953) and much later Brittan
(1970)).

Economists who supported floating were generally careful to stress that such a policy would give
autonomy in domestic policy use, rather than removing external constraints on policy entirely (e.g.
Brittan 1970, p.65, see also Brittan 1978, p.260).
However this seems to have been taken in some
circles as implying that floating could remove all
constraints on economic growth, that overnight the
much disliked balance of payments constraint could
be abolished. In Barber's Budget speech in March
1972 he argued that the "lesson of the international
balance of payments upsets of the last few years is
that it is neither necessary nor desirable to distort domestic economies to an unacceptable extent in
order to maintain unrealistic exchange rates...."
(House of Commons, 21 March; Hansard, Col. 1354).

Nevertheless it would be wrong to suggest that
the float of 1972 owed a great deal to the conversion of the institutions of economic policy to a new
theoretical stance. Officials commonly took the view
that fixed exchange rates were an important barrier
to inappropriate (i.e. inflationary) domestic
policies, providing a lever on policy agents. This
view was "voiced mainly by bankers and financial
officials, and economists seldom took it seriously"
(Hirsch and Higham 1974, p.14). Brittan (1970, p.62)
for example argued that "Under a floating rate the
real arguments against inflation - the internal
ones - will replace the external bogey, and the public will be able to judge the issue in the most
transparent and least technical form possible". In
addition to what might be called a gold standard
style defence of fixed parities, officials generally
viewed floating with trepidation because of expectations that floating rates would fluctuate wildly and
lead to different countries intervening in exchange
rate determination in contradictory ways.

The float of 1972 represented then not an
intellectual conversion so much as a combination of
lack of alternatives in the face of the break up of
the Bretton Woods system (only temporarily patched
up by the Smithsonian agreement) coupled with the
objective of 'going for growth'. Indeed the
Chancellor's speech in March 1972, in which he

stressed that his domestic policies would not be
inhibited by balance of payments problems, is seen
by some authors as directly contributing to the run
on sterling which culminated in the float in the
summer of that year (Hirsch and Higham 1974, pp.
8-9).

The floating of the pound broadly coincided
with a new emphasis on defeating inflation as a
policy objective. Initially these changes were not
closely related. The floating of the pound was
linked to a desire to maintain growth. The initial
weapon for defeating inflation was incomes policies.
In some views however, new attention to inflation
and floating of the exchange rate was paradoxical,
because it was held that the fixity of exchange
rates provided a lever (by the Central Bank on the
government, and/or by governments on sectors of the
electorate) which helped to limit inflation - the
pressure on the exchange rate could be used to argue
that policy was too inflationary. Thus the 'freedom'
from external pressure, which advocates of floating
rates was said by its proponents to entail, could be
seen as undesirable if domestic inflationary
pressures are strong. Thus Black (1977, p.115)
wrote:

> The U.K., by contrast, tried to gain freedom
> from the external constraint by floating from
> mid-1972 on. But the degree of freedom was mis-
> understood. Successive British governments
> allowed excessive monetary growth and public
> spending, generating rapid wage inflation.
> Inflation itself re-imposed the external con-
> straint, as a declining exchange rate of the
> pound made it more and more difficult to borrow
> abroad.

In the early years of the float (up to 1977)
the desire to maintain competitiveness largely over-
rode the hostility to inflation in exchange rate
policy. In other words exchange rate policy between
1973 and 1976 focussed mainly on smoothing and slowing, but not fundamentally trying to reverse, the
decline of sterling in line with the higher than
average rates of inflation in the U.K. Whilst there
was much hostility to inflation apparent in the
policy rhetoric of the period, the predominant
understanding seems to have been that the inflation
was causing an (undesirable) fall in the exchange
rate, rather than any idea that the exchange rate

could in any sense be seen as a weapon against inflation.

The exchange crisis of 1976 (like the accompanying public expenditure/deficit crisis) is crucial to the evolution of policy goals in the late 1970s and early 1980s. As so often in policy events it is difficult to disentangle the interwoven skein of events. But in the current context the following points seem most pertinent.

First of all the initial downward movement in the exchange rate in March 1976 was officially inspired, not produced in "the market". This of itself suggests that contemporary doctrinal changes concerning both the efficacy and possibility of exchange rate movements (see further below) were not significant for the authorities' actions at this time. The Bank believed in early 1976 that the pound was overvalued in relation to Britain's domestic competitive factors, and tried to push the exchange rate down.

This in turn precipitated a 'run' on sterling, which as in the late 1960s under fixed exchange rates, led ultimately to a package of borrowings from the I.M.F. and the usual kind of conditions attached to such borrowings. One of these conditions involved the use of money supply targets which then became a staple feature of British economic policy. This in many eyes could be seen as making impossible an exchange rate target. The argument being that a money supply target would determine the level of interest rates and these in turn would largely determine the relative attractiveness of the domestic currency and hence the exchange rate.[5] In other words if interest rates directly or indirectly are an instrument of domestic policy they cannot also be an instrument of external policy.

This dilemma however only exists given other policy assumptions. For example if domestic monetary policy was pursued via ceilings of bank credit rather than interest rates (as in, for example, Japan) the conflict could at least be reduced. Equally the members of the European Monetary System have committed themselves to a fixed exchange rate, without seemingly thereby giving up all attempts at domestic monetary control (Blackaby 1980, p.11). Part of the problem was of course the unwillingness of the authorities to actively dissuade inflows of capital by, for example, imposing taxes on non-resident holdings of sterling in the manner of those homes of financial rectitude, Switzerland and West Germany.

The Balance of Payments and the Exchange Rate

Initially in 1977 the Bank of England was very active in trying to hold the exchange rate down, reserves increasing by 75 per cent between June and October.

The abandonment of this attempt to hold to an exchange rate target from late 1977 seems to have rested largely on the irrepressible surge in purchases of sterling, but it also coincided with (and was to be rationalised by) certain doctrinal changes within the economics literature concerning the exchange rate. These doctrinal positions related to both the possibility of governments engineering exchange rate changes, and the effects of such changes (see also Eltis and Sinclair 1981).

Broadly speaking, in the new monetary approaches to the balance of payments, exchange rates were seen as determined by differential money supply growth, so that an exchange rate depreciation reflected excessive money supply growth in relation to domestic money demand, which would spill over into a balance of payments deficit and depreciation of the exchange. In this view governments could only effect the exchange rate indirectly, by controlling their domestic monetary policy.

Parallel to this was the view that exchange rate changes affected only the rate of inflation not real magnitudes. One strand of support for this view came also from the monetary theory of the balance of payments coupled with the "law of one price". This latter suggested that "Because the world market for manufactured goods is highly competitive each country must accept the world price for its tradeable goods and through competition in the labour market this will spread to non-tradeable products" (Ball, Burns, Lawry 1977, p.2). So a devaluation would be rapidly offset by a rise in domestic prices.

The same conclusion as to the ineffectiveness of exchange rate changes in shifting real magnitudes was derived by the Cambridge Economic Policy Group. Their theoretical stance was entirely different from the monetarist, being based on the view that devaluation would be unsuccessful because of "real wage resistance" leading to a rapid rise in costs to offset the devaluation. This led to the policy proposal for import controls as a way of evading the problem.

The question of the capacity of governments to alter exchange rates is returned to below, as this is clearly of prime importance in our discussion of policy objectives. But a few points may first of all be made about the effects of exchange rate changes. As so often in economic discussion the point hinges not on the principles of whether an effect exists, but its scale and timing. It would be difficult to argue that a devaluation of the exchange rate does not set up pressure tending to raise domestic prices and hence offset the effects of the devaluation. But this takes time - anything up to six years (Blackaby 1980, p.9). And whilst the competitive edge will eventually be lost, the consequence for output and productivity may be permanent.

Secondly the doctrine that changes in exchange rates only have effects on nominal not real magnitudes came to the fore when government policy was switching from a focus on real (employment) to nominal (inflation) magnitudes. Thus from late 1977 and especially after 1979 the rise in the exchange rate was presented as a means of reducing inflation, and hence something to be celebrated not bemoaned. For a very clear example under the Labour government, see CMND. 7405 (1978), paras. 37-45. Here as elsewhere it is difficult not to argue in a cynical manner that the governments of the day, having neither engineered nor in large part expected the rise in the exchange rate from 1977,[6] and being relatively unconcerned with its employment effects, were only too happy to adopt a doctrine which told them that this rise only impacted on the rate of inflation.

Like most cynical analyses this contains a deal of truth, but evades crucial points. Presented in this way economic theory simply acts as a cloak to defend policies taken on other grounds. But this is to ignore that the discourse of economics is at least part of the policy making process, and necessarily so; discussion of economic policy necessarily takes place in and through definite discourses provided partly by economic theory. But equally policy is also concerned with providing a range of rationales and defences for policies, and here economic theory may well be used in an ad hoc and fairly cynical manner.

Finally one may note on the question of the efficacy of exchange rate movements, that the evidence does not suggest that they have acted on their own as an anti-inflationary weapon. Rather rising exchange rates should be seen largely as a transmission belt from restrictive domestic policies to lower inflation rates (Higham 1981A).

The Balance of Payments and the Exchange Rate

"Confidence" and the Exchange Rate

This chapter has attempted to chart the changing emphases of balance of payments and exchange rate policy in the 1960s and 1970s. The focus has been on the way in which policy in this area has related to changes in domestic policy objectives. Only a little has been said about the constraints on policy in this area. Yet as has been argued elsewhere in this book it makes little sense to talk about objectives separate from the constraints on policy and how these are perceived. In this final section the events of 1976 are linked to the problem of the constraints on objectives in this area and the ways of dealing with those constraints.

In an important discussion of the events of 1976 Cobham (1982) has argued the case for a monetary explanation of the depreciation of sterling in that year. He points to the difficulties of alternative explanations in terms of the current account balance, or 'catching up' for past rates of inflation beyond the international average. He stresses that the evidence is not conclusive, but that there is a good case for saying that the continuation of the depreciation beyond the initial fall was the consequence of excessive Domestic Credit Expansion.

The significance of his article in the context of concerns of this chapter, is that he confronts directly the view, predominant in most accounts, that the fall of 1976 was due to a loss of confidence. He argues that whilst there _was_ a loss of confidence in sterling, this should best be seen as the transmission belt from excessive growth of D.C.E. to the exchange rate. In other words the loss of confidence was based on an 'objective' problem, not on simply the 'subjective' feelings of foreign exchange dealers. This argument has a clear political pay-off, which Cobham (p.452) summarises as follows:

> the implication of this paper is that the control of D.C.E., instead of being an insidious weapon wielded by that international capitalist policeman, the I.M.F., (for the purpose of bringing left-wing governments to heel), is in fact the best means for the government to prevent the development of a crisis and thereby prevent "outsiders" (the U.S.A., the I.M.F. or the City) from acquiring influences over its economic policies.

The Balance of Payments and the Exchange Rate

One doesn't have to accept Cobham's (undogmatic) view that the exchange rate fall of 1976 was a consequence of excessive D.C.E., to see that his emphasis on taking seriously the constraints on domestic policy, because of exchange rate consequences, is important. The constraints imposed on the British economy by the international movement of capital can be countered by taking seriously the features of the economy which capital flows respond to, and thus minimising the leverage of outside agencies. This would seem superior to both a focus on 'confidence' which tends to render the problem entirely arbitrary (who knows what effects that "confidence"?), and a focus on trying to prevent capital flows by methods such as exchange control. The difficulty with advocacy of the latter is that it doesn't take seriously the problem that much of todays capital flows are inextricably linked to ordinary commercial transactions, in which "leading and lagging" can have a substantial impact on exchange rates. It is very difficult to allow ordinary commercial transactions and control speculative flows when these are inextricably linked, and both take place within the same institutions, such as multinational corporations.

This links to the final broad theme, that the international constraints on domestic economic policy have increased of late, and this has not been offset by a floating exchange rate regime. Bryant's (1980, p.439) emphasis seems right, the degree of international economic integration affects the viability of an exchange rate regime, rather than exchange rate variability 'disintegrating' the world economy.

The integration of the world economy which is most important in the current context is that provided by the scale of international capital flows. (Though obviously these have tended to grow alongside, albeit at a faster rate, than movements of commodities).

The Governor of the Bank of England (B.E.Q.B., June 1972, pp.234-5) summarised the reasons for the growth of international capital flows from the early 1960s into three categories.

First, he emphasised the closer links of financial markets in different centres via the growth of international financial institutions and multinational corporations. Secondly the encouragement of such movements by international bodies such as the I.M.F. on the grounds that such free movement of funds to the highest profit areas will maximise

income growth. Thirdly the rise of inflation, and
with it the level of nominal interest rates, providing a greater scope for interest rate arbitrage
transactions.

In addition to these factors, there has been
the growth of the Euro-dollar markets, which has
functioned to rapidly bring into line interest rates
(or at least trends) in different centres, especially in Europe and the U.S.A. (Llewellyn 1980,
pp.185-7).

The implication of the growth of this integration is that the argument, popular under the
Thatcher government, that the exchange rate is
determined by the 'market' not the government,
should not be read as just 'ideological', as an
extension of that government's general rhetoric of
laissez-faire. The capacity of governments to pursue
an exchange rate target has been greatly reduced by
the kind of factors mentioned above. This means that
if a government is to have an exchange rate policy
it must take seriously these constraints, and not
retire into the belief that exchange controls can
easily extricate Britain from international constraints. This would be equivalent to the belief of
some of the original advocates of floating rates
that this would somehow allow the concentration on
domestic policy, letting the foreign account take
care of itself.

NOTES

1. One of the central questions asked of the
1964-1970 Labour government's policies in Beckerman
is "why did the balance of payments assume such an
important role and become an objective instead of
just a constraint on the extent to which more basic
objectives were pursued?". W. Beckerman (ed), The
Labour Government's Economic Record, (Duckworth,
London, 1972), p.11.
2. Strictly the Sterling Area was not synonymous with the Commonwealth. Up to 1972 the Overseas
Sterling Area consisted of the Commonwealth minus
Canada, plus South Africa, Iceland, Ireland, Kuwait,
Jordan and a few minor countries. This distinction
is ignored in the discussion here.
3. Though it may well be argued that the
competitiveness of British exports needs to be
judged in relation to all of Britain's balance of
payments objectives. "Britain's exports may have
been competitive, but still not competitive enough
to carry the burden of large military expenditures

abroad and capital outflows". R.N. Cooper, "The Balance of Payments" in R. Caves (ed), Britain's Economic Prospects, (Brookings Institution, Washington D.C., 1968), p.156.

4. For a contrary view to Thirlwall, stressing a secular decline in competitiveness, see for example G.D.N. Worswick "Trade and Payments" in A. Cairncross (ed), Britain's Economic Prospects Reconsidered, (Allen and Unwin, London, 1971), pp.61-100. There was also of course the fundamental problem of changes in the parity of the dollar, when that currency was functioning as the numeraire of the international currency system.

5. A complication here is that if as well as money supply targets a P.S.B.R. target is pursued (as in Britain), the money supply target may be undermined by capital inflows in response to the level of interest rates necessary to sell that debt. D.T. Llewellyn, International Financial Integration, (Macmillan, London, 1980), p.195.

6. Thus the White Paper The Challenge of North Sea Oil, CMND. 7143, (H.M.S.O., London, 1978) did not suggest any exchange rate effects from the discovery and exploitation of this resource. cf. F.T. Blackaby, "Exchange Rate Policy and Economic Strategy", Three Banks Review 126, (June 1980), p.5.

Chapter Eight

ANTI-INFLATION

By the end of the nineteen seventies inflation had
moved to the centre of the stage of policy makers'
concerns. In the 1979 election both political parties paraded their concern with inflation, and the
policies of both parties before and after this
election suggested that this concern was not merely
rhetorical (Post-1979 "monetarism" is looked at in
more detail in Chapter 10 below).

This increase in concern was no doubt in part a
reflection simply of the increase in the inflation
rate, as measured conventionally by the R.P.I.,
shown in Table 8.1. But such a view would clearly
not of itself be an adequate explanation. First, to
worry about inflation, at whatever pace it is pro-
ceeding, depends upon some conception of its effects,
and as suggested below changes in such conceptions
have been part and parcel of changes in policy on
inflation, operating substantially independently of
the rate of inflation.

Secondly, any assumption that the scale of concern with a problem is linked directly to the
measured incidence of a problem, must account for
the case of unemployment. In that case, a sharp
increase in the measured incidence of the problem,
over approximately the same period as the increase
in inflation, has been paralleled by a clear
decrease in policy concern (Chapter 6). So we cannot
understand what has happened to inflation or unemployment policy simply by reference to 'brute
reality', as represented by changes in the Retail
Price Index or the statistics of the numbers of
jobless.

Less importantly, the table shows the rather
odd point, that the 'take off' into emphasis on
inflation as a policy problem began when inflation
was at its post-war minimum, at the end of the

Table 8.1: Inflation Rates 1956-1980 (Retail Price Index)

1956	2	1969	5.4
1957	3.7	1970	6.4
1958	3.0	1971	9.4
1959	0.6	1972	7.1
1960	1.1	1973	9.2
1961	3.5	1974	16.1
1962	4.2	1975	24.2
1963	2.0	1976	16.5
1964	3.3	1977	15.8
1965	4.9	1978	8.3
1966	3.9	1979	13.4
1967	2.5	1980	18.4
1968	4.7		

Source: Economic Trends, (H.M.S.O., London, various dates).

fifties and beginning of the 1960s. Finally it may be argued that the data on inflation rates does not clearly justify the view that the post-war period has been one of secularly increasing inflation - in a simple statistical sense the time period is too short to disentangle convincingly trend and cyclical patterns.

Economists and Inflation
The increase in concern has no doubt partly reflected the changing views of economists. As suggested in Chapter 3, economists were only beginning to regard post-war inflation as a serious problem by the time of Radcliffe in the late 1950s. However, subsequently there has been both a shift in the seriousness with which inflation is viewed, and a related but not wholly consequential shift in the reasons why inflation is viewed as a problem.

Most important to the former shift has been a change in the weight given to unemployment and inflation. "In recent years, the economics profession seems to have modified its evaluation of the relative welfare loss from inflation and unemployment.... Estimates of the loss from unemployment have been lowered" (Wallich 1978, p.160). This change in assessment has involved both sides of the account, a re-assessment of the losses from both unemployment and inflation. In addition, there has been a shift in the emphasis on the nature of the

consequences of inflation, which has tended to some
degree to undermine the notion of a trade-off
between unemployment and inflation.

At the time of the Radcliffe Committee the
primary focus of economists' concern with inflation
(short of hyper-inflation), was with its redistributive consequences and its impact on the balance of
payments. Only a few mavericks stressed other
effects, and these contributions seemed to combine
enormity and vagueness in a manner few economists
found acceptable. By the end of the 1970s, however,
there had been a shift in emphasis, which whilst
still bringing out the probable redistributive
consequences of inflation now also suggested substantial consequences for output and employment. The
locus classicus of this view is Friedman (1977), and
its arguments returned to below in the last section
of this chapter.

Whilst this shift in economists' perceptions of
the problem of inflation has not been without its
policy effects, this chapter suggests it has been
only at most a relatively small part of the basis
for changes in policy. So whilst these and other
aspects of economists' discussion of inflation need
to be borne in mind in trying to answer the question
"why do governments worry about inflation?", we
should not conflate that question with "why do
economists worry about inflation?".

In particular any account of changes in policy
towards inflation in the 1960s and 1970s needs to
take account of the means that governments associated with this objective - especially incomes
policies and demand deflation. The weight attached
to the conquest of inflation depended to a considerable extent on the perceived consequences of the
means to be employed in this conquest. Such an
argument may also be used to contest the view that
the rate of inflation can be seen as the consequence of maximising calculations by governments as
to its costs and benefits to them.

The Means to Beat Inflation
Already by the time of the Radcliffe discussions two
clear means to reduce inflation had been adduced by
economists: incomes policies and deflation. Whilst
the Phillips curve trade-off (Phillips 1958) seemed
to offer a relatively easy policy option in the
sense that the unemployment "price" to be paid for
reducing inflation was quite small, the governments'
policies moved towards incomes policies. In the

short-run this may have been influenced by the publication of the O.E.E.C. report on Inflation
(O.E.E.C. 1961) which endorsed such policies. Such
endorsement was also evident in the 4th Report of
the Cohen Council, which notably differing from the
1st Report, stressed not monetary policy but general
restraint in money incomes as an appropriate method
of dealing with inflation (compare 1st Report (1958),
paras. 116 and 147, and 4th Report (1961), paras. 8
and 36).

Clearly such switches in emphasis may be put
down to short-run factors - how far either 'excess
demand' or 'cost push' was seen as contributing to
inflation in the particular period under review (see
for example Paish's surprising willingness at least
to countenance incomes policy in 1970 and 1971
because inflation in that period was mainly 'cost
push', Paish (1971). More generally, however, the
willingness to use incomes policy or deflationary
measures to counter inflation may be linked both to
the importance given to unemployment as a policy
objective and to the perceived other consequences of
incomes policies.

No government until the mid-1970s has ever said
explicitly that it is pursuing policies that will
increase unemployment in order to contain inflation.
Such views have been enunciated by economists,
starting with the well-known advocacy of Paish in
the 1950s (Paish 1962, esp. Ch. 7). Obviously this
disparity may be explained by the governmental
commitment to full employment, or to put it less
vaguely, the governmental perception that the
formal commitment was electorally vital.

Incomes policies popularity was clearly in
general that it promised a lessening of inflation
without abrogating responsibility for full employment. This has persistently been argued to be a
mirage - a desire for a cure for the disease of
inflation, without the willingness to suffer the
pain of the bleeding such a cure demands. Yet this
desire to evade the unemployment consequences of
anti-inflationary measures seems to be much more
important in explaining the persistent attachment to
incomes policy that intellectual woolly-mindedness,
which is given pride of place in most attacks on
incomes policy (e.g. Brittan and Lilley 1977,
Ch. 1). One might also note that this persistent
attachment is also related to the fact that,
certainly up to the mid-1970s, an increasing proportion of all employees were in the public sector, so
that governments which in any way wanted to control

government expenditure were forced willy-nilly to
have an incomes policy for a major part of the work-
force.

However, whilst a seeking after incomes policy
had become in the 1960s and 1970s a standard part of
the reportoire of macro-economic policy, and one
enthusiastically pushed by the Treasury (Ham 1981,
pp.20-1, 34, 112), it was pursued fitfully and
consequently rather unsuccessfully, and this in turn
impacted on the seriousness with which the objective
at which it was aimed, reducing inflation, was
pursued.

It is obvious enough that at one end of the
political spectrum the Labour Party's difficulties
with incomes policies arose from the attachment to
free collective bargaining amongst trade unions.
This attachment arose not only from the hostility of
trade unions to profits, which were seen as increased by incomes policies, but also from the well-
founded belief that such bargaining was a raison
d'etre of British trade unionism (Stewart 1977,
pp.38-9). It also arose from the belief that free
collective bargaining was a fundamental political
right in a capitalist society - a view which united
Left and Right in the trade union movement - and one
which had proved its efficacy in raising real
standards of living in the post-war period. The
post-war expansion of such bargaining had unambiguously coincided with the most sustained rise in
living standards that the British working class had
ever attained, and clearly this could be argued to
be no mere coincidence but a fundamental cause and
effect.

Unsurprisingly, therefore, the successful pursuit of incomes policy by Labour governments was
crisis based; such policies could only gain enough
support to be viable under conditions of severe
economic constraint, to be effectively repudiated
once that period had passed. (This pattern was perhaps emphasised by the fact that the share of
profits in National Income tends to rise in the
recovery phase of the cycle, apparently supporting
the view of those that incomes policies have redistributed incomes from wages to profits). Thus
incomes policies under Labour governments in the
1960s and 1970s had an ad hoc character, were used
in unprincipled ways, and rested not on ideological
commitment, but on the passing fears of the possibly
worse alternatives. This is true despite the fact
that both in 1964 and 1974 the incomes policies were

supposed to be well thought out and permanent policies; but this was true only in their rhetoric.

The major attempt to grapple with this problem
came with the Labour government from 1974 in which
the government under the name of the 'social
contract' offered a series of concessions to the
unions on other aspects of policy in return for
agreement on restraint in wage bargaining.

A number of points may be made about this.
First attacks on it as somehow against the principles of parliamentary democracy appear to rest on a
doctrine of parliamentary sovereignty which is
unsustainable (see Thatcher's response to Healey's
1976 budget, Hansard, 6 April 1976, Col. 285;
Phelps Brown 1981). As modern 'pluralist' democracy
rests on continual government bargaining with
interest groups, it may well be argued that it is
better if these bargains are public and explicit as
the social contract bargain was.

However the character of the policy was not as
radically different from what went before as its
proponents hoped, especially in the sense of moving
towards a long-term policy in this area. First the
social contract was a contract between the T.U.C./
individual trade union leaders and the Labour government which remained very much a contract between
leaderships. It could be 'sold' to the rank and file
in the unions as long as the crisis of the mid-
seventies appeared severe and compelling enough.
But it involved no fundamental institutional or
attitudinal change on the part of union members.
Secondly the capacity and/or willingness of the
government to deliver on the public expenditure and
macro-economic aspects of the 'deal' declined
rapidly from 1976 with the exchange rate and public
borrowing crisis of that year. Whilst it should
perhaps be stressed that in certain areas, notably
in strengthening trade union bargaining rights, the
government did 'deliver' its part of the contract,
its failure on the macro side laid it open to a
charge of having reneged on the agreement.

On the Conservative side a similar fitful
commitment to incomes policy is apparent, albeit
with wholly different reasons. Incomes policies have
commonly been attacked by economists, especially
Conservative economists, for their impact in dis-
torting wage bargaining, in preventing wages from
fulfilling their allocative function in the labour
market (Brittan and Lilley 1977, Ch. 8). However the
attachment of Conservatives to incomes policies was
weakened not so much by attachment to this view on

their effects, but perceptions of their <u>political</u>
consequences, coupled with a greater liking for
another means of countering inflation, restrictive
monetary policy.

Politicians on the Right in Britain have
correctly perceived that incomes policies in a
country with a strong established trade union movement are likely to have political consequences which
they dislike. They are likely in a general sense to
require an increase in trade union power, as unions
provide an input into determining the shape of any
policy on incomes. Equally they are likely to
require some <u>quid pro quo</u> in the form of other policies which are hardly likely to be amenable to
Conservatives:

> Still more important is the price that is paid
> to obtain union consent for incomes policy.
> This requires so much in the way of policies
> which depress profits and interfere with the
> workings of the labour and product markets that
> the longer-term effects on employment is
> certainly detrimental (Brittan and Lilley 1977,
> p.25).

On the other side of the Conservative assessment of incomes policy has been the perception that
the alternative, deflation, was both less politically horrific in its own right than Labour was
inclined to belief, and also that it fitted in with
the general Conservative perception that public
expenditure should be reduced. For in Britain monetary and fiscal policy have been inextricably
intertwined (unlike, on occasion, the U.S.A.) so
that deflationary monetary policies have almost
always been coupled with public expenditure restraint (usually cuts in the rate of growth). Thus
British macro policy in the 1960s and 1970s usually
consisted of package deals, in which in the restrictive phases fiscal deflation was coupled with
monetary restraint, nicely linking (from the view-
point of Conservative ideology) attacks on the size
of the public sector and on inflation, without the
political danger of incomes policies. This policy
drift only came to fruition after 1979 (see below
Chapter 10) - before then it remained hidden
beneath the public consensus on the unacceptability
of mass unemployment.

All this is very general, but it does I believe
provide a necessary background to understanding why
concern with inflation fluctuated so much in Britain

over the 1960s and 1970s, apart from changes in the
rate of that inflation. Labour was unhappy with a
permanent incomes policy and the alternative of
deflationary policies; Conservatives were unhappy
with the former and only gradually overcame the
belief that politically the latter would be disastrous. With both parties only employing incomes
policies on an 'emergency' basis, and deflation when
all else seemed to fail, inflation crept up along
with unemployment and there grew up an "implicit
Paishism"; whilst no government would proclaim the
desirability of more unemployment to cure inflation,
it would not strenuously resist the drift in that
direction.

The Costs and Benefits of Inflation
All this is very different from the argument that
governmental acceptance of inflation (or unwillingness to combat it with adequate vigour) was based on
a rational calculation as to its costs and benefits
to government. In the 'economics of politics'
approach to government activity, it is pointed out
that looking upon government as a sector of the
economy amongst others, it is the sector where gains
from inflation most clearly arise. Most importantly
this is because of the position of government as the
largest nominal debtor in the economy, which nominal
position is reduced and may be reversed in real
terms under conditions of inflation (Taylor and
Threadgold 1979). Governments also gain from inflation in the sense that it raises tax revenues without explicit increases in tax rates, insofar as
nominal tax bands are not adjusted in line with
inflation.
    These processes would imply a direct gain to
government from inflation. In a related way it may
be argued that inflation is a consequence of a
political calculation rather than a direct object of
such calculation. If governments are seen as gaining
politically from public expenditure, but losing from
explicit taxes, it may be argued that they will
therefore tend towards budget deficits, which will
then in turn cause inflation (Gordon 1975).
    The first prong of this argument, which sees a
direct link between the financial gains to government and inflation, is similar to much neo-classical
argument in that the postulate of a rational calculation and a consequence, are not linked in any way
by an account of the institutional mechanism within
which that calculation is made and that effect

generated. Where exactly the cost benefit calculation is made that underlies inflation generation by
governments is not shown.

It may be thought absurdly naive to ask for
evidence that governments or government departments
(the Treasury?) have calculated in this way. Plainly
they would not have proclaimed such discreditable
practices from the rooftops. But equally if such
were the forms of calculation is it not a 'Machiave-
llian' view of government policy making that it is
aiming at one thing but proclaiming the exact
opposite? Such a view of government does seem to
have been held by some commentators. Parkin (1975,
p.200) for example wrote with reference to incomes
policies "The fact that governments repeatedly turn
to such policies even though they, and everyone
else, know how impotent they are, lends major support to the basic thesis that inflation is caused by
governments for their own benefit".

This is a curious form of "major support"; we
know governments want inflation because they hide
behind incomes policies which they know to be
ineffective. As suggested above, attachment to
incomes policies can be explained without recourse
to such incredibly rationalistic arguments. Governments no more than individuals can helpfully be
understood as "dessicated calculating machines".

The 'government sector' may in certain national
accounting contexts be sensibly used as a unitary
category; it does not make sense to talk about it as
if it were an economic agent with a unified will
guided by a unified form of calculation, and the
capacity to make that will be effective. It may be
an interesting paradox that governments talk a lot
about defeating inflation and yet are its main bene-
ficiaries, and it may be a paradox that particularly
worries economists who work with simple notions of
economic agents and their calculations. But it is a
paradox which should be not resolved by recourse to
wholly unconvincing accounts of how government
policy is made.

The view that inflation is an unintended consequence of actions of governments on such things as
public expenditure is clearly not subject to such a
criticism. Nevertheless, such analysis does not take
sufficient account of the means - incomes policy and
deflation - discussed above. In other words it is
not just that governments are not too unhappy to
resolve their problems in other areas (e.g. raising
explicit tax rates) by inflation, but that there is
a clear problem in the means assumed to be necessary

to directly confront that inflation. Inflation is
not just something which 'unfortunately' happens as
a side product of other policies, governments do
'really care' about inflation, but they are (or
generally were in the 1960s and 1970s) unwilling to
bear the perceived cost of the means necessary to
its defeat.

The Rise in Importance of Inflation

The above remarks apply to the general pattern of
policy in the 1960s and early 1970s. But it should
be said that they tend to obscure the important
shift in the policy perception of inflation which
occurred in the mid-1970s, and which gave the price-
level and pre-eminence in policy making that it had
never had before in the era of economic management.

As always such a shift in perception is both
difficult to locate with precision and difficult to
explain. But one clear index of its evolution may be
found in the budget statements of the Chancellor
(Denis Healey) in the mid-1970s.

In the first budget of his period as Chancellor,
Healey placed a considerable emphasis on inflation
as a problem, albeit the consequences were perceived
in a trivialised (and sexist) way. "Faced with the
prospects of inflation on the present scale, we cannot afford to leave aside any measure which the
government can take to help the housewife where it
matters" (Hansard, 26 March 1974, Col. 283). But the
defeat of inflation could not be secured at the cost
of full employment. "I totally reject the philosophy
that would cure the high blood pressure in the
economy by bleeding it to death" (Ibid., Col. 290).

It was precisely in the context of movements in
this perceived trade-off between inflation and
unemployment that the new emphasis on inflation as
primary is apparent.

In November of 1974 Healey was still able to
say "Yet there is no real evidence that in this situation the adoption of deflationary policies will
produce a worthwhile impact on the rate of inflation
- at any rate within a time scale that democracy
will tolerate" (Hansard, 12 November 1974, Col.
244). "Deliberately to adopt a strategy which
requires mass unemployment would be no less an
economic than a moral crime" (Ibid., Col. 253).

By early 1975 however the emphasis had clearly
shifted:

> I fully understand why I have been urged by so
> many friends both inside and outside the House
> to treat unemployment as the central problem
> and to stimulate a further growth in home
> consumption, public or private, so as to start
> getting the rate of unemployment down as fast
> as possible. I do not believe it would be wise
> to follow this advice today .... I cannot
> afford to increase demand further today when
> 5p. in every £ we spend at home has been
> provided by our creditors abroad and inflation
> is running at its current rate (Hansard,
> 15 April 1975, Col. 282).

The statement accepted that the price of defeating
inflation was higher unemployment - the first time
this had been explicitly stated and stated to be
acceptable.

By early 1976 the conversion to the new orthodoxy was apparent "This is above all a budget about
jobs and about inflation, which is the main threat
to jobs in Britain today" (emphasis added; Hansard,
6 April 1976, Col. 232).

Clearly Chancellor's speeches are only the tip
of an iceberg, and a tip which may not in all
respects be the same as what remains hidden. Nevertheless I think these changing emphases are an index
of a general change in perception of what macro-
economic policy is trying to do.

This change can be treated as a shift in the
ideologies underlying policy. Ham (1981), for
example, treats policy in this period as a reassertion of the Treasury's unfortunate adherence to
retrograde 'abstract doctrine'. Ham, however, has
problems with this period, because his general
thesis that the Treasury has consistently pursued a
line in which "manufacturing and industrial interests have been consistently sacrificed to abstract
doctrine and, above all, the strength of the pound"
(p.7) is hardly consistent with the events of 1975
and 1976 when as he himself stresses the Treasury
deliberately initiated a fall in the value of the
pound, albeit one which eventually got out of hand
(pp.123-5; p.128). Whilst it would be difficult to
argue that the Treasury has been the site of all
wisdom in economic matters in the last fifty years,
it equally seems exaggerated to see every policy
problem as the result of the "personnel, culture and
attitude" of this one institution (Ibid., p.2). (For
a defence of the Treasury in this period see Burnett

1982). How otherwise might this evolution to be
explained?

First of all there was of course an upward
shift in the price level. However as asserted at the
beginning of this chapter, to view the acceleration
of inflation at the time as the main explanation of
the growing concern with inflation sidesteps the
problem that the response to such an acceleration
depends upon the mode in which it is perceived. Two
particular features of the perception of inflation
of this period probably greatly added to the
seriousness with which it was viewed, creating something like a 'moral panic' in the mid-1970s over
inflation somewhat akin to that over "mugging" at
the end of the decade. These two elements were,
firstly, the economists' belief that as long as
macro policy attempted to maintain unemployment
above its 'equilibrium' level, then inflation would
consistently tend to accelerate. This was a point
emphasised by Britain's two most important indigen-
ous monetarists in their popular presentation of the
monetarist case (Laidler 1972; Parkin 1974).

Secondly there was a growing literature which
tried to argue that this inflation was a structural
feature of democratic societies, which could only be
restrained by constitutional changes which would
establish certain policies (monetary and fiscal) as
outside the competence (in both senses) of elected
governments (Friedman 1975; Brittan 1977). In this
view the emergence of rapid inflation in the 1970s
was a delayed effect of the post-war commitment to
full employment, a delay caused either by slowly
adapting expectations or to the "irrational"
adherence to fixed exchange rates which meant that
inflation was effectively avoided by policies
ostensibly designed to deal with balance of payments
crises.

Taken together these two trends turned what was
arguably a short-term phenomenon, with a short-term
cause, the oil crisis, into both manifestation and
cause of fundamental social disintegration. Probably
the best example of this is Rees Mogg (1974). "The
insanity of inflation leaves a mark of insanity on
society; it changes a good society into one which,
so long as inflation lasts, is wholly and fradulent-
ly unjust" (p.13).

Secondly, the focus on inflation as the policy
problems seems to have represented a rationalisation
for the seeming incapacity of governments to cope
with the 'alternative' major problem, unemployment.
That is to say, the undoubted difficulties of

governments in dealing with unemployment seems to
have made it easier to argue that dealing with this
problem should be a 'medium-term' objective, the
short-term focus to be on inflation.

Thirdly there were of course the direct
pressures from governmental creditors - domestic and
international - to make inflation a priority, at
least indirectly via a stress on public borrowing.
Domestic borrowers were probably strongly influenced
by Friedman's acolytes in the financial and serious
press - Brittan, Jay, Rees Mogg, and this was
probably a major conduit of monetarist ideology into
policy making.

Fourthly the 'public expenditure crisis' of the
mid-1970s reduced governmental fears of the political consequences of deflationary fiscal policies by
bringing out the scale of popular opposition to
public expenditure and taxation (see Ch. 6 above).
This latter may have been particularly important in
the Treasury, whose traditional concern for the
management of public finance came under great strain
in this period. Perhaps most famous was the suggestion that £5 billion of government expenditure
growth had been unplanned (Godley 1976). On 'objective' criteria there was not obviously a problem.
Government expenditure in Britain was not out of
line with other O.E.C.D. countries (Neild and Ward
1978, Appendix B), nor was PSBR (Economic Trends,
May 1976). However what mattered was the view taken
by the government's creditors, increasingly
influenced by the monetarists and the general
alarmist talk of the time.

These features taken together forced unemployment from the centre of concern and inflation in the
opposite direction. This was obviously apparent in
Callaghan's famous speech to the Labour Party
conference in 1976, which his son-in-law (Peter Jay)
announced in the Times as "the most breathtakingly
frank public pronouncement since St. Paul's First
Epistle to the Corinthians". As we have seen the
shift had already taken place in the Chancellor's
public posture.

Inflation and Unemployment
But even this statement did not go as far as the
view that the Phillips Curve was not only <u>vertical</u>
(no unemployment/inflation trade-off) but positively
sloped - inflation causes unemployment. Prior to
Friedman's (1977) statement of this, it had normally
been argued by non-economic 'mavericks' (see Ch. 3

below) and by economists only in the context of
hyper-inflations. Now Friedman claimed that even at
the relatively moderate levels of inflation suffered
by the advanced capitalist countries in the 1960s
and 1970s unemployment was a consequence.

Friedman stressed that it is only unanticipated
inflation that reduces unemployment. He argued that
we would expect to see a link between high inflation
and high unemployment because as inflation rises so
does the volatility of inflation. This is said to
decrease employment in two ways. First increased
volatility of price movements shortens the optimum
length of unindexed commitments and renders indexation more advantageous. This implies a shortening of
time horizons, and even where indexation is introduced this is always imperfect and introduced with a
lag. Therefore "An additional element of uncertainty
is, as it were, added to every market arrangement"
(Friedman 1977, p.466). The effects of this on
employment are unclear. "About all one can say now
is that the slow adjustment of commitments and the
imperfections of indexing may contribute to the
recorded increase in unemployment" (Ibid., pp.
466-7).

Increased volatility of the price level is also
argued to render market prices a less efficient
system for co-ordinating economic activity. There is
an increased amount of 'noise' in market signals.
Again Friedman argues:

> the effect on economic efficiency is clear, on
> unemployment less so. But, again, it seems
> plausible that the average level of unemploy-
> ment would be raised by the increased amount
> of noise in market signals, at least during
> the period when institutional arrangements are
> not yet adapted to the new situation (Ibid.,
> p.467).

Friedman attempts to back these rather general
formulations with empirical evidence from seven
major countries over the period 1956-75, and attempted to show that increasingly over this period
unemployment was positively rather than negatively
correlated with inflation. The exercise is not
convincing - the range of countries is small, the
unemployment data are not standardised, and as
Friedman himself notes, the strongest evidence of his
thesis is in the early 1970s when the data are distorted by the oil crisis. A rise in oil prices which
is only partly accommodated by the monetary authori-

ties will raise both the rate of inflation and the level of unemployment in all the countries affected. The more systematic evidence in Higham and Tomlinson (1982) does not support the Friedman thesis. Nevertheless, the Friedman argument was used by politicians to argue that, despite appearances, concern with inflation was also concern with unemployment.

In the context of the current book what is particularly important to note is that the concern with inflation, by generating deflationary policies, leads to a self-fulfilling prophecy about high inflation causing unemployment, as the deflationary policies pursued to defeat that inflation add to the job queues.

This means that whatever the reason why government's worry about inflation, that worry is likely to lead to increased unemployment. In that sense the conjuring up of the Weimar Republic as the analogy for what was happening in "inflation ridden" Britain in the mid-1970s, was important in paving the way back to the mass unemployment of the early 1980s.

Chapter Nine

GROWTH

Growth played little explicit part in policy debates in the late 1960s. The July measures of 1966 aborted the National Plan, and effectively with it the rhetoric of the "New Britain". The devaluation of 1967 was (after some delay) followed by a further severe 'stop' under Chancellor of the Exchequer Jenkins, which eventually brought a massive improvement in the balance of payments, at the price of abandoning any attempt to make the economy expand.

Yet the very multiplicity of goals to which growth could be posed as the solution meant that it would not for ever be muted, especially in a competitive political system. It re-emerged, albeit with considerable vagueness, in the Conservative policy proposals which were generated by that party in its opposition years after 1964. As in the early 1960s the growth objective was not only profoundly "polyvalent' but imbued with tremendous moralism, a central feature of almost all British political debate. Thus whilst Conservative advocacy of growth involved a rejection of the dirigisme of economic planning, its most striking characteristic was not the means envisaged in any mechanical sense but the emphasis on growth through something akin to 'moral regeneration'.

This view is aptly summed up by the head of the Conservative Research Department 1965-70:

> No-one was so naive as to believe the once fashionable theory that economic progress could be accelerated by increasing the pressure of demand. Something far more fundamental was required. The strategy was no less than an attempt to change the whole attitude of mind of the British people: to create a more dynamic thrusting "go-getting" economy on the American

or German model; to create not merely new
material wealth but also a new pride in
achievement (Harris and Sewill 1975, p.30).[1]

This commitment to growth became more explicit
in 1972, but this time the means were much more
explicit. In this chapter I want to examine the
evolution of the argument for economic growth in the
early 1970s focussing on the two separable periods
before and after 1972. This period is primarily
important here for the re-orientation it saw in
policy objectives, and the eventual demise of growth
as a significant policy objective for a considerable
period. A less important but still significant element was the way in which policy evolution in this
period was taken by many to indicate the final bank-
tuptcy of the existing means of economic management,
providing the basis of more than one Damascus road
conversion to a new brand of conservatism (see e.g.
Pringle (1977), for such an interpretation; and
Joseph (1975) for the most famous such conversion).

Dashing for Growth, Again

Retrospectively the first half of the Conservative
government's period of office at the beginning of
the 1970s has been seen as a precursor to
'Thatcherism' - a commitment to 'laissez-faire' and
'right wing' policies blown off-course by a rising
tide of inflation. Whilst there are clear parallels
between the rhetoric of "Selsdon man" and "Grantham
woman" the differences are probably more significant. First, whilst the government of 1970 was
committed to reducing taxation, its main thrust was
towards tax reform, aimed at creating incentives,
but not involving (in rhetoric at least) the kind of
rolling back of the public sector envisaged in 1979
and afterwards.[2] Secondly, whilst the rhetoric of
hostility to trade unionism was powerful in both
periods, the Heath government did perceive unions as
having an important albeit restricted and redefined
role in the economy, rather than seeing them as
essentially damaging and destructive. Whilst the
1971 Industrial Relations Act ignored some of the
recommendations of the Donovan Commission (e.g. on
strike ballots), it shared that Commission's view on
the desirability of co-operation and dialogue with
'responsible' trade unions. (Holmes, 1982).
In these ways, Heath's policy thrust can be
reasonably described as "technocratic" (Butler and
Pinto-Duschinsky 1971, p.70; Ramsden 1980, pp.250-2),

rather than in the mould of later conservative whiggism. Also different was Heath's whole hearted commitment to membership of the E.E.C. as the best policy for Britain. Here there seems to have been a clear running together of ends and means. As the immediate economic costs of joining the E.E.C. were clearly adverse (Britain a free trading, small but efficient agricultural producer was ill-fitted to the E.E.C.'s foundation on heavily protected, large and inefficient agricultural sectors), the pro-E.E.C. economic arguments had to focus on long-term "dynamic" benefits. Thus economic growth was argued as a consequence of membership of the E.E.C., resulting from the enlarged market, with the economies of scale and increased competition this would bring (see for example CMND. 4715, 1971, paras. 41, 46-57). Whilst this view was no doubt seriously believed at the time, it conveniently conjured up a (vague and unquantifiable) economic benefit to be used to weigh against the obvious costs. This fitted in with established British political argument, in which almost every policy had to be justified in economic terms, though it is clear that for many of the proponents and opponents of E.E.C. entry the fundamental arguments were political.

By these technocratic changes, plus the competitive environment consequent on E.E.C. entry, economic growth was to be attained.[3] The objective of growth seems to have been seen as above all to reduce inflationary pressures by reducing incompatible demands in national output, and providing greater resources to combat "social problems" (Harris and Sewill 1975, pp.29-30). But in addition, whilst moral or morale changes were seen as aiding growth, they were also seen as its consequence:

> there were many who saw in the creation of new prosperity the means of achieving not only social and environmental improvement but also a revival of national purpose and self confidence (Ibid., p.31).[4]

The incoming government of 1970 probably had economic policies which were unusually well worked out for an opposition party acceding to power. But these policies were mostly concerned with the areas of tax reform, industrial relations, and the machinery of government. There was no clear policy on macroeconomic issues and in particular on growth. As one sympathiser has summarised the position, the Conservatives' programme in 1970:

was, collectively a much more elaborate and sophisticated policy of "setting the people free". It had, however, several weaknesses. It did not in reality deal with the problem of "steering" the economy, and the emphasis on the rewards to be obtained from structural reforms was excessive. Heath was personally committed to economic growth, but the Party's economic policy gave no clear indication of how this was to be achieved without relapsing into the familiar "stop-go" cycle" (Rhodes-James 1972, p.136).

Thus the objective of economic growth, unlike in the early 1960s, was not tied to any specific mechanism or institutional loci. Government, trade union and tax reform, plus E.E.C. membership were to generally improve the performance of the British economy, but the precise link between cause and effect was not spelt out.

This is not the place to give a blow by blow account of the first two years of the 1970 government's policies (see on this Stewart 1977, Ch. 5; Blackaby 1978, pp.52-62). But as far as objectives of policy are concerned there are several points of importance.

First inflation was not given a high priority in the policies of the incoming government - or indeed by the defeated government. As Stewart notes (p.115) little was said about prices in the main parties' election manifestos, even though it did become a central issue in the election campaign.

This is an interesting instance in the study of policy objectives. The Conservative Party was certainly aware of public concern over the rate of inflation. As the official Conservative Party Research Department put it in its report on the 1970 election, despite this concern

"due probably to the traumatic experiences of incomes policy into the early 1960s, there was a remarkable reluctance by the Shadow Cabinet during the years of Opposition to discuss any policy for dealing with inflation..... The result was that the Research Department had, at the very last moment, to invent a policy for dealing with inflation; and this was spatchcocked into the manifesto after the seventh draft when it was in final proof stage" (cited Ramsden 1980, p.227).

Similar difficulties existed for the Labour Party.
Labour had political problems with the means
(incomes policies) commonly deemed necessary to deal
with inflation, the Conservatives ideological
problems with the same means.

Whilst the Conservatives did adjust their
policies to take account of public perceptions of
the inflation problem, it was not until late 1970
and early 1971 that inflation moved to the centre of
policy making, and it was only in the latter years
that Britain's performance in this respect became
notably worse than that of major competitor
countries.

Secondly, there was as yet no questioning of
the status of the full employment commitment in the
mainstream of Conservative policies. Whilst unemployment had been rising fast in the late 1960s
there was neither an attempt to either shrug this
off, nor explicitly discount it as a problem, until
such work as that of Wood in 1972 (see also Chapter
6 above).

Thirdly, whilst there was no explicit attack on
the conduct of macro policy as there had been in the
'growth' period in the early 1960s, as Rhodes-James
suggests in the quotation above, macro-management
was not given a high priority by the government.
Like the government of 1964, faith was placed in
institutional reform rather than improved management
in the orthodox post-war sense.

Thus, for example, the first budget of the new
government, 27th October 1970, was not primarily concerned with demand management but with tax reform
and changes in the level and type of state intervention in the economy. A roughly neutral budget was
justified by not wishing to give a boost to inflation, but this was a minor part of the exercise.
Equally the budget of 1971 was mainly concerned with
tax reform - the introduction of V.A.T., changes in
income and corporation tax being the centrepieces.
Economic growth played no direct part in budgetary
calculations. It was rising inflation and unemployment which triggered a reversal of policy, at first
gradual but from the beginning of 1972 more marked.
Up until then the drift of policy had been to hold
unemployment at around half a million until the rise
in wages reduced. In addition, in the public sector
a policy of each successive settlement being lower
than the previous one was pursued. The first policy
foundered on the rise in unemployment to almost a
million in the winter of 1971/2, the second on the
miners' settlement after a seven week strike ending

in February 1972. Hurd suggests (1979, p.90) that it
was inflation rather than unemployment that
triggered the "U turn", growth being seen as a means
of defeating inflation (see further below).

It was this failure which set the scene for the
gradual but eventually radical reversal of policy
which was to place economic growth at the centre of
the policy agenda in a much more "active" way than
in 1970 to 1972.

After the U-Turn

The change in focus which emerged from early 1972
involved, firstly, a much greater reliance on traditional macro management so far as fiscal and monetary policy was concerned, coupled with a new stance
on the balance of payments. Essentially the policy
was one of reflation with the intention of "riding
through" any balance of payments difficulties by
allowing the pound to float. This was however
expressly portrayed not as one more "go" period but
as a policy of growth. Reflation (i.e. changes in
capacity utilisation) were to lead to growth (i.e.
changes in capacity) by government stressing that it
would not be deflected from its course. In this way
it was hoped that investment would be encouraged,
and the economy enabled to continue to expand.

Inflation was to be dealt with by incomes
policies. The policy of allowing the pound to float
was not seen as significant in its effects on
inflation, but was seen as a means only of breaking
out of stop-go into the sunny uplands of sustained
growth. Growth was also to be functional to reducing
inflation; growth was to be "offered" to the trade
unions in return for their acceptance of incomes
policy. This is important to the argument that what
changed policies in 1972 was not so much the rising
tide of unemployment as the rise in inflation.
Whilst increased growth would clearly reduce unemployment, the government also believed that it would
create the right environment in which successful
negotiation could be conducted with the Trade
Unions. Heath did not seem to understand how far the
Industrial Relations Act made it impossible for the
T.U.C. to co-operate closely with his government.
Thus the previous attempt to deal with inflation via
trade union legislation rebounded against using the
carrot of growth to change union behaviour. As in
other areas growth was not the panacea its protagon-
ists hoped.

In the budget of March 1972 the Chancellor announced that:

> The measures I shall put to the House are intended to ensure a growth of output at an annual rate of 5 per cent between the second half of last year and the first half of next ....if my expectations are correct, output will have risen by 10 per cent over the two year period from the first half of 1971 to the first half of 1973 (Col. 1353).

In the same speech (Col. 1354) the Chancellor stressed that "it is neither necessary nor desirable to distort economic economies to an unacceptable extent in order to maintain unrealistic exchange rates, whether they are too high or too low".

Some of the origins of this decision to 'float' the pound have been outlined in Chapter 7. What is important in the context of the policy of economic growth is twofold. First it meant that the exchange rate was to be subordinated to <u>growth</u> in a manner unprecedented in the post-war period.

Secondly the commitment to growth unlike either in the early 1960s or, in more muted form, in the early 1970s, was not predicated on a break with the previous format of economic management as far as the domestic economy was concerned. Growth was not to come from a break with "stop-go" by institutional changes, but rather from a massive and unprecedented "go". In other words reflation of a traditional kind was to be pursued, but a reflation to be sustained through thick and thin.

The emphasis on growth from 1972 may then be seen as in part a logical consequence of pre-exist- ing debates on economic policy. Economic growth in 1970 was deemed highly desirable, but something to be attained by institutional changes which would make the private sector deliver growth, and thus an objective without the quantitative targets as well without the dirigisme of "economic planning". When by 1972 this policy had clearly failed to cope with the problems of inflation and unemployment, and at the same time there were a number of pressures to allow the exchange rate to float, going for growth via direct macro-economic means and allowing the float to "take care" of the balance of payments appeared a logical policy. So the "U turn" of 1972 was not so much from "free market" to "intervention- ist" policies, as a switch from technocratic solu- tions to a combination of traditional macro policy

coupled with the 'freeing' from the traditional constraint on reflation, the balance of payments.

Of course the policy failed. Whether this was
due to its inherent defects (e.g. Pringle 1977),
world conditions, or simply bad macro management,
especially too rapid a <u>pace</u> of expansion (Blackaby
1979) is not directly of concern here. But the
consequences of this failure for the objective of
economic growth are important.

For many both in and, increasingly, beyond the
Conservative party, the two periods when great
stress had been put on growth as an objective had
both ended disastrously. In 1964 Labour had won an
election as the more natural pursuer of the "economic growth by planning" inaugurated by its Conservative predecessor. After 1972 growth through reflation had proved to be a mirage. Demand management
could not deliver growth.

Proponents of this latter view tended to play
down the 'planning' aspect of the 1960s commitment
to growth (e.g. Pringle 1977, p.11). This fits in
with the argument that in both cases growth was
pursued by (inappropriate) macro-economic policies
and that this reflected the domination of a
(mistaken) neo-Keynesian consensus especially amongst economists and the media.

This interpretation raises a number of problems. First, as argued in Chapter 4, the commitment
to growth in the early 1960s simply cannot be understood except in relation to the notion of planning.
Of course 1963-4 did see a massive reflation of the
economy but this owed much more to short-term
electoral calculations than the preceding commitment
to growth (such calculations did not weigh anything
like as heavily in 1972).

Secondly, the initial growth commitment of the
Conservatives in 1970 did not at all rely on macro
management, rather on a range of institutional
changes as suggested above. Thirdly the growth
policy after 1972 involved a sharp break with old
policies, notably on the exchange rate rather than
being a continuation of them. (Floating was a policy
more popular on the right than amongst the "neo-
Keynesian" consensus).

In any case Pringle exaggerates the role of
economists and the media in bringing this stress on
growth. As Hurd (1979, p.89) points out, businessmen
were major agitators for growth, and the Heath
government was very sensitive to this constituency.

Equally the Treasury's support for economic
growth was based on the understandable view that

this would provide the resources for financing the expenditure programmes for which it was constantly being pressed by other departments. Thus the Treasury's position was not simply a desire to increase the "size of the public sector and thus in its power" (Pringle 1977, p.16), but to resolve the conflicting pressures upon it as guardian of the public purse and provider of the revenue of government programmes.

The Bank of England's position is also important. Pringle's account (pp.25-32) rightly stresses that the Bank did not wholeheartedly embrace control of the money supply in the early 1970s, retaining a concern to manage interest rates (especially for debt purposes). Also it does seem to be the case that once the exchange rate was floated the Bank of England lost its central strategic goal of the whole post-war period. This made its policies much less clearly directed, though the centrality of inflation as a concern is clear, coupled with a focus on incomes policies as the solution to this problem (see B.E.Q.B., December 1970, pp.473-5). Indeed in April 1972 the Governor of the Bank spoke of the dangers of floating the pound because of the possible impact on the rate of inflation (B.E.Q.B., June 1972, p.229).

However, as far as growth is concerned, the role of the Bank in fuelling the demand expansion after 1972 seems to have been a largely inadvertent one. Whilst it is true that the Bank was unhappy about rising interest rates because of their impact on debt management, and also on the housing market, the expansion in the money supply of this period seems to have been an unintended consequence of Competition and Credit Control. This was a policy which fitted in with the commitment to a more competitive environment in the policies of 1970.

Competition and Credit Control (see Blackaby 1978, pp.238-40) was aimed at ending the interest rate cartel of the Clearing Banks, and ending the process whereby controls fell most heavily on those banks, who in turn responded by aiding the growth of institutions whose activities fell outside government control. Controls were no longer to be focussed on banks' and other financial institutions assets, but on their lending. The actual method of doing this - at 12 per cent reserve asset ratio - greatly increased the liquidity of the banks who responded by an enormous increase in their lending, which doubled between mid-1971 and mid-1973. Whilst this kind of response was expected, its scale was not.

The general point here is that the Bank's policies were not aimed at the kind of money supply growth which occurred in 1972/3. Rather this was the consequence of Competition and Credit Control, which had quite a different rationale, plus the attachment to low interest rates. Even on this latter point there are some suggestions that the Bank would have liked to see higher interest rates in the early part of the Competition and Credit Control experiment (B.E.Q.B., December 1972, pp.516-7).

Finally, it should be stressed that, apart from the arguments of economists and the institutional character of the Bank of England and the Treasury, the growth of the 1972-3 period was a political programme. It was not a pre-election boom as in 1963/64, but was aimed at winning acceptance for government policies, especially by the unions, and also to a lesser extent providing a strong platform for Britain within the E.E.C.

Nevertheless it is not surprising that for many the 1972-73 period marked the end of the road for growth policies. The epitaphs were written:

> During 30 years we have tried to force the pace of growth. Growth is welcome, but we just do not know how to accelerate its pace. Perhaps faster growth, like happiness, should not be a prime target but only a by-product of other policies (Joseph 1975, p.7).

This disillusion with growth it should perhaps be stressed (cf. Arndt 1978) owed little to the impact of ecological arguments. Whilst these came with growing intensity in the 1970s, there were compelling reasons for politicians to take little note. Firstly much of the propaganda for 'no growth' came from those who were already well off, and thus had acquired most of the benefits of high living standards. For the mass of the population, or governments trying to appeal to that mass for electoral support, such arguments could be seen as elitist and always likely to be a minority concern (see Blackaby 1974). Secondly, the appeal of growth lay precisely in its 'all purpose' character, and thus was unlikely to be given up for the politically much less appealing task of the tricky allocation of resources from a cake of constant size. Finally, whilst the importance for policy debate of point should not be exaggerated, the arguments for no-growth were often economically illiterate, in particular ignoring the capacity of markets and governments to change the relative prices and therefore the production and consumption of finite resources.

More important than ecological arguments against growth was the disillusion suggested above about the means tried to attain it. In addition the seventies saw a renewed emphasis on stability, in the face of external shocks of unprecedented severity. This view was well summed up by Sewill (in Harris and Sewill 1975, p.57):

> Growth has been one of the main aims of the political parties, and the raison d'etre of many policies. We have .... sought it with Neddy, with tax reform, with local government reforms, with Royal awards and with training boards. But it must now be recognised that, even if economic growth is still desirable, it is no longer a viable political aim - in the sense that it can no longer be a central theme with which to inspire the nation.

What was needed instead was a concentration on stability - "price stability and social stability".

Growth was not undesirable, but could only be regarded as something of a vain hope left over from more optimistic days. One day it might return, but in the meantime more serious problems had to be tackled.

NOTES

1.   Sewill was also assistant to the Chancellor of the Exchequer (Barber) from 1970 to 1974.

2.   It is notable that a Conservative policy sub-committee on taxation in 1965 suggested a wealth tax to replace revenue lost by reducing higher levels of income tax. This was supported by a majority of a high-powered cross-sectional committee in the Party, including Edward Heath, but was eventually rejected as unacceptable to the Party as a whole (J. Ramsden, The Making of Conservative Party Policy, (Longman, London, 1980), pp.244-6.

3.   Growth was sometimes linked to the E.E.C. in the opposite way "should our aim be to increase our national efficiency so that we can enter Europe from strength and not from weakness, so that we can hope to lead Europe when we are in?" (Ramsden, Ibid., p.247).

4.   Heath personally seems to have viewed the possibility of mass participation in his favourite relaxations - sailing and music - as dependent upon

growth, D. Hurd, <u>An End to Promises. Sketch of a
Government 1970-74</u>, (Collins, London, 1979),
pp.84-9.

Chapter Ten

MONETARISM: DESPERATE REMEDIES?

The self-proclaimed radicalism of the Conservative
Government of 1979 opened up a series of questions
previously muted about the formation of policy
objectives. This was a government which in its own
view was to reverse the decline of post-war Britain
by breaking with the previous consensus policies and
embarking on a new road. It pronounced itself bent
on a strategy which would relegate most of the
policy debates discussed elsewhere in this book to
the dustbin. In their stead would be a policy which
at least in outline was as coherent and logical as
it was radical. The prime direct objective of macro-
economic policy would be the defeat of inflation.
The other "post-war consensus" objectives, concerning the balance of payments, growth and above all,
full employment could not be achieved in any positive sense by government. "The short-term stabilisation of output, employment and external account were
deliberately de-emphasised" (Buiter and Miller 1981,
p.316). The most that government could do would be
to remove the canker of inflation and the other
obstacles that lay in the way of the private economy
generating these desirable ends. "The government has
deliberately not seen its targets in terms of the
ultimate objectives of price stability and high output and employment because these are not within its
direct control" (H.M.S.O. 1980, p.9).
     The macro policy of the government focused
therefore on a Medium Term Financial Strategy. (For
a succinct outline of this strategy see Howe's
letter to the Chairman of the Treasury and Civil
Service Committee, H.M.S.O. 1980, pp.3-5). This gave
priority to defeating inflation, by means of a
decline in the growth of the money supply, coupled
with a decline in the growth of the P.S.B.R. Thus M3
(the chosen target for money supply) and the

P.S.B.R., would be the central target variables in the endeavour to attain the objective of defeating inflation. This macro strategy would be coupled with a focus on improving the 'supply side' of the economy which involved increasing the role of 'market forces' in the economy especially by means of changes in the laws regarding trade union activity, public expenditure cuts and reductions in government intervention in private sector economic activity.

For those unsympathetic to the government's approach this package posed problems of understanding and analysis of a severe kind, and it is the attempts to grapple with these problems which are focussed on in this chapter. It is right to focus on these problems in the context of this book precisely because they were explicitly aimed at comprehending the <u>objectives</u> the government set itself. Thus they brought into play arguments about the formation of economic policy objectives which had remained largely muted under the blanket of the post-war consensus. Looking at the analytic responses to "Thatcherism" means grappling with general problems about the formation of economic policy objectives, albeit by focussing on a particular episode in policy formation.

Responses to 'Thatcherism'

Clearly any attempt to summarise the response by its opponents to the post-1979 economic strategy must simplify in order to get any purchase on the arguments. Nevertheless underlying all the many analyses which have been offered[1] seem to be two basic positions.

On the one hand is the view that the Thatcher strategy is a form of madness or insanity, with no rational basis. Alternatively, there is the view that the strategy is a coherent and rational one (albeit risky), but one whose objectives are obscured by its rhetoric, that rhetoric operating only to obscure underlying realities.

The first argument is probably more common in popular discussion than the latter. In public speeches there are frequent references to "mad monetarism", "insane policies", the "mad axewoman". Peter Shore (in Gould, Mills and Stewart 1981, p.ix) has written of the need for a policy of "sanity and realism" arguing that the Thatcher government "took office and took leave of its senses". Amongst economists the argument has been

sustained by reference to the incoherence of monetarism as an economic doctrine, with the implication
that attachment to its precepts by the post-1979
government can only be explained as a species of
madness. Thus John Hughes (1980) in an article
entitled "The Economics of the Madhouse" can doubt
whether there is anything in government policy
"capable of rational examination" (p.4) and suggest
that "the government however needs scapegoats. It is
moving beyond rational discussion" (p.9).

The alternative view is that, far from mad, the
strategy of Thatcherism is a coherent set of policies to achieve definite objectives. Thus for example Aaronovitch and Smith (1981) list these objectives, giving pride of place to an attempt "to shift
the balance of strength further towards capital and
away from labour" (p.369). Glyn and Harrison (1980,
p.138) have argued that "The core of Thatcherism is
a coherent set of policies aimed at enabling market
forces to restore adequate conditions for producing
surplus value. All other considerations are subordinated to this aim". Rowthorn (1981, p.4) has
written of the Thatcher government as "consciously
promoting an economic crisis as a way of restoring
the primacy of market forces in economic life".

In this view talk of the money supply, public
sector borrowing requirement etc. is essentially
ideological camouflage, which once removed will
reveal a strategy by capital or the ruling class to
gain its interests at the expense of the working
class. Thus Kaldor (1983, p.62) argues that "The
centrepiece of the government's economic strategy,
the control of the money supply, however genuinely
believed in by some people, is really only a facade
or a smokescreen".

Now clearly these two arguments can be run
together. Some, who devote their time to showing the
irrationality of Thatcherism, at the same time 'in
passing' suggest that attachment to this irrationality may be explained by the view that the government
is 'really' trying to attain something different
from its proclaimed aims (e.g. Coutts, Tarling, Ward
and Wilkinson 1981, p.88, footnote 1). And indeed it
would seem to be a severe intellectual problem for
those who take the first view to explain this
attachment. Without some notion of collective
delusion, the attachment of a government to demon-
strably false propositions about the economy seems
hard to understand. One possible way is to stress
the role of economic theory in policy making, and
thus to explain Thatcherism as the putting into

practice of monetarist theory. In this view post-1979 policy reflects the displacement of one economic ideology, Keynesianism, by another, Monetarism. The argument poses two serious problems. First the policies of the post-1979 government have not followed the theories of monetarism as expressed by Friedman and his followers. As Friedman himself made clear (Friedman 1980) the focus on the P.S.B.R. and interest rates, crucial components of the governments' strategy, was in his view mistaken. Most especially, because it implied attempting to control the money supply by controlling the demand for money, a policy vigorously denounced (Friedman 1980).

Secondly, those opposed to post-1979 policies commonly sought explanations of this policy which went beyond "mere words" i.e. they desired a "material" explanation which would locate the economic ideology of the argument in relation to some underlying real force. Thus Kaldor (1982, p.xi) sees the rise of monetarism in Britain as linked to the growing importance of the City as well as "the floods of increasingly obscurantist literature from America". This underlying force of course was what the second argument was only too willing to supply. Behind the ideology of monetarism lay the very material forces of the ruling class. Unsurprisingly, therefore, most oppositional writing on the Thatcher experiment has favoured a version of the latter explanation, where the rhetorical objectives of reducing inflation and improving the supply-side of the economy have hidden the real objectives, those of inflicting upon the working class a historic defeat in the class struggle with capital.

Thatcherism and the Class Struggle

Such an approach raises a series of problems about the formation of policy objectives. Some of these are very general problems about social theory which will only be touched on here. The focus will be on the more specific aspects, though in my view the former are vital to understanding the latter. First of all the approach depends upon identifying, indeed stressing, the gap between the proclaimed objectives of policy and their real objective. This discrepancy is accounted for by use of the category of "ideology".

This concept is central to many sociological and Marxist accounts of societies functioning. In debates in these areas in recent years the category has been argued about at great length, and its severe limitations made apparent (Hirst 1979). But these debates do not seem to have registered very much in discussions of economic policy. Here the notion of ideology is often used as a way of avoiding problems, rather than trying to solve them.

One of the central problems of the notion of ideology is how far it is to be seen as a set of ideas which are deliberately propagated by those who know them to be false. This view of ideology was long ago satirised by Marx, as the belief that priests are really atheists who lie about their beliefs. Yet such a crude view of ideology is deployed in accounting for the 1979 government's attachment to monetarism. Harris for example (1982, p.20) suggests that this government had to find a way of selling its real objective of "crashing the economy" to the electorate "This is where the academic doctrine of monetarism comes in. By claiming that all governments can control its money and that all money affects is prices, this doctrine furnishes a good sales pitch". Monetarism is thus used deliberately to obscure the real objectives of the government.

This view if ideology as a surface veneer of beliefs, which hide deeper motives, makes it impossible in general to understand the strength of adherence of individuals or groups to any particular ideology even when it would no longer seem functional for them to do so. More particularly it raises a tricky problem for the analysis of policy - who are those who are making this deliberate obfuscation, and how do they come to agree how and where and when these lies are to be propounded? In other words this view of ideology must ultimately rest on a conspiracy theory of policy making, but fails to show how this conspiracy is organised and functions. [2]

Obviously not all writers will be so crude in their deployment of the category of ideology. In particular, there is a large school of Marxists who want on the one hand to maintain the central Marxist premise of fundamental class interests in shaping society, but who want also to argue that ideology is "relatively autonomous" from these interests. This provides a merely verbal solution to the problem, because it still must leave some role for these interests which is not ideological but "real" - otherwise the whole notion of real interests prior to any ideology in which they are articulated would collapse. To illustrate this

point let us quote from a recent attempt to link
economic theories to interests:

> In the first place, policy makers are usually
> committed to a view of their interests and will
> use (even seize on) theories that justify or
> legitimise the policies they wish to pursue.
> The theories play an ideological role and some-
> times leave the theoreticians protesting that
> they are misrepresented by what is done in
> their name. But there is a second aspect, which
> is that policy makers even in formulating their
> interests must draw on visions of the world
> available to them providing these are not self-
> evidently destructive of the society they
> identify with (Aaronovitch and Smith 1981,
> p.373).

The second part of this quotation seems on the
one hand to accept that interests have to be formu-
lated (i.e. do not exist separate from the ideas
that embody them), but then tries to couple this
with the idea that those interests may sometimes be
"self-evident" i.e. exist separate from and prior to
the ideas that embody them.

Unsurprisingly, from these rather confusing
general propositions about the relation between
economic ideology and interests, emerges a rather
confusing account of the policies of the 1979
Conservative Government. This "claimed monetarism as
a justification for its policies (the ideological
role referred to above) but it also believes that
the mechanisms and relationships presented by monetarists....will hold if used in determining policy".
Such a formulation clearly fails to come to grips
with the concept of ideology in understanding policy
making.

The second problem is related to the first.
Behind the smokescreen of ideology is the reality of
class interest. Now at one level it is impossible to
'disprove' that class interests are at play in each
and every policy decision. But there are a series of
problems with such an approach. First, it needs to
be recognised that there is an important difference
between arguing that the outcome of every policy can
be construed as a victory or defeat for a particular
class, and the view that the effect was calculated
in advance by that class. The first view is simply a
mode of political analysis which, whatever its
problems or shortcomings, is in principle irrefut-
able. If the initial postulate that society is

essentially organised around the conflicting interests of two classes is granted, it logically follows that each and every policy can be analysed as having consequences for these interests. But the second kind of argument is clearly more problematic. In part this is recognised by Marxism, when it points to the class struggle as meaning that class interests will not always be realised, but may be defeated by the opposition of the other class.

But a crucial problem remains. Where is this class interest decided upon, and how does it make itself felt i.e. how does it get itself represented? The answer to the first question in Marxism is via the notion of class interests prior to ideology, which as suggested above is a tricky notion to sustain. How are interests 'known' except through 'ideas', and if, as Marxists argue, ideology is all pervasive in society how are these ideas to avoid being "ideological"? The answer to the second part of the question is even more of a problem. How does capital (or the working class) make its interest felt given that classes are not directly social actors? By means of definite institutions - the CBI, Conservative Party etc. But how are these representatives held to their "brief" to represent these interests? In other words the mechanisms of tying class to institutions are never spelt out and this is unavoidable, it is inherent in the notion of representation. This concept means that the presence of something which is also absent. The class (working or capitalist) is absent from parliament or other arenas of decision-making but present through its party representative. But this sets up an insoluble opposition. For if the process of representation is to have any effect of itself, and it must do or the class would itself be present, then how is this process constrained to always represent that interest?

To summarise these rather abstract but crucial points. The notion that economic policy and the ideologies that surround it can function to serve class interests can be used as a post hoc way of understanding policy. It may be an unhelpfully reductive way of understanding policy i.e. every policy decision is reduced to a single problem of class struggle, but it is not illogical. On the other hand attempts to show that policy represents the prior decisions of a class, must ultimately reduce to a conspiracy theory of policy making, dependent upon mechanisms which are never, and can never, be specified.

The third central problem of the manner of analysing policy outlined above is that in elevating the role of interests to a central position, it neglects the role of constraints. This point needs to be spelt out carefully.

The focus on class interests at work in policy making means that the problems of national economic management are not taken seriously. "The nation" is viewed as an ideological construct which itself serves only to confuse discussion of policy and serve the interests of capitalists (see for example Panitch 1976; Harris 1972; Radice 1984). Thus each and every economic problem only exists in relation to a particular ideology linked in turn to class interests. This framework makes it literally unthinkable that policy problems might exist independently of the ideology of policy makers, i.e. would exist for any government whatever its political complexion.

In the next section I want to try and show that in fact many of the features of 'Thatcherism' can be understood as a particular type of response to constraints of the British economy, constraints which would have to be grappled with by any conceivable government whatever its ideological predilictions (cf. Thompson 1981).

Constraints on Economic Policy

Opponents of the post-1979 policies have had to account for the primacy given in those policies to the defeat of inflation. This has required an analysis of what inflation is. The overwhelming majority of these opponents have argued that inflation is fundamentally a consequence of distributional struggles (Rowthorn 1977; CSE/LWG 1980; Aaronovitch and Sawyer 1981). These distributional struggles produce inflation when fought out in a context of full employment (which strengthens labour's bargaining power), and slow growth (which makes the struggle between the contending interests much sharper).

It is not surprising that this is the predominant explanation of inflation offered by the Left. It reduces inflation more or less directly to the class struggle. This in turn allows anti-inflationary policies, e.g. incomes policies, to be interpreted as just one more weapon of the class enemy. Inflation is thus often just another misleading slogan in the class war:

Monetarism: Desperate Remedies?

> Inflation has been presented as a generalised
> threat....in order to enlist under the banner
> of the fight against inflation a broad range
> of support for policies designed in practice
> to curb real wages and undermine trade union
> rights (CSE/LWG 1980, p.117).

In pursuit of such a line of argument the following
is offered:

> Incomes policies, with the exception perhaps
> of the third stage of Heath's policy in 1973
> when wages were linked to prices, have been
> policies of wage restraint designed to reduce
> the share of wages and increase the share of
> profits. The assertion is evidenced by the
> fact that between 1948 and 1976 there were
> fourteen years in which incomes policies were
> operated, and over these periods net real
> income of the man with two children fell by
> 2 per cent. In the periods without incomes
> policy net real income rose by over 4 per
> cent (CSE/LWG, p.127).

But this will not do as an argument. Changes in
the growth rate of real wages are not direct evidence of the wage/profit split of national income.
As is well-known incomes policies in Britain have
usually been introduced in times of crisis when the
rate of growth of national income has usually slowed
down. In other words the slow growth of real wages
has reflected not a redistribution of national
income but a slow down in its aggregate growth. One
would not guess from the sentence quoted above that
the share of profits in national income has more or
less consistently declined over most of the post-war
period (Scott 1978).
These points are made to suggest that the discussion of inflation as a solely distributional
phenomena is always likely to lead to unacceptable
arguments. Fundamentally, this is because such
approaches attempt to evade any specific problem of
national economic management in the name of the
reality of the class struggle. Thus Left accounts of
inflation have few specific national referents -
whilst they are presented as analyses of Britain
they could be talking about almost any (capitalist)
country. In particular such approaches must discount
any important role for monetary policy as an independent element in inflation precisely because

monetary policy is by and large <u>national</u> policy,
irreducible to a general category of class struggle.
    Another point about Left analyses of inflation
is that by focussing on the distributional struggle
between capital and labour as a cause, they sidestep
the difficult distributional problems that may
accompany inflation. For as we have already suggested, there is no evidence that inflation has led to
a shift in resources from wages to profits, but it
has certainly redistributed resources amongst wage
earners. There is no clear evidence that inflation
has disrupted the normal, well entrenched patterns
of relative wages (Routh 1980, Ch. 4), but the
redistribution has been via negative interest rates
on savings. Throughout most of the inflation of the
late 1960s and 1970s nominal interest rates failed
to match inflation rates, and so real interest
rates were negative. This acted as a major source of
redistribution, especially from building society
depositors (who are relatively old and poor) to
building society borrowers (who are relatively young
and affluent) (Foster 1976).
    The point here is not that such a process could
not be overcome, by indexation, though there would
be substantial political obstacles. Rather, the
difficulty is that focussing on capital/labour
struggles as the source of inflation understate its
effects on the large number of people who are either
directly part of neither capital nor labour, of who
whilst workers, have also accumulated substantial
savings.
    Because of the kinds of arguments outlined
above the Left has not usually ignored the need to
tackle inflation. The CSE/LWG (1980, p.117) stresses
the need to "take into account the strong popular
aversion to inflation even where we cannot find a
clear rational basis for it". As already suggested
the 'material basis' is stronger if one looks away
from the direct capital/labour struggle. But more
generally any analysis which suggests that inflation
is not a 'real' problem but an 'ideological' one is
likely to lead to a <u>de facto</u> downgrading of its
importance.

<u>Controlling the Money Supply</u>
As already suggested, the Left has generally presented attempts to control inflation by controlling the
money supply as ideological camouflage, as irrelevant to the real issue. Partly this argument is
based on arguments that the relationship between

money supply growth and inflation is extremely problematic, and that in any case the money supply is difficult to control. These points have considerable force.

On the first point Kaldor (1980, Table 4, p.303; reprinted in his 1982 Table VII, p.85) has offered data for a range of countries on the relation between M3 and inflation. His main point is that these data show no stable lag between M3 growth and inflation. Secondly it is clear that the attempts to control M3 in Britain in the late 1970s and early 1980s were very unsuccessful (Thompson 1981, pp.53-62). This was indeed recognised by the government in March 1981 when it 'rebased' its money supply targets, which had been announced in the Medium Term Financial Strategy of 1980, to take into account the above-target growth of M3. (Until then the government had simply rolled forward the monetary targets inherited from the Labour Government).

This is not the place to address the complexities of money supply growth and control. (For a good survey of the problem see Artis and Lewis 1981). Rather the question here is what conclusions are to be drawn from the lack of a simple relationship between the money supply and inflation, and the difficulties of the authorities in actually controlling the money supply.

One possible conclusion to be drawn is that these difficulties are merely evidence of the purely ideological, obfuscatory character of monetarism. However Aaronovitch (1981, p.23), unlike many on the Left has accepted that "the money supply does play a part in the inflationary process", but then goes on to argue that this does not mean support for a policy of controlling the money supply because it is "hard to define, even harder to actually measure, and much harder still to control" (Ibid., p.23).

Now if the first postulate is accepted, i.e. that money supply growth is part of the inflationary process, this clearly means that control of the money supply is not just an ideological obfuscation but a 'real' problem, i.e. one which exists independently of the ideological views of monetarists. This conclusion is in fact accepted by Kaldor (1980, p.315) "Of course control is necessary to prevent an undue expansion of credit to the private sector, particularly for speculative purposes or for consumer credit. But for this purpose it is best to go back to some improved and more comprehensive version of the lending controls abandoned in 1971". In other words acceptance of the need for control of credit creation in no sense implies acceptance of the nostrums of monetarism (see also Miller 1981).

Once it is accepted that there is a 'real' problem of money supply/credit control then the implication is clearly that the problem for non-monetarists is one of finding more successful, and more politically acceptable, mechanisms for achieving this objective than those employed by monetarist governments. Aaronovitch's points about the difficulties of controlling the money supply should then point to the need for radical policies to achieve these objectives, rather than their abandonment.

One may note more generally that Aaronovitch's accurate strictures on the difficulties of money supply control could be applied to more or less any policy instrument. None of them (fiscal policy, interest rates, exchange rates for example) is a straightforward instrument which governments can simply wield to attain objectives. It is only in the light of an implicit contrast with an untenable view of easily manipulated, always effective policy instruments, that the undoubted problems of money supply control are seen as implying abandoning attempts at such control. Economic management is always the use of imperfect weapons to attain proximate and compromised goals. There are never solutions to economic management problems, only varying degrees of failure.

The more specific problem of what alternative mechanisms of credit control might look like is addressed by Thompson (1981, pp.62-8). The points will not be repeated here. Suffice to say that they involve attempting to by-pass the role of the private financial system in the process of credit control. In particular, by making the Central Bank a real bank, advancing credit directly both to public and private economic agents, rather than simply acting as an intermediary between the public sector and private financial institutions. This would provide no easy solutions but would at least recognise the significance of credit control for <u>any</u> attempt to manage the British economy.

The P.S.B.R. and Taxation

The second major component of the post-1979 economic strategy was control of the Public Sector Borrowing Requirement. Here again the Left often suggested that concern with the P.S.B.R. was purely "ideological". For example the CSE/LWG (p.43) document argues that "the monetarist case against the

P.S.B.R. is largely fabricated". This is based on
the arguments that there is no relationship between
P.S.B.R. and money supply growth, nor is it the
case, as monetarists have argued, that public
borrowing "crowds out" the private sector for example by driving up interest rates.

Again we may accept these arguments without
accepting the conclusion drawn from them. Artis and
Lewis (1981, Table 4.1, p.69) show for the period
1963 to 1980 the absence of any clear link between
the P.S.B.R. and sterling M3. Equally, as Taylor and
Threadgold (1979) have made clear, what matters for
any possible 'crowding out' of private by public
sector debt is the real value of the P.S.B.R., (a
point made, also, by Friedman 1980, pp.55-61) which
in fact because of inflation has been radically
reduced of late.

Yet can we draw from these points that control
of the P.S.B.R. is not a problem for governments not
committed to monetarism? Arguably not. On the
contrary, concern with the P.S.B.R. under anything
like existing institutional arrangements is
unavoidable. The size of the P.S.B.R. functions as
an index of the financial 'responsibility' of
national financial policy, so that with the growth
of the scale of international capital flows the
size of the P.S.B.R. can act as a major stimulant to
inflows and outflows of funds. This then poses
serious problems for economic management. In other
words, any government concerned with economic
management could not ignore the P.S.B.R.

If the size of the P.S.B.R. is not to be ignored then this has clear implications for public
expenditure and its financing.

First, there is plainly a problem about discussion of the public sector which treat that sector
as undifferentiated in its effects. For example,
discussion of the public sector must take into
account that many parts of the public sector are
regressive in terms of their impact on the vertical
distribution of incomes (Le Grand 1982). Thus
defences of the public sector are deeply problematic
where they rely primarily on arguments about promoting income equality (see Heald 1983, Ch. 6). On the
other hand this is clearly not the only aspect of
public sector. In addition to the traditional social
cost benefit style of arguments, there is the
question of employment creation, which under British
circumstances may well be envisaged as most easily
attained in the public sector. Few elaborated
socialist accounts of the public sector treat it as

unproblematically a "good thing". On the other hand
there is both a defensive "anti-cuts" rhetoric which
seems to imply precisely this, and on the other hand
an unwilligness to probe some of the divergent
effects of the currently existing public sector for
socialist politics.

Treating the P.S.B.R. as a problem to be taken
seriously, and at the same time defending the existence of a large public sector, means taking the
problem of taxation as <u>central</u> to economic management.

Socialists have not been prolific in their
writings on taxation. Much work that has appeared
has focused on the distributional consequences of
the British tax system (e.g. Field, Meacher, Pond
1977). Whilst this is explicable, and of itself
desirable, it locates the problem of taxation only
in one context, not primarily in that of revenue
raising as an aspect of national economic management. The danger here is that these traditional
distributional concerns will be made compatible with
revenue raising concerns only by conjuring up the
possibility of finding a 'pot of gold', which can
allow large revenues to be raised whilst reducing the
tax burden of the average worker.

Day and Pond (1982), for example, point out how
corporations have reduced their tax payments of
late, and how wealth taxation could be extended.
Whilst such taxation must be reformed to make sure
that "the burden of financing public expenditure is
not concentrated on the working class alone" (p.164)
the capacity of such reforms to yield enormous
revenues should not be exaggerated. On the other
hand reductions of tax expenditures (e.g. mortgage
interest relief), may well be sensible proposals,
and may be progressive in <u>over all</u> effect, nevertheless their abolition would <u>clearly</u> increase the tax
burden on many working class households. So it is
one thing to ensure that the tax burden is "fairly"
distributed, but another "to ensure that this burden
(of taxation on working people) is not increased
still further under the A.E.S." (Ibid., p.157).

Finally there is the problem of the supply
side. In many accounts of the post-1979 governments,
the concern of policy with the supply side is
treated as a code word for attacks on trade unions,
public expenditure and the welfare state. Here
again, we may note that whilst obviously monetarist
governments will construe supply side problems in a
particular manner, they are not simply the creation
of monetarist ideology. By and large the Left has

recognised this, and has identified two main kinds of solutions to Britain's productive inefficiencies. One is to raise the level of investment via increases in demand and controls over corporations, and the other is some version of industrial democracy/workers control.

Neither of these emphases appears adequate. The focus on the volume of investment ignores the fact that Britain uses existing investment much less efficiently than competing countries (e.g. Caves and Krause, 1980, Ch. 3). Whilst few would doubt the need for higher levels of investment in Britain, as an accompaniment to economic expansion and improved efficiency, it is far from clear that the focus on this as Britain's central "supply-side" problem is appropriate.

Secondly the stress on industrial democracy as a source of increased efficiency raises difficult problems. As Hodgson (1984, Ch. 9) powerfully points out, many experiments in participation and industrial democracy have resulted in efficiency gains. However, what is much less clear, is whether such gains would necessarily arise where such democracy was present at the level of overall corporate strategy, as radical measures of industrial democracy via, say, workers directors, imply. The fundamental difficulty of tying advocacy of industrial democracy to efficiency is that it ties the process of democracy to an end which may not be realised. And in doing so it necessarily devalues the process itself. In other words it does not make democracy an objective in its own right, whose effects may be extremely difficult to calculate separate from the highly specific institutional framework in which they exist (see also on this Tomlinson 1982, Ch. 7).

The Left's focus on investment volume and industrial democracy is explicable in terms of the political consequences of focussing on the major alternative problem area. This area may be summarised as 'enterprise practices', where this covers everything from managerial strategies through to trade union organisations to questions of worker motivation. Whilst this is an extremely heterogeneous set of problems it is unified by being linked to politically highly problematic questions about union roles in management, the limits of collective bargaining, the status of management as a practice which raise a host of political problems for the Left. This is registered by the fact that attempts to take detailed enterprise practices seriously are notable by their absence in socialist accounts of economic strategy, and are commonly seen as threatening the sins of "corporatism" and "syndicalism". These slogans are entirely destructive of serious argument about enterprise level policies, and make entirely rhetorical references to enterprise democracy. Any serious enterprise level democracy would precisely imply workers involvement in management, which raises a host of problems which cannot even be discussed whilst these slogans are taken seriously.

The Character of Monetarism

The central thrust of the above arguments is that monetarism addresses in its own peculiar way problems of the British economy which are irreducible to the ideology of those determining policy. In other words the task for those who dislike monetarism is not to 'reveal' the spurious nature of monetarism's problems, but to develop superior ways of formulating and dealing with those problems.

Of course these problems are not the products of nature, they are historical products which can be reformed. To take one example. The P.S.B.R. is mainly a problem because of the scale of international capital flows and the institutional regime which makes these flows possible. Neither the flows nor the institutions are immutable. But equally they are very deeply embedded aspects of the current economic organisation of the Western world. Changing them would be a long-term policy, with many problems arising, and it is far from clear that the gains from such a policy would outweigh the costs. A sensible policy may therefore be to go for a long-term reduction of the P.S.B.R. to a negligible amount and/or a change in its forms of financing to insulate fiscal policy from the constraint of private financing of the fiscal deficit.

The Monetarism of 1979 presented itself as a coherent strategy, with the instruments of policy logically arranged to attain pre-given ends. The opponents of this policy have by and large taken this notion of strategy seriously usually regarding it as a coherent strategy but with other than the manifest objectives (e.g. Harrison 1982, p.20). Indeed the notion of strategy in a very similar sense is used by the Left in its notion of the 'Alternative Economic Strategy'.

Strategy both in the form of the M.T.F.S. and A.E.S. imply similarities with military strategy, where a central General Staff directs the deployment of policy instruments in order to attain pre-determined objectives. Policy intentions are translated into action through a clear hierarchy of decision agents.[3] Now what should be strikingly clear from the experience of the post-1979 government is that economic policy cannot helpfully be conceived as functioning in this fashion.

For example, it is clear that the Thatcher governments have found it almost impossible to cut public expenditure, despite the significance attached to this task.[4] Equally the authorities' capacity to control the money supply, as already noted, was greatly exaggerated, especially in 1980-81 when the scale of the depression led to a large leap in company borrowing.

Indeed one may suggest that there was, at least on the surface, striking paradox in the government's incapacity to control government expenditure and the money supply coupled with an eventual success (at least in 1982-3) in controlling inflation.[5] Proponents of the view that the government's "real objective" was to increase unemployment to break labour resistance to capital's objectives will argue that the fall in inflation was the consequence of unemployment, and that this was what the government intended all along.

But this view does not seem to be justified. Firstly there seems little doubt that the government was genuinely surprised by the rise in unemployment under its policies. Whilst it did expect some rise, it expected this to be "transitional", as the publics' expectations and behaviour adjusted to the new policies. Thus in the 1980 Budget Report it was assumed that G.D.P. would fall by 2 per cent in that year and then grow at 1 per cent per year in the next three years. In fact G.D.P. fell about 3 per cent in 1980 and continued to fall through most of 1981. Of course, once it had risen, the government was more than willing to use unemployment as a lever in wage bargaining, but it is difficult to sustain the view that this was their prime objective all along. Rather it may well be the case that certain of the most obviously anti-labour aspects of the policy of the 1979 government's policies, e.g. its stress on anti-union legislation, reflected the failure of the policies of the 1979 manifesto (Thompson 1981).

Secondly, like almost everyone else in Britain in 1979, the Conservatives seem to have believed that 3 to 4 million unemployed would be electorally disastrous, and hence hardly to be advocated. And thus was probably a correct calculation - without the Falklands War and the break-up of the Labour Party, the level of unemployment probably would have been electorally disastrous for the Conservatives.

Overall, when talking about policy since 1979, it is important to stress that this has not been a well-defined and successful strategy, clear in its objectives and the means to their achievement. The government's policies have been much more ad hoc, contradictory and problematic than a grand term like strategy suggests. Equally, they have not been the outcome of any single source - insanity or the interests of capital - understanding which provides the easy way to comprehending those policies.

NOTES

1. An exception to this is Jones, though in retrospect its judgement may have underestimated the capacity of the Thatcher government to manage the contradictions of its policies. P. Jones, "The Thatcher Experiment: Tensions and Contradictions in the First Year", <u>Politics and Power</u>, 2, (1980).

2. This is not to say of course that Marxists are not sensitive to this problem. Rather it is to say that ultimately a Marxist analysis must perceive <u>classes</u> acting as conscious decision agents, which problem no amount of sensitivity can overcome.

3. This of course is <u>not</u> an adequate account of military strategy. See for example J. Keegan, <u>The Face of Battle</u>, (Penguin, Harmondsworth, 1976).

4. By spring 1984 this seems to have been accepted by the government, with both Thatcher and Lawson saying publicly that their aim now was to stabilise government expenditure, allowing it to fall as a share of National Income as growth took place.

5. This paradox was in part at least more apparent than real, because measured by other indices, M1, real interest rates and general indicators of financial stringency, monetary policy was highly restrictive despite the failure to attain M3 targets. W. Buiter and M. Miller, "The Thatcher Experiment: The First Two Years", <u>Brookings Papers on Economic Activity</u>, 2, (Fall 1981), pp.342-9.

Chapter Eleven

SUMMARY AND CONCLUSIONS

At the end of the Second World War the major concerns
of British macroeconomic policy were twofold. All
informed observers saw that the major short-run
impact of the war had been to radically undermine
Britain's international payments position. Hence
there was great trepidation about how Britain would
be able to finance its necessary level of imports
with the return to peace time conditions. Domestically, the major concern was Britain's ability to
live up to the promised "high and stable" levels of
employment promised by the war time Coalition.
    In fact, narrowly interpreted, neither of these
problems proved very difficult to deal with.
Britain's exports expanded rapidly from the late
1940s, and, helped in the 1950s by a favourable
movement in the terms of trade, financing commodity
imports caused no greater difficulties in the 1950s
and early 1960s. Even more rapidly after the war,
full employment was attained, and except briefly
during the fuel crisis of 1947, was maintained with
no great difficulty for two decades.
    Of course Britain did have balance of payments
problems in the 1950s, but these reflected the over
ambitious investment and government spending
objectives of the time, coupled with the problems of
coping with the decline of sterling as a world
currency, rather than any difficulty in financing a
full employment level of commodity imports. Whilst
balance of payments and exchange rate difficulties,
in various guises, are an almost constant feature of
modern British economic policy, the defining feature
of the post-war policy regime was the commitment to,
and achievement of, full employment.
    To many people, then and since, full employment
appeared unproblematic as a goal - its benefits
obvious, the costs of its absence manifest. The

purpose of the discussion of full employment in this book has not, of course, been to argue the desirability of mass unemployment. (For the contrary case, see e.g. Tomlinson 1983A). Rather the argument has been that the commitment to full employment was fragile, partly (though not only), because that commitment was not based on an extended discussion and acceptance of the benefits it would bring, nor the difficulties its pursuit would entail under circumstances less propitious than those of the 1950s and 1960s.

The second thrust of the argument on unemployment is that its achievement in the 1950s and 1960s owed much more to non-policy circumstances than is commonly accepted. The belief in, and pursuit of, management of the economy since 1945, important as it has been, should not blind us to the severe limits of economic management, especially in the international circumstances of the 1980s. (A point returned to below).

Britain shared a commitment to full employment with many other advanced capitalist countries. But the means used to pursue that end in Britain were highly specific, and tied much more to a particular version of fiscal management than any other country. The problem was that the commitment to full employment as an objective then became seemingly inextricably entangled with those particular means, so that the fiscal crisis of the 1970s was also a crisis of employment policy. This is not to deny that there were other reasons why full employment became more difficult to achieve in the 1970s. But the point to be stressed is that the will to deal with that difficult environment was weakened by the peculiar policy regime, which was seen as having delivered full employment in the preceding decades.

The "fiscal crisis" of the mid-1970s was perceived as such largely because of the acceleration of inflation, and the widely held, if vague, belief that government profligacy was at the root of the inflation problem. The chapters on inflation have argued for a considerable scepticism on the economic damage likely from inflation. This is not, of course, to deny that as experienced in Britain inflation did considerable harm by redistributing private sector wealth either to the government or to other parts of the private sector. But the reasons for this are both specific and avoidable. In other words, most of the redistribution arose from the failure to index financial assets, and this partly reflected the very newness of the experience of

inflation on the scale of the 1970s. It is far from
clear that this failure to index reflected fundamental features of the political system, i.e. the
political weight of debtors. Certainly the evidence
of the early 1980s is that the issue of indexed
government debt and a rise in real interest rates
can move the balance sharply in favour of lenders
surprisingly easily.

If the redistributive effects of inflation can
largely be avoided, are the effects on output and
employment substantial enough to justify a sharply
deflationary policy? As argued above (Chapter 8)
this has not been demonstrated. Rising unemployment
has been <u>associated</u> with inflation, but the main
causal sequence seems to be from inflation to
government policy, i.e. deflation, to unemployment.[1]
In other words the reason why inflation is linked to
higher unemployment is mainly because of the
political reaction to inflation on the part of
government. This is not to argue that governments in
deflating their economies are being irrational.
Their perception may accurately be that inflation
arouses almost all the electorates fears, whilst the
costs of unemployment are borne by a relatively
small proportion of the populace. (Though this
perception appears to have come <u>post hoc</u>, rather
than being the origin point of deflationary
policies). Nevertheless, it is important to stress
that of itself inflation has not been clearly shown
to undermine the workings of a capitalist economy in
the radical way many commentators have feared (and a
few hoped) that it would.

It is appropriate to note that such scepticism
about the harms of inflation is not the consensus
view of economists. Broadly speaking, it is probably
right to say that the majority of economists in
Britain believe that it is important to reduce
inflation, albeit most would not pursue such an
objective as vigorously as the Thatcher government
have done. The basis of the views expressed in this
book is that the evidence of the harms done by
inflation is not compelling, whilst the costs of
pursuing strong anti-inflationary policies is all
around us.

From the mid-1950s economic growth has been one
of the constants of economic policy (and even in the
1970s and 1980s has been little undermined by envi-
ronmentalist attacks). Yet its active pursuit has
been extremely episodic. Neither of thee two features is really surprising.

The commitment to growth would seem to arise logically from a combination of belief in the capacity of government to control the economy, coupled with full employment. If the economy can be controlled then the many benefits of higher incomes appear to be within the government's gift. If full employment has been achieved, then higher output can only be attained by greater output from a given labour force, no longer from increased employment of that work force.

On the other hand the episodic nature of the active pursuit of economic growth derives from the lack of clarity about the causes of such growth, and hence cycles of faith and loss of faith in various policies for its attainment. In particular there has been the recurrent question whether <u>macroeconomic</u> policy can have much effect as the rate of economic growth. Here a number of points need to be distinguished.

First, it does <u>not</u> seem to be the case that the macroeconomic policies of the 1950s and 1960s, in the form of "stop-go", greatly affected the rate of economic growth in Britain in that period. "Stop-go", despite much criticism, did not lead to particularly sharp fluctuations in the British economy.

Secondly, however, there is no doubt that the macro environment <u>can</u> substantially affect the growth performance of the economy. Thus the sharply deflationary policies after 1979, whatever their effects on short-run productivity, seem to have dealt a substantial blow to long-run output growth, by a once-and-for-all destruction of much manufacturing capacity.

Thirdly, it may well be that the effects of macroeconomic policy on economic growth are asymmetrical. Whilst incompetent macro policy may damage economic growth, it is much less clear that such policy can shift a growth path upwards. Hence the search for various "structural", "institutional" etc. alternative policies to increase growth may in a general sense be appropriate, though this is not the place to discuss what exactly those terms might mean and what kinds of reforms might be successful.

The overall point to be stressed here is that the pursuit of economic growth has often been rhetorical, and that when more substantive efforts have been made, these have been largely unsuccessful. Yet this commitment remains a powerful one in the sense that the perceived benefits are so substantial. Above all rapid economic growth seems to

promise an avoidance of hard political choices by
financing more of everything.

The final point about economic growth is that
it is largely in this context that the perception has
arisen that postwar British economic policy has
failed. Before "league tables" of growth appeared in
the 1950s, there were periodic worries about
Britain's economic performance, dating back to at
least the "Made in Germany" panic of the 1890s. But
the widespread notion that the British economy was
performing substantially and consistently worse than
other advanced capitalist countries only became
established from the late 1950s. Paradoxically this
was also of course the beginning of the "never had
it so good" years. The point is that in historical
context these <u>were</u> the good years. It is only in the
context of international comparisons that British
performance was plainly poor. This is perhaps worth
stressing, as a background to the strident rhetoric
about Britain's long-run failures which has formed
part of the background to Mrs. Thatcher's economic
policies.

Probably no area of policy is more difficult to
summarise than the balance of payments. Perhaps the
most one can say in one sentence is that, after
surprising success in the 1940s and 1950s, Britain
has had persistent difficulties since the early
1960s in financing a full employment level of
imports. However this must be immediately qualified
by saying that other objective than the simple
financing have almost always obtruded. On the one
hand in the 1950s and for much of the 1960s there
was the commitment to a scale of overseas investment
and foreign military expenditure which may be seen
as an attempt to maintain an unsustainable burden
for the British economy (e.g. Strange 1971). Equally
there was the commitment during the same period to a
fixed sterling exchange rate until this became
totally unworkable in 1967.

The view that the British economy was internationally over-committed became generally accepted in
official circles only after the devaluation of 1967.
The devaluation also marked the end of the belief
that ill-defined "structural" reforms could avoid
the necessity for having a lower exchange rate. More
generally the devaluation of the pound opened the
way for pressure on the dollar and ultimately on the
Bretton Woods system as a whole.

Two points should be stressed about this
collapse in the context of Britain's policy objectives. On the one hand, the growing volume and

volatility of short-term capital flows was a crucial part of the reasons for the collapse of Bretton Woods, and this growth was to continue post-Bretton Woods, and to provide a much less favourable climate for every countries national economic management. Equally the collapse of Bretton Woods, whilst inaugurating a general system of floating exchange rates, was interpreted and coped with in different ways in different countries. In Britain the floating of the exchange rate resulted from a lack of a clear alternative, given the break-up of Bretton Woods, coupled with the objective of "going for growth".

Whilst "going for growth" quickly disappeared, the legacy of a floating exchange rate was central to the evolution of policy objectives in the 1970s and 1980s. Above all, the exchange rate could now come to be seen as a weapon, albeit an unruly one, in the battle against inflation. Movements in the exchange rate became central to the inflation/employment trade-off, so that in 1979-81 the appreciation of sterling was a major source of output and employment collapse in the U.K., but greatly aided the anti-inflationary objectives of the government.

However, the extent to which governments embraced the effects of (some) movements in the exchange rate does not mean, of course, that they effectively controlled that rate, certainly in any direct manner. For if the overarching feature of economic policy in the 1950s and 1960s was the commitment to and achievement of full employment, the most striking feature of the 1970s and 1980s has been the difficulty of domestic economic management in attaining any objective. In other words the international integration of the capitalist economies has both increased their interdependence and raised the cost of any policy of "going it alone". This is not to endorse the view that management of the national economy is a "myth", a chimera (Radice 1984), but it is to emphasise the difficulties and limits of such management, in comparison with the balmy days of the 1950s and early 1960s.

The decline in Britain's capacity to attain macroeconomic policy objectives since the mid-1960s is clear. It is much less clear that this can be ascribed to any single cause. In part Britain has had a history shared with others of the less successful advanced capitalist economies, though by most indices Britain has been closest to worst even amongst those poor performers. Perhaps the best way of summing up the reasons for this would be to say that Britain's absolutely low and slow growing productivity in most manufactured goods has exacerbated every problem, even those originating externally (e.g. the two oil crises of 1973/4 and 1979/80). Manufacturing performance remains crucial about all because of its central role in Britain's balance of payments, and despite its much-noted small and declining role in total employment, (see Williams et al 1983, Introduction).

To emphasise the crucial role of manufacturing efficiency in Britain's economic predicament is not to imply that microeconomic policy aimed at increasing efficiency (in all its variants) is all that matters. Rather it is to emphasise that macroeconomic policy has a crucial but necessarily limited set of effects. Great damage can and has been done by inappropriate macro policy. But, equally, the best macro policy in the world cannot deliver everything, and is in any case conditioned in its success by other non-macro events and policies. The early post-war years did engender an exaggerated belief in the capacity of governments to manage their economies, and that management has become more difficult over time because of growing interdependence between nations. However, that is no good reason for arguing that governments can do nothing to affect real variables, as is currently fashionable. Intentionally or not, government policy since 1979 has affected real variables in a very striking manner.

This book began by stressing that in the early postwar years the commitment to and achievement of full employment can helpfully be seen as the defining aspect of economic policy. This is clearly no longer true today. In Britain in 1984 there is plainly a lack of commitment to full employment as a goal, as well as obviously a lack of achievement of such an objective. Those (like the author) who would put great emphasis on the achievement of fuller employment, may be tempted to ascribe that lack of commitment a central role in the failure in achievement. In other words, with the will, could not governments readily re-establish much fuller employment? Whilst political will is always important, a focus on the desires of government should not be allowed to obscure the fact that this lack of will is linked to a realistic perception of the difficulties of attaining full(er) employment.

Here the previous point about the very strong stress in Britain on fiscal policy as the means to full employment is very important. Undoubtedly the sharp rise in unemployment since 1979 owes a great deal to deflationary fiscal policy (e.g. Buiter and

Miller 1983). But one must note that unemployment has been rising almost continually since 1967, long before deflation became the centrepiece of policy. Equally, it does not follow that the effects of a fiscal deflation can be simply reversed by a fiscal expansion.

If the question is posed, can Britain get back to much fuller employment, then the answer can probably best be divided into two. Britain has been pursuing a much more deflationary fiscal policy (measured by the size of the public sector deficit) than most O.E.C.D. countries. Its unemployment rate is also higher. This suggests that there is scope for a less deflationary policy i.e. one more akin to the O.E.C.D. average, and this would in turn bring unemployment closer to the O.E.C.D. norm. The exact amount of change in fiscal stance possible before a loss of financial confidence would occur is very difficult to estimate. But, paradoxically perhaps, it would be easier for a Conservative government to pursue such a relaxation than a more left-wing government. Financial markets would be less suspicious of a right-wing government, compare, for example the recent experience of France (e.g. Cobham 1984), with the current American policy. In the first case the policies and the rhetoric led to a quick reversal of reflation, in the second case a record deficit has been tolerated, albeit helped by a tight monetary policy and very high interest rates. To get unemployment down to the O.E.C.D. average would at the present (autumn 1984) reduce unemployment by around 1½ million - a substantial cut. But plainly this is nowhere near full employment in the sense of the 1950s and 1960s. The possibility of achieving that kind of unemployment level simply by expansionary fiscal policy appears extremely remote. Such policies of expansion would quickly lead to higher inflation, balance of payments difficulties and loss of financial confidence. Hence to pursue fuller employment further, even given a less deflationary macroeconomic environment, would require other radical changes in economic institutions and policy.

The case against a radical change towards a "seige economy" solution is not that it is necessarily economically illogical, but that its political consequences are likely to quickly undermine its pursuit. In other words, radical controls on imports might, at least in the short-run, be a way of generating domestic employment, but at a substantial cost to the standard of living of the employed. Whilst such a policy may well be morally defensible, any government pursuing such a policy is unlikely to stay in power long.

For good or ill Britain is inextricably linked to the international economy in a multitude of ways and on a scale that means any policy must, for the foreseeable future, work broadly within those links. This does not mean reform isn't possible, but it does mean that isolation is not a viable option.

Incomes policies have been at the centre of pre-Thatcher attempted solutions to Britain's macro-economic problems. The failure of such policies in the past is not evidence of their undesirability, only their difficulty of achievement. The search for such policies, it may be argued, should be encouraged by the demonstration, since 1979, of the alternatives. Incomes policies are obviously not 'radical' in the context of most of the postwar history of policy in Britain. But what would be radical would be an attempt to couple such policies with a reform of trade union practices, a re-orientation of those away from collective bargaining over pay, and a focus on employment. In other words a successful policy on employment may require acceptance that governments, however well-intentioned, cannot deliver full employment. They can avoid creating a deflationary environment, but private economic agents, especially unions and employers, must accept they too have a substantial role in the pursuit of fuller employment.

Hence, in brief conclusion, it may be argued both that a more expansionary fiscal and general macroeconomic environment is a necessary condition for fuller employment, but that it cannot be sufficient. Sufficient conditions would embrace both a different international environment (e.g. more autonomy of the European economies from the influence of the U.S. economy) and domestic changes. These domestic changes would, above all, have to challenge the still predominant postwar consensus that the responsibility for full employment both can, and should, lie with government, whilst responsibility for wages should be left largely with employers and unions. Whilst this division of labour remains, it is difficult to see much progress towards fuller employment.

NOTES

1.   The main exception to this would seem to be
the effect of inflation in shifting the savings
ratio upwards and hence depressing demand. However
this can be fairly readily offset by government
action to increase its own expenditure or reduce its
own saving.

Note that prior to the inflation of the 1970s
it was generally believed that inflation would
reduce savings, and this figured strongly in the
more dramatic views about the effects of inflation
on a capitalist economy (see Chapter 3). The fact
that the redistributive effects of inflation did <u>not</u>
have this consequence, may partly account for the
relative lack of concern with inflation in government policy in the period when the redistributive
aspects were most concentrated upon.

REFERENCES

Aaronovitch, S. (1971) The Road from Thatcherism,
    Lawrence and Wishart, London
Aaronovitch, S. and Smith, R. (1981) The Political
    Economy of British Capitalism, McGraw Hill,
    London
Abrams, M. (ed) (1946) Britain and Her Export Trade,
    Pilot Press, London
Abrams, P. (1963) 'The Failure of Social Reform
    1918-20', Past and Present, 24, 43-64
Addison, P. (1977) The Road to 1945, Quartet, London
Aldcroft, D.H. (1962) 'The Early History and
    Development of Export Credit Insurance in Great
    Britain 1919-39', Manchester School, XXX(1),
    69-84
Alexander, J. and Toland, S. (1980) 'Measuring the
    Public Sector Borrowing Requirement', Economic
    Trends, 322, 82-98
Amery, L.S. (1947) The Awakening: Our Present Crisis
    and the Way Out, Macdonald, London
Andrzejewski, S. (1954) Military Organisation and
    Society, Routledge and Kegan Paul, London
Apple, N. (1980) 'The Rise and Fall of Full Employ-
    ment Capitalism', Studies in Political Economy,
    4, 5-39
Arndt, H.W. (1978) The Rise and Fall of Economic
    Growth, Longman Cheshire, Melbourne
Arndt, H.W. (1981) 'Economic Development: A Semantic
    History', Economic Development and Cultural
    Change, 29(3), 457-66
Artis, M. (1973) Economists and Inflation, The
    University, Swansea
Artis, M. and Lewis, M. (1981) Monetary Control in
    the U.K., Phillip Allan, Deddington
Atkin, J. (1970) 'Official Regulation of British
    Overseas Investment 1914-31', Economic History
    Review, 23(2), 324-35
Bach, G.L. and Ando, A. (1957) 'The Redistributional
    Effects of Inflation', Review of Economics and
    Statistics, XXXIX(1), 1-13
Bacon, R. and Eltis, W.A. (1976) Britain's Economic
    Problem: Too Few Producers?, Macmillan, London
Ball, R.J. (1967) 'The Case Against Devaluation of
    the Pound', Bankers Magazine, April, 230-35
Ball, R.J., Burns, T. and Lawry, J.S.E. (1977) 'The
    Role of Exchange Rate Changes in Balance of
    Payments Adjustment - the U.K. Case', Economic
    Journal, 87(1), 1-29

References

Barnett, J. (1982) _Inside the Treasury_, Andre
    Deutsch, London
Beck, M. (1979) 'Public Sector Growth: A Real
    Perspective', _Public Finance_, 34, 313-56
Beckerman, W. (1972) _The Labour Government's
    Economic Record 1964-70_, Duckworth, London
Beckerman, W. (1974) _In Defence of Economic Growth_,
    Cape, London
Beveridge, W. (1942) _Social Insurance and Allied
    Services_, CMD. 6404, H.M.S.O., London
Black, J. (1979) _The Economics of Modern Britain_,
    Martin Robertson, Oxford
Black, S. (1977) _Floating Exchange Rates and
    National Economic Policy_, Yale U.P., New
    Haven
Blackaby, F.T. (1976) 'The Target Rate of Unemploy-
    ment' in G.D.N. Worswick (ed), _The Concept and
    Measurement of Involuntary Unemployment_, Allen
    and Unwin, London
Blackaby, F.T. (ed) (1978) _British Economic Policy
    1960-74: Demand Management_, C.U.P., Cambridge
Blackaby, F.T. (1979) 'The Economics and Politics
    of Demand Management: The British Experience',
    in S.T. Cook and P. Jackson (eds), _Current
    Issues in Fiscal Policy_, Martin Robertson,
    Oxford
Blackaby, F.T. (1980) 'Exchange Rate Policy and
    Economic Strategy', _Three Banks Review_, 126,
    3-17
Bloomfield, A.I. (1945) _The British Balance of
    Payments Problem_, Essays in International
    Finance No. 6, Princeton University, Princeton
Boltho, A. (1983) 'Is Western Europe Caught in an
    Expectations Trap?', _Lloyds Bank Review_, 148,
    1-13
Booth, A. (1983) 'The "Keynesian Revolution" in
    Economic Policy-Making', _Economic History
    Review_, XXXVI(1), 103-23
Booth, A. (1984) 'Defining a Keynesian Revolution',
    Economic History Review, XXXVII(2), 263-7
Boyd Orr, J. (1936) _Food, Health and Income_,
    Macmillan, London
Brittan, S. (1967) _Inquest on Planning in Britain_,
    P.E.P., London
Brittan, S. (1970) _The Price of Economic Freedom_,
    Macmillan, London
Brittan, S. (1971) _Steering the Economy_, 3rd edition,
    Penguin, Harmondsworth
Brittan, S. (1975) _Second Thoughts on Full
    Employment Policy_, Centre for Policy Studies,
    London

References

Brittan, S. (1978) 'How British is the British Sickness?', Journal of Law and Economics, 21(1), 245-68

Brittan, S. and Lilley, P. (1977) The Delusions of Incomes Policy, Temple Smith, London

Brodie, R. (1959) Strategy in the Missile Age, Princeton U.P., Princeton

Brown, A.J. (1955) The Great Inflation 1939-51, O.U.P., London

Brunner, J. (1967) 'The Plan that Failed' in I.E.A., Growth Through Industry, Institute of Economic Affairs, London

Bryant, R.C. (1980) Money and Monetary Policy in Interdependent Nations, Brookings Institution, Washington D.C.

Buchanan, J. and Wagner, R. (1977) Democracy in Deficit: The Political Legacy of Lord Keynes, Academic Press, London

Buchanan, J., Burton, J. and Wagner, R.E. (1978) The Consequences of Mr. Keynes, Institute of Economic Affairs, London

Budd, A. (1978) The Politics of Economic Planning, Fontana, London

Buiter, W. and Miller, M. (1981) 'The Thatcher Experiment: The First Two Years', Brookings Papers on Economic Activity, 2, 315-79

Buiter, W. and Miller, M. (1983) 'Changing the Rules: Economic Consequences of the Thatcher Regime', Brookings Papers on Economic Activity, 2, 305-79

Burnett, J. (1966) Plenty and Want, Nelson, London

Butler, D. and Pinto-Duschinsky, M. (1971) The British General Election of 1970, Macmillan, London

Cairncross, A. (1975) Inflation, Growth and International Finance, Allen and Unwin, London

Cairncross, A. (ed) (1970) The Managed Economy, Blackwells, Oxford

Cairncross, A. (ed) (1971) Britain's Economic Prospects Reconsidered, Allen and Unwin, London

Cairncross, A. and Eichengreen, B. (1983) Sterling in Decline, Blackwells, Oxford

Cairncross, F. (ed) (1981) Changing Perceptions of British Economic Policy, Methuen, London

Calder, A. (1969) Peoples War, Panther, London

Carroll, B. (1968) Design for Total War, Mouton, The Hague

Carr, E.H. (1966) The Bolshevik Revolution 1917-23, Vol. 2, Penguin, Harmondsworth

Castles, F. (1978) The Social Democratic Image of Society, Routledge and Kegan Paul, London

References

Catherwood, H.F.R. (1966) _Britain with the Brakes Off_, Hodder and Stoughton, London

Caves, R. (ed) (1968) _Britain's Economic Prospects_, Brookings Institution, Washington D.C.

Caves, R. and Krause, L. (eds) (1980) _Britain's Economic Performance_, Brookings Institution, Washington D.C.

C.S.O. (1951) Central Statistical Office _Statistical Digest of the War_, H.M.S.O., London

Chelliah, R.J. (1971) 'Significance of Alternative Concepts of the Budget Deficit', _I.M.F. Staff Papers_, 20, 741-84

Chester, D.N. (ed) (1951) _Lessons of the British War Economy_, N.I.E.S.R., London

Clark, C. (1961) _Growthmanship_, Institute of Economic Affairs, London

Clarke, W. (1967) _Report of the Committee on Invisible Exports: Britain's Invisible Earnings_, British National Export Council, London

Coats, A.W. (1974) 'Inflation in Perspective - A Historian's View' in _Inflation: Causes, Consequences, Cures_, Institute of Economic Affairs, London

Coats, A.W. (1981) 'Britain: The Rise of Specialists', _History of Political Economy_, 13, (3), 365-404

Cobham, D. (1982) 'Domestic Credit Expansion, Confidence and the Foreign Exchange Market: Sterling in 1976', _Kredit und Kapital_, 15(3), 434-53

Cobham, D. (1984) 'French Macroeconomic Policy Under President Mitterand: An Assessment', _National Westminster Bank Quarterly Review_, February, 41-51

Cohen Council _Council on Productivity, Prices and Incomes_, 1st Report 1958, 4th Report 1961, H.M.S.O., London

Cole, G.D.H. (1944) _How to Obtain Full Employment_, Post War Discussion Pamphlets No. 4, London

CMD. 6527 (1944) _Employment Policy_, H.M.S.O., London

CMD. 9725 (1956) _Economic Implications of Full Employment_, H.M.S.O., London

CMND. 3787 (1968) _The Basle Facility and the Sterling Area_, H.M.S.O., London

CMND. 4715 (1971) _The U.K. and the European Communities_, H.M.S.O., London

CMND. 5157 (1972) _White Paper on Unemployment Statistics_, H.M.S.O., London

CMND. 7405 (1978) _The European Monetary System_, H.M.S.O., London

References

Conan, A.R. (1968) 'Restructuring the Sterling Area',
     The Banker, May, 429-36
C.S.E./L.W.G. (1980) Conference of Socialist
     Economists/London Working Group The Alternative
     Economic Strategy, C.S.E., London
Cook, S.T. and Jackson, P. (eds) (1979) Current
     Issues in Fiscal Policy, Martin Robertson,
     Oxford
Corden, W.M. (1965) Recent Developments in the
     Theory of International Trade, Princeton
     University, Princeton
Coutts, K., Tarling, R., Ward, T. and Wilkinson, F.
     (1981) 'The Economic Consequences of
     Mrs. Thatcher', Cambridge Journal of Economics,
     5(1), 81-94
Crick, B. (1964) In Defence of Politics, Penguin,
     Harmondsworth
Crosland, A. (1956) The Future of Socialism, Cape,
     London
Crosland, A. (1962) The Conservative Enemy, Cape,
     London
Cunliffe (1918) 1st Interim Report of the Committee
     on Currency and Foreign Exchanges after the
     War, Cd. 9182, H.M.S.O., London
Cutler, A., Hindess, B., Hirst, P., and Hussain, A.
     (1976 and 1977) Marx's Capital and Capitalism
     Today, (2 Vols.), Routledge and Kegan Paul,
     London
Day, A.C.L. (1954) The Future of Sterling, Clarendon
     Press, Oxford
Day, L. and Pond, C. (1982) 'The Political Economy
     of Taxation and the Alternative Economic
     Strategy', Socialist Economic Review, Merlin,
     London
Deacon, A. (1981) 'Unemployment and Policies in
     Britain Since 1945' in B. Showler and
     A. Sinfield, The Workless State, Martin
     Robertson, Oxford
Dean, A.J.H. (1975) 'Earnings in the Public and
     Private Sectors 1950-75', National Institute
     Economic Review, 74, 60-70
Dow, J.C.R. (1964) The Management of the British
     Economy 1945-60, C.U.P., Cambridge
Duboff, R.B. (1977) 'Full Employment: The History of
     a Receding Ideal', Politics and Society, 17(1),
     1-25
Dunning, J. (1979) 'The U.K.'s International Direct
     Investment Position in the mid-1970s', Lloyds
     Bank Review, 132, 1-21

References

Economic Trends (1976) 'International Comparisons of Public Sector Financial Balances', Economic Trends, 271, 82-8

Eltis, W.A. and Sinclair, P. (1981) The Money Supply and the Exchange Rate, O.U.P., Oxford

Employment Policy (1944) White Paper on Employment Policy, CMD. 6527, H.M.S.O., London

Estrin, S. and Holmes, P. (1983) French Planning in Theory and Practice, Allen and Unwin, London

Fetter, F.W. (1977) 'Lenin, Keynes and Inflation', Economica, 44, 77-80

Field, F., Meacher, M. and Pond, C. (1977) To Him Who Hath, Penguin, Harmondsworth

Fishman, D. (1980) 'A Radical View of the European Monetary System', Politics and Power, 1, 175-83

Foot, K.D.K.W. (1972) 'The Balance of Payments in the Inter-War Period', Bank of England Quarterly Bulletin, 12(3), 345-63

Ford, A. (1962) The Gold Standard 1880-1914: Britain and Argentina, Clarendon Press, Oxford

Foster, J. (1976) 'The Redistributive Effect of Inflation on Building Society Shares and Deposits 1961-74', Bulletin of Economic Research, 28(2), 68-75

Foucault, M. (1979) The History of Sexuality, Vol. 1, Allen Lane, London

Friedman, M. (1953) 'The Case for Flexible Exchange Rates' in Essays in Positive Economics, C.U.P., Chicago

Friedman, M. (1974) Monetary Correction, Institute of Economic Affairs, London

Friedman, M. (1975) Unemployment versus Inflation?, Institute of Economic Affairs, London

Friedman, M. (1977) 'Nobel Lecture: Inflation and Unemployment', Journal of Political Economy, 85(3), 451-72

Friedman, M. (1980) Memorandum of Evidence to the Treasury and Civil Service Committee: Monetary Policy, HC 720, H.M.S.O., London

Friedman, M. (ed) (1966) Studies in the Quantity Theory of Money, Chicago U.P., Chicago

Fry, R. (1968) 'Government Spending Overseas', The Banker, June, 493-500

Gardner, R.N. (1956) Sterling-Dollar Diplomacy, Clarendon Press, Oxford

Glyn, A. and Harrison, J. (1980) The British Economic Disaster, Pluto, London

Godley, W.A.H. (1974) 'Memorandum of Evidence' in House of Commons 1st Report From the Expenditure Committee, HC 69 I, H.M.S.O., London

References

Godley, W.A.H. (1976) 1st Report from the Expenditure Committee: The Financing of Public Expenditure, HCP 69 II, H.M.S.O., London

Gordon, R. (1975) 'The Demand for and Supply of Inflation', Journal of Law and Economics, 18(4), 807-36

Gould, B., Mills, J. and Stewart, S. (1981) Monetarism or Prosperity, Macmillan, London

Ham, A. (1981) Treasury Rules, Quartet, London

Hancock, W.K. and Gowing, M.M. (1949) The British War Economy, H.M.S.O., London

Harris, J. (1977) William Beveridge: A Biography, Clarendon Press, Oxford

Harris, N. (1972) Competition and the Corporate Society, Methuen, London

Harris, R. and Seldon, A. (1979) Over-Ruled on Welfare, Institute of Economic Affairs, London

Harris, R. and Sewill (1975) British Economic Policy 1970-74: Two Views, Institute of Economic Affairs, London

Harrison, J. (1982) 'Thatcherism: Is it Working?', Marxism Today, July, 19-25

Harrod, R. (1952) The Life of John Maynard Keynes, Macmillan, London

Harrod, R. (1963) The British Economy, McGraw-Hill, New York

Hayek, F. (1933) Prices and Production, L.S.E., London

Hayek, F. (1960) The Constitution of Liberty, Routledge and Kegan Paul, London

Hayek, F. (1972) A Tiger by the Tail, Institute of Economic Affairs, London

Heald, D. (1983) Public Expenditure, Martin Robertson, Oxford

Heathfield, D. (1979) Perspectives on Inflation, Longman, London

Heclo, H. and Wildavsky, A. (1981) The Private Government of Public Money, 2nd ed., Macmillan, London

Henderson, P.D. (ed) (1966) Economic Growth in Britain, Weidenfeld and Nicolson, London

H.M.S.O. (1980) Treasury and the Civil Service Committee Memoranda on Monetary Policy, HC 720, H.M.S.O., London

Higham, D. (1981) The Effect of Exchange Rate Changes on the U.K. Balance of Payments, with Special Reference to the Devaluation of 1967, Unpublished D.Phil. Dissertation, Oxford University

References

Higham, D. (1981A) 'Strong Currencies and Economic Performance', Three Banks Review, 130, 3-22

Higham, D. and Tomlinson, J. (1982) 'Why Do Governments Worry About Inflation?', National Westminster Bank Review, May, 2-13

Hindess, B. (1977A) Philosophy and Methodology in the Social Sciences, Harvester, Brighton

Hindess, B. (ed) (1977B) Sociological Theories of the Economy, Macmillan, London

Hirsch, F. (1965) The Pound Sterling: A Polemic, Gollancz, London

Hirsch, F. and Higham, D. (1974) 'Floating Rates - Expectations and Experience', Three Banks Review, 102, 3-34

Hirst, P. (1979) On Law and Ideology, Macmillan, London

Holmes, M. (1982) Political Pressure and Economic Policy: British Government 1970-74, Butterworth's, London

House of Commons (1976) 1st Report from the Expenditure Committee, HC 69 I and II, H.M.S.O., London

Howson, S. (1975) Domestic Monetary Management in Britain 1919-38, C.U.P., Cambridge

Howson, S. and Winch, D. (1977) The Economic Advisory Council 1930-39, C.U.P., Cambridge

Hughes, J. (1980) 'The Economics of the Madhouse', Workers Control Bulletin, 1, 4-9

Hurd, D. (1979) An End to Promises: Sketch of a Government 1970-74, Collins, London

Hutchinson, T.W. (1968) Economics and Economic Policy 1946-66, A.M. Kelley, New York

Hutchinson, T.W. (1977) Knowledge and Ignorance in Economics, Blackwells, Oxford

Jackman, R., Mulvey, C. and Trevithick, J. (1981) The Economics of Inflation, 2nd ed., Martin Robertson, Oxford

Jackson, P. (1980) 'The Public Expenditure Cuts: Rationale and Consequences', Fiscal Studies, 1(2), 66-82

Johnson, H. (1967) 'A Survey of Theories of Inflation' in Johnson (ed), Essays in Monetary Economics, Allen and Unwin, London

Jones, H. (1975) An Introduction to Modern Theories of Economic Growth, Nelson, London

Jones, P. (1980) 'The Thatcher Experiment: Tensions and Contradictions in the First Year', Politics and Power, 2, 137-68

Joseph, K. (1975) Reversing the Trend, Centre for Policy Studies, London

References

Joseph, K. (1978) Towards Fuller Employment, Centre
    for Policy Studies, London
Kaldor, N. (1959) 'Economic Growth and the Problem
    of Inflation', Part I, Economica, 26(3),
    212-26 and Part 2, 26(4) 287-98
Kaldor, N. (1964) Essays on Economic Policy, Vol. I,
    Duckworth, London
Kaldor, N. (1980) 'Monetarism and U.K. Monetary
    Policy', Cambridge Journal of Economics, 4(4),
    293-318
Kaldor, N. (1982) The Scourge of Monetarism, O.U.P.,
    Oxford
Kaldor, N. (1983) The Economic Consequences of
    Mrs. Thatcher, Duckworth, London
Kaldor, N. (ed) (1971) Conflicts in Policy
    Objectives, Basil Blackwell, Oxford
Kalecki, M. (1943) 'Political Aspects of Full
    Employment', Political Quarterly, 14(4),
    322-31
Kay, J. and King, M. (1978) The British Tax System,
    O.U.P., Oxford
Keegan, J. (1976) The Face of Battle, Penguin,
    Harmondsworth
Keegan, V. and Pennant-Rea, R. (1979) Who Runs the
    Economy?, Temple Smith, London
Keynes, J.M. (1971) Collected Writings, Vol. I:
    Indian Currency and Finance, Macmillan, London
Keynes, J.M. (1971A) Collected Writings, Vol. II:
    The Economic Consequences of the Peace,
    Macmillan, London
Keynes, J.M. (1971B) Collected Writings, Vol. IV:
    The Tract on Monetary Reform, Macmillan, London
Keynes, J.M. (1971C) Collected Writings, Vol. VI:
    Treatise on Monday, Vol. 2, Pure Theory of
    Money, Macmillan, London
Keynes, J.M. (1972) Collected Writings, Vol. IX:
    Essays in Persuasion, Macmillan, London
Keynes, J.M. (1978) Collected Writings, Vol. XXII:
    Activities 1939-45: Internal War Finance,
    Macmillan, London
Keynes, J.M. (1980A) Collected Writings, Vol. XXVII:
    Activities 1940-46: Shaping the Post-War World
    Employment and Commodities, Macmillan, London
Keynes, J.M. (1980B) Collected Writings, Vol. XXVI:
    Activities 1941-46: Shaping the Post-War World:
    Bretton Woods and Reparations, Macmillan,
    London
Keynes, J.M. and Henderson, H. (1929) 'Can Lloyd
    George Do It?' in Keynes (1972), Collected
    Writings, Vol. IX: Essays in Persuasion,
    Macmillan, London

References

King, M. (1975) 'The United Kingdom Profits Crisis: Myth or Reality?', Economic Journal, 85(1), 33-54

Kirby, M.W. (1981) The Decline of British Economic Power, Allen and Unwin, London

Labour Party (1976) Report of the Annual Conference of the Labour Party, Labour Party, London

Laidler, D. (1972) 'The Current Inflation: Explanations and Policies', National Westminster Bank Review, November, 6-21

Laidler, D. (1975) Essays on Money and Inflation, Manchester U.P., Manchester

Laidler, D. and Parkin, M. (1975) 'Inflation: A Survey', Economic Journal, 85(4), 741-809

Le Grand, J. (1982) The Strategy of Equality, Allen and Unwin, London

Leruez, J. (1975) Economic Planning and Politics in in Britain (translated by M. Harrison), Martin Robertson, Oxford

Leyland, N.H. (1952) 'Productivity' in Worswick, G.D.N. and Ady, P., The British Economy 1945-50, Clarendon Press, Oxford

Lindert, P.H. (1969) Key Currencies and Gold 1900-13, Princeton Studies in International Finance No. 24, P.U. Press, Princeton

Lipton, M. (1968) Assessing Economic Performance, Staples Press, London

Little, I.M.D. (1964) 'Review of Dow (1964)', Economic Journal, 74(4), 983-5

Llewellyn, D.T. (1980) International Financial Integration, Macmillan, London

Macmillan Committee (1931) Committee on Finance and Industry: Report, CMD. 3897, H.M.S.O., London

Marwick, A. (1964) 'Middle Opinion in the 1930s: Planning, Progress and Political Agreement', English Historical Review, 79(2), 285-98

Matthews, R.C.O. (1968) 'Why has Britain had Full Employment Since the War?', Economic Journal, 78(3), 555-69

Matthews, R.C.O. (1969) 'Post-War Business Cycles in the U.K.' in Bronfenbrenner (ed), Is the Business Cycle Obsolete?, S.S.R.C., New York

Matthews, R.C.O. (1970) 'Full Employment Since the War - A Reply', Economic Journal, 80(1), 173-6

Meade, J. (1951) The Theory of International Economic Policy, Vol. I, The Balance of Payments, O.U.P., London

Meade, J. (1966) 'Exchange Rate Flexibility', Three Banks Review, 70, 3-27

Meade, J. (1982) Stagflation, Vol. I, Wage-Fixing, Allen and Unwin, London

References

Meyer, F.V., Corner, D.C. and Parker, J.E.S. (1970)
    Problems of a Mature Economy, Macmillan,
    London
Meynaud, J. (1958) Technocracy, Faber and Faber,
    London
Middlemas, K. (1978) Politics in Industrial Society,
    Deutsch, London
Middleton, R. (1982) 'The Treasury in the 1930s:
    Political and Administrative Constraints to
    Acceptance of the "New Economics"', Oxford
    Economic Papers, 34(1), 48-77
Miller, M. (1981) 'Monetary Control in the U.K.',
    Cambridge Journal of Economics, 5(1), 71-9
Milward, A.S. (1965) The German Economy at War,
    Athlone Press, London
Milward, A.S. (1970) The Economic Effects of the
    World Wars on Britain, Macmillan, London
Mitchell, J. (1966) The Groundwork to Economic
    Planning, Secker and Warburg, London
Moggridge, D.E. (1972) British Monetary Policy
    1924-31: The Norman Conquest of $4.86, C.U.P.,
    Cambridge
Mosley, P. (1984) The Making of Economic Policy,
    Wheatsheaf, Brighton
National Economic Development Council (1963A) Growth
    of the U.K. Economy to 1966, N.E.D.O., London
National Economic Development Council (1963B)
    Conditions Favourable to Economic Growth,
    N.E.D.O., London
National Economic Development Council (1976)
    Cyclical Fluctuations in the U.K. Economy,
    Discussion Paper No. 3, N.E.D.O., London
Neild, R. and Ward, T. (1979) The Measurement and
    Reform of Budgetary Policy, Heinemann, London
Nurske, R. (1944) International Currency Movements,
    League of Nations, Geneva
Nutter, G.W. (1978) Growth of Government in the
    West, American Enterprise Institute, Washington
    D.C.
O'Brien, D.P. (1970) J.R. McCulloch: A Study in
    Classical Economics, Allen and Unwin, London
Organisation for European Economic Co-operation
    (1961) The Problem of Rising Prices, O.E.E.C.,
    Paris
Oxford (1944) Oxford University Institute of
    Statistics, The Economics of Full Employment,
    O.U.P., Oxford
P.R.O. (1940A) CAB 87, WA 40(3), no date (but 1940)
    War Arms Committee

References

P.R.O. (1941A) CAB 87/4, IEP 41(3). Internal
    Measures for the Prevention of General
    Unemployment, 3 November 1940
P.R.O. (1941B) CAB 87/4, 1, 11 November 1941,
    Appendix C
P.R.O. (1941C) PREM 4, 100/5, 24 May 1941
P.R.O. (1943A) CAB 87/63, EC 43/6, 16 October 1943
P.R.O. (1944A) PREM 4, 96/6, 6 January 1944.
    Cherwell to Churchill
P.R.O. 123/48, CAB 123/48. No date. Robbins to
    Lord Present of the Council
Paish, F.W. (1956) 'Britain's Foreign Investments:
    The Post-War Record', Lloyds Bank Review, 41,
    23-39
Paish, F.W. (1962) Studies in an Inflationary
    Economy, Macmillan, London
Panitch, L. (1976) Social Democracy and Industrial
    Militancy, C.U.P., Cambridge
Parkin, M. (1974) 'U.K. Inflation: The Policy
    Alternatives', National Westminster Bank
    Review, May, 32-47
Parkin, M. (1975) 'The Politics of Inflation',
    Government and Opposition, 10(2), 189-202
Peacock, A. and Shaw, G.K. (1981) The P.S.B.R.,
    University College of Buckingham, Occasional
    Papers in Economics, No. 1, The University,
    Buckingham
Peden, G. (1979) British Rearmament and the Treasury,
    Scottish Academic Press, Edinburgh
Peden, G. (1980) 'Keynes, the Treasury and Unemploy-
    ment in the Later 1930s', Oxford Economic
    Papers, 32(1), 1-18
Phelps-Brown, H. (1981) 'Incomes Policy Revisited',
    Fiscal Studies, 2(3), 1-9
Phillips, A.W. (1958) 'The Relation Between
    Unemployment and the Rate of Change in Money
    Wage Rates in the U.K. 1861-1957', Economica,
    25, 283-99
Pitkin, H. (1967) The Concept of Representation,
    University of California Press, Berkeley
Pliatzky, L. (1982) Getting and Spending: Public
    Expenditure, Employment and Inflation, Basil
    Blackwell, Oxford
Polanyi, G. (1967) Planning in Britain: The
    Experience of the 1960s, Institute of Economic
    Affairs, London
Political and Economic Planning (1947) Britain and
    World Trade, P.E.P., London
Political and Economic Planning (1960), Growth in
    the British Economy, P.E.P., London

References

Rowthorn, B. (1977) 'Conflict, Inflation and Money', Cambridge Journal of Economics, 1(3), 215-39

Rowthorn, B. (1981) 'The Politics of the Alternative Economic Strategy', Marxism Today, January, 4-10

Sayers, R.S. (1956) Financial Policy 1939-45, H.M.S.O., London

Sayers, R.S. (1976) The Bank of England, Vol. 2, C.U.P., Cambridge

Scammell, W.M. (1980) The International Economy Since 1945, Macmillan, London

Scott, M. (1978) Can We Get Back to Full Employment?, Macmillan, London

Shanks, M. (1961) The Stagnant Society: A Warning, Penguin, Harmondsworth

Shonfield, A. (1959) British Economic Policy Since the War (revised edition), Penguin, Harmondsworth

Shonfield, A. (1965) Modern Capitalism, O.U.P., London

Sinfield, A. (1976) 'Unemployment and the Social Structure' in G.D.N. Worswick (ed), The Concept and Measurement of Involuntary Unemployment, Allen and Unwin, London

Sinfield, A. (1981) What Unemployment Means, Martin Robertson, Oxford

Skidelsky, R. (1970) Politicians and the Slump, Penguin, Harmondsworth

Smith, K. (1982) 'Why Was There Never a Keynesian Revolution in Economic Policy? A Comment', Economy and Society, 11(2), 223-8

Speer, A. (1972) Inside the Third Reich, Sphere, London

Stewart, M. (1977) The Jekyll and Hyde Years: Politics and Economic Policy Since 1964, Dent, London

Stone, R. (1977) Inland Revenue Report on National Income 1929, C.U.P., Cambridge

Stout, D. (1976) International Price Competitiveness, Non-Price Factors and International Trade, N.E.D.O., London

Strange, S. (1971) Sterling and the British Policy, O.U.P., London

Sweezy, P. (1968) The Theory of Capitalist Development, Monthly Review, New York

Swenarton, M. (1981) Homes Fit for Heroes, Heinemann, London

Taylor, A.J.P. (1970) English History 1914-45, Penguin, Harmondsworth

References

Taylor, C.T. and Threadgold, A.R. (1979) "Real" National Savings and its Sectoral Composition, Bank of England Discussion Paper No. 6, Bank of England, London

Tew, B. (1982) The Evolution of the International Monetary System 1945-81, Hutchinson, London

Thirlwall, A.P. (1980) Balance of Payments Theory and the U.K. Experience, Macmillan, London

Thompson, G. (1978) 'Capitalist Profit Calculation and Inflation Accounting', Economy and Society, 7(4), 394-429

Thompson, G. (1979) 'The Growth of the Government Sector', Unit 3 of Open University Course, Political Economy and Taxation, Open University Press, Milton Keynes

Thompson, G. (1981) 'Monetarism and Economic Ideology', Economy and Society, 10(1), 27-71

Thompson, G. (1982) 'The Firm as a "Dispersed Social Agency"', Economy and Society, 11(3), 233-50

Tinbergen, J. (1950) Economic Policy: Principles and Design, North-Holland, Amsterdam

Titmuss, R. (1963) Essays on the Welfare State, Allen and Unwin, London

Titmuss, R. (1976) Problems of Social Policy, (Annotated edition), H.M.S.O., London

Tobin, J. (1977) 'How Dead is Keynes?', Economic Inquiry, XV(4), 459-68

Tomlinson, J. (1981A) Problems of British Economic Policy 1870-1945, Methuen, London

Tomlinson, J. (1981B) 'Why was there never a Keynesian Revolution in Economic Policy?', Economy and Society, 10(1), 72-87

Tomlinson, J. (1981C) 'The Economics of Politics and Public Expenditure: A Critique', Economy and Society, 10(4), 383-402

Tomlinson, J. (1982) The Unequal Struggle? British Socialism and the Capitalist Enterprise, Methuen, London

Tomlinson, J. (1983) 'Where do Economic Policy Objectives Come From?: The Case of Full Employment', Economy and Society, 12(1)

Tomlinson, J. (1984) 'A Keynesian Revolution' in Economic Policy-Making', Economic History Review, XXXVII(2), 258-62

Trevithick, J. (1975) 'Keynes, Inflation and Money Illusion', Economic Journal, 85(1), 101-13

Tribe, K. (1978) Land, Labour and Economic Discourse, Routledge and Kegan Paul, London

Viner, J. (1937) Studies in the Theory of International Trade, Harper, New York

References

Waight, L. (1939) The History and Mechanism of the Exchange Equalisation Account 1932-39, C.U.P., Cambridge

Wallich, (1978) 'Stabilisation Goals: Balancing Inflation and Unemployment', American Economic Review, Papers and Proceedings, 68(2), 159-64

Walters, A. (1978) Economists and the British Economy, Institute of Economic Affairs, London

Ward, T. (1977) Cambridge Economic Policy Review, 3, Gower, Aldershot

Wass, D. (1978) 'The Changing Problems of Economic Management', Economic Trends, 293, 97-104

Webster, C. (1982) 'Healthy or Hungry Thirties?', History Workshop, 13, 110-29

Whiting, A. (1976) 'An International Comparison of the Instability of Economic Growth', Three Banks Review, 66, 26-46

Williams, K. (1981) From Pauperism to Poverty, Routledge and Kegan Paul, London

Williams, K., Williams, J. and Thomas, D. (1983) Why Are the British Bad at Manufacturing?, Routledge and Kegan Paul, London

Williamson, O.E. (1981) 'The Economics of Organisation: The Transaction Cost Approach', American Journal of Sociology, 87(3), 548-77

Wilson, H. (1971) The Labour Government 1964-70 - A Personal Record, Weidenfeld and Nicolson, London

Winch, D. (1972) Economics and Policy, Fontana, London

Wintringham, T. (1942) Peoples War, Pilot Press, London

Wood, J. (1972) How Much Unemployment?, Institute of Economic Affairs, London

Wood, J. (1975) How Little Unemployment?, Institute of Economic Affairs, London

Worswick, G.D.N. (1970) 'Fiscal Policy and Stabilisation' in Cairncross (ed), (1970)

Worswick, G.D.N. (ed) (1976) The Concept and Measurement of Involuntary Unemployment, Allen and Unwin, London

Worswick, G.D.N. and Ady, P.H. (1952) The British Economy 1945-50, Clarendon Press, Oxford

Worswick, G.D.N. and Ady, P.H. (1962) The British Economy in the 1950s, Clarendon Press, Oxford

Wright, A.W. (1979) G.D.H. Cole and Socialist Democracy, Clarendon Press, Oxford

Wright, J.F. (1979) Britain in the Age of Economic Management, O.U.P., Oxford

References

Wright, M. (1977) 'Public Expenditure in Britain:
    The Crisis of Control', _Public Administration_,
    55, 143-69.

INDEX